DISCOUNTING THE FUTURE

ALSO IN THE *NEAR FUTURES* SERIES

Discounting the Future: The Ascendancy of a Political Technology

Liliana Doganova

ZONE BOOKS

near futures

Printed in the United States of America.
Distributed by Princeton University Press Press,
Princeton, New Jersey, and Woodstock, United Kingdom

Excerpt from Kim Stanley Robinson, *The Ministry for the Future*
    (New York: Orbit Books, 2020), pp. 129–32.
Reproduced with permission of Little Brown Book Group Limited.

Library of Congress Cataloging-in-Publication Data
Names: Doganova, Liliana, 1980– , author.
Title: Discounting the future : the ascendency of a political technology /
    Liliana Doganova.
Description: Brooklyn, New York : Zone Books, [2024] | Series: Near futures |
    Includes bibliographical references and index. | Summary: "Through
    the historical sociology of discounting as a valuation technique, this
    book explores the defining traits and contradictions of our relationship
    to the future" — Provided by publisher.
Identifiers: LCCN 2023032355 (print) | LCCN 2023032356 (ebook) |
    ISBN 9781942130918 (hardcover) | ISBN 9781942130925 (ebook)
Subjects: LCSH: Policy sciences. | Forecasting. | Sociology. |
    BISAC: BUSINESS & ECONOMICS / Environmental Economics |
    SOCIAL SCIENCE / Sociology / General
Classification: LCC H97 .D634 2024 (print) | LCC H97 (ebook) |
    DDC 320.6 — dc23/eng/20230825
LC record available at https://lccn.loc.gov/2023032355
LC ebook record available at https://lccn.loc.gov/2023032356

CONTENTS

Introduction

In the summer of 2022, climate change seemed more palpable than ever. As I was writing these lines, fires were consuming the French Landes, Europe's largest artificial forest. Apocalyptic images of raging blazes, displaced people and animals, devastated land, and burned trees fed the news. For the public, forest fires incarnated global warming: they blended the temporality of a threatened future and the causality of heat waves and drought. In the media, experts described forest fires as both a cause and consequence of global warming: "while global warming explains why forest fires are becoming more frequent and intense, such fires can in turn accelerate the rise in temperatures," warned a professor of environmental geography; the thousands of hectares of forest going up in smoke are like "a carbon bomb exploding," alerted a forest scientist (Seibt 2022). When fires resumed less than a month after they had been controlled by firefighters, French Prime Minister Élisabeth Borne declared in front of journalists the "urgency" of the situation and the will "to act on all fronts, in order to fight even better in the future and prepare ourselves for events that we know very well are related to climate change" (*Le Monde* 2022).[1]

If forest fires incarnated global warming, reactions to them bore resemblance to what is often referred to as climate action (or, more critically, inaction) and its temporalities. Firefighter's interventions signaled the urgency of action to be taken. Questions about whether the fires could have been avoided led to doubts about current forest

management practices, revealed the fragility of monocultural planta-
tions, and pointed to the likely adaptability of certain kinds of vegeta-
tion to global warming. Discussions focused on the urgency of saving
the present and the preparedness for a warming future. As in debates
on climate change (in)action, the possibility that this future could be
acted upon was blurred.

This book is devoted to one of the reasons why we can or cannot act
on the future. It is a reason at once mundane and highly technical and
thus seemingly both beneath notice and difficult to grasp. One objective of this book is to show that it nevertheless deserves our scrutiny.
The reason why we can or cannot act on the future is embodied in
an instrument we use to look to the future. It is a technical approach
to dealing with what may come—to which I will nevertheless refer
under its vernacular name: *discounting*. Discounting is an economic
calculation that companies and governments (some would say individuals, too) make to decide about things by determining how valuable
they are. The value of things, the calculation goes, comes from the
flows of costs and revenues or benefits that they are likely to generate in the future. As future flows are brought in the present, they are
devalued due to their distance in time and their uncertainty. Discounting deserves our scrutiny, this book argues, because its mundaneness
hides significant consequences for how we have come to conceive of
the future and because its technical aspects hide fundamental political questions about the capacity of certain actors and the incapacity of
others to picture the future and act on it.[2]

I will not start this introduction by describing discounting; its
description, both as a theory of action and a theory of value, is the
object of the first chapter of this book.[3] In this introduction, I will
acquaint the reader with discounting in two steps. First, and briefly, I
will present one instance in which discounting came under the spotlight and became explicitly the object of a debate—highly technical but
at the same time blatantly political—that revolved around the problem
of climate (in)action. Second, and at more length, I will discuss the

three troubles with discounting that this debate quite readily reveals. These can be formulated as the following three questions: Is the future worth less than the present? Is the future what matters? Should everybody look to time and to value in that way? In other words, I will discuss discounting as a mode of valuing the future, as a way of futureing value, and as a general form of action. Finally, I will explain how these problems—the definition of and the troubles with discounting— are addressed in the five chapters of the book.

DISCOUNTING AND THE PUZZLE OF CLIMATE (IN)ACTION

One of the rare moments in which the economic technique of discounting came under the spotlight was in a heated debate on climate (in)action known as the Stern/Nordhaus controversy. The story starts with the following paradox: while today climate change is supported by sound scientific evidence and materialized in observable and impressive events such as forest fires, we seem incapable of taking action against it. The "we" in question encompasses a wide range of people and institutions in developing and developed countries, Europe and the United States, older and younger generations, right and left governments, that vary in their willingness and ability to act.[4] The interesting question for us here is not who acts or does not act, but how and why they do so. And the interesting finding is that climate inaction is perfectly justified by the tools and procedures that governments use for the sake of making decisions with objectivity and for the general interest. In other words, climate action is at odds with rational decision-making. How come?

Today, public policies are analyzed in terms of their costs and benefits: a good policy, or rather a policy worth implementing, is a policy whose benefits outweigh its costs. Through the lens of cost-benefit analysis, climate change policy would incur, for example, the costs of reforming production processes and consumption patterns in order to reduce emissions. It would be worth implementing if the costs are at

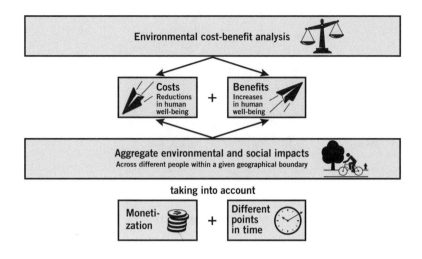

Figure I.1. Illustration of cost-benefit analysis in environmental policy (OECD 2018). Redrawn by Virge Kask.

least compensated by the benefits it will generate in the future. But how to compare future benefits and present costs? How to *balance* them, as suggested by the weighing scales image recurrent in expositions of cost-benefit analysis in public policy (fig. I.1)?

In order to treat as commensurate benefits and costs that occur in different points of time more or less distant in the future, standard cost-benefit analysis makes use of discounting. The monetary value of an event (a cost or a benefit) that occurs at a certain point in time is reduced by a certain factor called the discount rate. The logic is the same as that of the rate of interest: money set aside today is equivalent to "more money in the future," because it can be put in a savings account and multiplied by the rate of interest. In discounting, however, the arrow of time is reversed: money expected in the future is equivalent to "less money today," because this "less money today" is supposed to be able to produce that "more money in the future."

The logic is certainly not easy to grasp when one is not familiar with discounting, but let us try to embrace it in order to follow its implications. Reversing the arrow of time entails reversing the arithmetical operation. Moving from the present to the future, one multiplies by the rate of interest; moving from the future to the present, one divides by the discount rate. Moving from the present to the future, value expands: this reflects ideas of economic growth and technological progress. Moving from the future to the present, value shrinks: it is "capitalized," as I will explain below, that is, folded back into the capital that is supposed to produce it. As the table that accompanies the weighing scales in Figure I.2 explains, there is a "time cost of money" that reflects "the impact of time on the value of future benefits and costs": "Money spent or earned today is more valuable than the same amount of money promised in a future year since the money earned today can be invested and earn additional revenue in the interim years. Therefore benefits and costs accruing in later years of an analysis are often valued at a discounted rate" (Sallman et al. 2012, p. 14).

Usually, the discount rate used for events occurring at different points in time is the same, but the power given to the discount rate is greater the more distant an event is in time. With a discount rate of say 5 percent, the monetary value of an event worth $100 is reduced by 1.6 (1.05 to the power of 10) if the event occurs in 10 years. However, it is reduced by 132 (1.05 to the power of 100) if the event occurs in 100 years. As a result, $100 in 10 years is worth $63 today, but $100 in 100 years is worth $0.80 today. In other words, the "present value" of $100 in 100 years is $0.80. The reduction effect is dramatic. Climate change policies incur costs that are proximate in time ("act now...") and generate benefits that are very distant in time ("...to save the future") and are therefore heavily discounted. The value of such policies—obtained by subtracting discounted future costs from discounted future benefits—turns out to be null, if not negative. Hence, they are not worth implementing. This is how rational decision-making leads to climate inaction.

The *Stern Review on the Economics of Climate Change* (Stern 2007), a 700-page report released for the government of the United Kingdom in 2006 by economist Nicholas Stern, spotted the problem and created a commotion by proposing a fundamental change in discounting to allow for reaching the conclusion that it is worth acting now to save the future. As the review's summary of conclusions explains, "there is still time to avoid the worst impacts of climate change, if we take strong action now." The costs of inaction are estimated: "if we don't act, the overall costs and risks of climate change will be equivalent to losing at least 5% of global GDP each year, now and forever" (p. vi). And so are the costs of action: "the costs of action—reducing greenhouse gas emissions to avoid the worst impacts of climate change—can be limited to around 1% of global GDP each year" (p. vi). The result of the math is that "the benefits of strong, early action considerably outweigh the costs" ("Summary of Conclusions," p. vi, and "Executive Summary," p. ii).

The trick that allowed the *Stern Review* to reach such a conclusion lay in the redefinition of the discount rate. Discounting, the review explains, has two justifications in the theory of economics: one relates to the idea that in the future, people will be richer and will therefore give less worth to an additional amount of money; the other relates to the idea of "pure time preference," according to which "people prefer to have good things earlier than later" (p. 31). The problem, the *Stern Review* notes, is that when it comes to climate change, the "people" in question are not the same. We are not in a situation in which one individual is deciding whether she should consume now or save for later. We are in a situation in which current generations are deciding to consume now and thereby depriving not themselves, but future generations, of the possibility to consume later, the "later" of current generations being actually the "now" of future generations. Therefore, the review proposes, "we have to ask how [future generations] should be represented in the views and decisions of current generations." For both ethical and logical reasons, and referring to the work of economists such as Frank Ramsey, Amartya Sen, and Robert Solow, the review formulates the following solution:

We take a simple approach in this Review: if a future generation will be present, we suppose that it has the same claim on our ethical attention as the current one.

Thus, while we do allow, for example, for the possibility that, say, a meteorite might obliterate the world, and for the possibility that future generations might be richer (or poorer), we treat the welfare of future generations on a par with our own. (Stern 2007, p. 31)

This methodological choice results in a lower discount rate and in the possibility to conclude that the benefits of climate change policy, albeit distant in the future, can compensate its costs, overvalued by their proximity in time. Climate action is thus justified. More than that, it becomes urgent.

Climate policy clearly is viewed in current approaches to it as an investment strategy.[5] The *Stern Review* makes that point when exposing its conceptual framework: "Mitigation—taking strong action to reduce emissions—must be viewed as an investment, a cost incurred now and in the coming few decades to avoid the risks of very severe consequences in the future" ("Executive Summary, p. i). However, viewed as an investment strategy, its treatment of discounting was deemed "extreme" by another leading economist, William Nordhaus (2007). In an article published in *Science*, Nordhaus argued that the *Stern Review*'s conclusions "about the need for urgent and immediate action will not survive the substitutions of assumptions that are consistent with today's marketplace real interest rates and savings rates" (p. 202). For him, the discount rate "that enters into the determination of the efficient balance between the cost of emissions reductions today and the benefit of reduced climate damage in the future" should be "the return on capital." And this return on capital, "which measures net yield on investments in capital, education and technology," is "observable in the marketplace."

What does one see when she "observes" the discount rate "in the marketplace," as Nordhaus suggests doing? A number much higher than the *Stern Review*'s, which was 1.014 per cent. The difference between the *Stern Review*'s "prescriptive" rate and Nordhaus's "descriptive" rate—for it is supposed to be observed in the market—accounts for the discrepancy between the *Stern Review*'s proposal, which suggests "global emissions reductions of between 30 and 70% over the next two decades, objectives consistent with a carbon tax of around $300 per ton today," and standard economic models, whose recommendations lead to a ten times lower carbon tax and a gradual tightening of climate policy over time (Nordhaus 2007, p. 201).

The Stern/Nordhaus controversy, and more broadly the debate over prescriptive versus descriptive discounting, has been widely analyzed in the literature of economics and law (Goulder and Williams 2012; Kelleher 2017; Weisbach and Sunstein 2009). When Nordhaus won the Nobel Prize in Economics in 2018, the debate spilled over in the broader literature. The levels and the theoretical justification of the discount rates defended by Nordhaus were not the only things that were criticized, either. Joseph Stiglitz commented that Nordhaus's economics of climate change is not only "badly flawed," but in fact "dangerous because we don't have another planet we can go to if we mess this up" (AFP 2020). The very idea that climate change policy can be treated in the terms of cost-benefit analysis appeared puzzling. Are cost-benefit analyses appropriate when "we are considering the possibility of human extinction" (Mann 2022)? Can we consider that "reducing CO_2 emissions is but an element in a strategy of investment in the future, next to capital accumulation: one sacrifices a few points of GDP now in order to gain other points of GDP in hundred years"? (Pottier 2018)

THE TROUBLES WITH DISCOUNTING

In a critical discussion of Nordhaus's legacy in the debate over discounting, Geoff Mann writes that while "discounting is a crucial element in all investment decisions," even "at first glance, there's something troubling about discounting. On what grounds can future states of the world be considered less important, less valuable, than the present" (Mann 2022)? Thus, as we've seen, discounting is troubling, first, because it rests on the questionable assumption that the future is worth less than the present—an assumption that, as the Stern/Nordhaus controversy indicates, becomes even more perplexing today, in an epoch permeated by concerns such as climate change and sustainable development, which are all about making the future count. However, there are also (at least) two more troubles with discounting.

The second trouble is at odds with the first: although discounting devalues the future, it nevertheless assumes that it is the future that counts—that it is the future that we should look to when we make decisions about the present and when we search for the value of things. Consequently, discounting also erases the past and the present as guides for action and sources of value. In other words, if discounting is troubling due to how it values the future, it is no less troubling because of how it futurizes value, that is, treats the future as the locus of value.

The third trouble with discounting is its association with investment as a way to think about making decisions. It assumes everyone behaves or is to be made to behave like an investor and that looking to the future to make decisions about different courses of action always means considering these courses of action and the things upon which they bear as *investments*. Corporations have their discount rates, indicated by their financial departments. Likewise, governments have their social discount rates, which they may observe in the market (as Nordhaus suggests) or decide upon themselves (as Stern suggests).[6] Individuals, too, according to economic science, have their own discount rates, which explain their decisions about the more or less "green" qualities of the goods that they purchase and more broadly about the amount of money that they save, consume, or keep for investment.[7] As I will argue below, the pervasiveness of investment as a worldview and a style of action is thus entangled with discounting as a general form. But first, let us consider each of these troubles in more depth.

IS THE FUTURE WORTH LESS THAN THE PRESENT?

Why is the future assumed to be worth less than the present? This is the first thing that troubled me about discounting when I encountered this technique. I was studying the biotechnology market and wondering how, practically, biotech start-ups and pharmaceutical companies could agree on a price when they were exchanging, for millions of dollars, promises—in PowerPoint presentations, pitches, and business plans—about future drugs that barely existed at the moment when the transaction was taking place. The price of a future drug, I was explained, is based on the calculation of its "net present value" (NPV), defined as the sum of the flows of costs and revenues that the drug will generate in the future, discounted at the proper discount rate. The trouble, my interviewees added, is that when the drug development projects that are being bought and sold are at an early stage, and the hoped-for resulting drugs are distant in time—sometimes as long as ten years from the moment of the transaction—the future revenues that they are expected to yield get discounted so much that they cannot weigh against the development costs more proximate in time.

The problem that these managers formulated was akin to the problem encountered by climate change policy that I discussed above. Certainly, the time scale was shorter: ten instead of a hundred years. And the consequences seemed less dramatic: the risk that discounting made humanity run was not extinction, but less innovation. Because discounting gave less weight to the future than to the present, it automatically favored projects that were less innovative and quicker to bring to market. It threatened innovation and instituted short-termism.

I was sensitive to this critique of discounting and was happy to discover it resonating in the literature. In the practitioner literature devoted to the pharmaceutical industry or to the valuation of investment projects more broadly, I found that discounting calculations triggered controversies, that the definition of the discount rate and the treatment of uncertainty were far from settled, and that other techniques, such as real options valuation,[8] were put forward as substitutes for discounting and the calculation of net present value. (See Doganova 2011, 2015.) Discounting created real troubles in the pharmaceutical industry. For some, discounting did not impede companies from engaging in long-term projects, but it made managers feel uncomfortable with the decisions that they were making and that looked like "bad" decisions, giving birth to projects with no apparent or even "negative" value. A manager from the research department of a pharmaceutical company complained in the pages of *Drug Discovery Today*: "Companies have undertaken negative NPV (net present value) projects consistently, citing strategic importance. These were not intrinsically 'bad' business decisions, but the valuation methodology produced negative figures. Correspondingly, however, some were uncomfortable with the purely subjective decisions taken in the face of negative valuations" (Pandey 2003, p. 968). Others attributed a stronger effect to discounting, arguing that it actually blocked long-term innovative projects. An article published in the *Harvard Business Review* and coauthored by the Harvard Business School strategy professor Clayton Christensen, the father of "disruptive innovation," listed discounting as one of the three "innovation killers" that "destroy your [company's] capacity to do new things." Among the three financial tools that act "as an accomplice in the conspiracy against successful innovation," the "indiscriminate and oversimplified use" of the net present values calculated through discounting was depicted as "a root cause of companies' persistent underinvestment in the innovations required to sustain long-term success" (Christensen et al. 2008, pp. 100–101).

Such accusations were not new. Already in the 1980s, as discounting was making its way into companies' decision-making practices until it became the most widespread tool for assessing investments, strategy scholars were whistleblowing. Again in the pages of the *Harvard Business Review*, two other Harvard Business School professors established the link between discounting and insufficient investment. Through tools such as discounting, they argued, we—the United States, in this case—are "managing our way to economic decline" (Hayes and Abernathy 1980). This and related articles attracted a lot of attention among the readers of the *Harvard Business Review* and reached the pages of *The New York Times* (Wayne 1982).

Discounting thus weighs the present against the future in such a way that the present defeats the future. Far removed from companies' investment decisions and concerned with the future of democracy, rather than with economic growth and innovation, philosopher Daniel Innerarity identifies the problem of our relationship to the future as "the tyranny of the present":

> We find ourselves in a regime of historicity where the present is lord and master. This is the tyranny of the present, in other words, the tyranny of the current legislature, of the short term, consumerism, our generation, proximity, etc. This is the economy that privileges the financial sector, profits over investments, cost reduction over company cohesion. We practice an imperialism that is no longer related to space but to time, an imperialism of the present that colonizes everything. There is a colonization of the future that consists of living at its expense and an imperialism of the present that absorbs the future and feeds off it parasitically.... This present replaces the long term with the short term, duration with immediacy, permanence with transience, memory with sensation, vision with impulse. (Innerarity 2012, p. 8)

Innerarity attributes the tyranny of the present to an overall trend that characterizes our epoch, captured by notions such as presentism (Hartog 2003) and acceleration (Rosa 2013). The expansion of discounting clearly functions as one of the drivers or consequences of these phenomena. Discounting literally devalues the future and gives priority to the present, inducing short-termism or myopia, as with of the managers I described above. The discount rate creates an almost automatic link between valuation through discounting and shorter periods for realizing value because time is viewed as something that has a cost. However, discounting could also be analyzed in exactly the opposite terms: as futurism, as opposed to presentism, because it posits the future as the ultimate source of rewards in the present, and as deceleration, as opposed to acceleration, because it delays action that we should take now to save the long-term future, waiting for more efficient future technologies and smarter and richer future generations to arrive.

The curious thing with discounting is thus that it can be and do many different, even opposite things. Following the development of this peculiar object requires us to abandon grand historical narratives about change in our experience of time or about the temporal structures of our societies and to examine, in moments when discounting is put forward as a solution to a problem or criticized and contested and transformed, how the relationship between the past, the present, and the future and the very matter of which these temporalities consist are put to trial and performed. As I will argue in the chapters that follow, viewed in this way, *discounting is a political technology* and *the future is a political domain*—that is, a domain over which actors struggle to acquire the capacity to act.

IS THE FUTURE WHAT MATTERS?

In light of its Janus-faced nature, it is no surprise that the second trouble with discounting is the opposite of the first. Discounting can devalue the future in relation to the present, but it also tells us that to know what we should do now, we should look to the future for the consequences of these decisions, expressed as flows of value. This second trouble is less palpable, though. I became sensitive to it as I was studying the early uses of discounting in forest management in the eighteenth and the nineteenth centuries in Europe, which I will discuss in Chapter 2. Discounting was open to criticism because it entailed envisaging the forest as capital and the forest owner as an investor, and in doing so, it entailed acceleration: the forest seen as capital, processed through the gaze of the investor for whom time has a cost, was a forest managed with shorter rotation lengths, that is, a forest whose trees were felled at an earlier age. But forests also were the birthplace, or at least an early test bed, of the notion of sustainability (Hölzl 2010; Warde 2011) and of future-oriented valuation and management practices at odds with discounting's discounting of the future (Doganova 2018). The ensuing debates on the public versus private ownership of forests raised the following question: Who has a stake in the long-term management of the forest (Nordblad 2016; Vatin 2008)? Could the private owner, in spite of having a life span much shorter than that of the trees, manage a forest in line with the general interest of society? Or is the state the only "imperishable being," as one protagonist put it, to whom forests and their long-term futures could be entrusted?

In the mid-nineteenth century, scientific forestry, from which the first formulations of discounting, known as "the Faustmann formula" (Faustmann 1968), emerged, offered the hope to provide a clear answer to these questions by determining, by means of mathematics, the correct calculation of the value of a forest and hence its optimal management, in particular, the right moment to fell the trees and sell wood and timber on the market. At that time, this optimal management came to be defined as what maximized the "present value" of the forest, calculated by the flows of costs and revenues and discounted at the rate of interest, that it was likely to produce in the future. As the introduction to the English translation of the article in which the Faustmann's formula was published in 1849 notes (Gane 1968), the novelty of discounting as a valuation technique lay in the idea that the value of the forest stemmed from the future, rather than the present or the past.

This turn to the future was accompanied by a critique of the relevance of other temporalities to thinking about the value of forests. The critique took two different forms. The first was addressed to the present of the market (Muniesa and Doganova 2020): the value of the forest, the argument went, cannot be captured in the price of land, timber, or wood that the market displays at the moment when the valuation is made. The market's "principle of instantness" (Vatin 2005) produces a price that is different from what Faustmann called the forest's "economic value" and that finance later called "fundamental value" (Bryan and Rafferty 2013), a value that encompasses its future.

The second critique was less explicit, but more violent. It was addressed to the present of the poor people who lived nearby the forest (fig. I.2). As an editor of the *Rheinische Zeitung*, in 1842, the young Karl Marx involved himself in the debates on a "law on the theft of wood" that defined the gathering of fallen wood as "theft." Marx formulated the conflict that he observed in terms of rights and property: the conflict between "the right of human beings," whom the law deprived from their customary rights, and that of trees, behind which stood forest owners and the state." (Marx 1842).

Historian Richard Hölzl describes how future-oriented scientific forestry, supported by judicial and military interventions, affected the present practices of local populations:

> For the local population the new measures meant that it was increasingly denied access to a resource vital for its daily "politics of survival" (Shiva 1991). Without access to agricultural forest resources the people's ability to secure their livelihood in times of crisis shrank to a minimum. Long cycles of timber production guided the felling plans; coppices were eradicated; financial revenue became the guiding principle for the distribution of forest products and replaced the early principle of "necessity" (*Notdurft*).... Cultivation plans for afforestation meant that ever more patches of grassland...were closed to pasture, grass-cutting or litter collecting. (Hölzl 2010, p. 445)

We can reformulate the conflict described by Marx in terms of temporalities: the future of trees, forest owners, and the state, on one side, and the present of the poor, on the other. This conflict is very different from the one between present and future generations. It opposes those who live in the present, engaged with the necessity of survival, and

Figure I.2. Hunting the wood gatherers. *Le Petit Parisien*, March 3, 1895 (Bibliothèque nationale de France).

those who can afford to look to the future. Keeping trees for the future is certainly an act of sustainability, but it is at the same time an act of extraction from the present. Here, reversing Innerarity's terms, it is the future that colonizes the present.

DISCOUNTING AS A GENERAL FORM

The endless expansion of discounting is troubling, too. Discounting can be found at the intersection of several trends whose universalizing and structuring ambition has been captured in the literature in terms of "the capitalization of almost everything" (Leyshon and Thrift 2007), "the value of everything" (Mazzucato 2018), "the asset condition" (Birch 2018), the "financialization of valuation" (Chiapello 2015), or "the time of investees" (Feher 2017, 2018). These terms signal that the configuration of things in view of them producing future flows of costs and revenues (things that can then be called capital, assets, or investments) is a transformation that is *general*, insofar as it affects "everything" (or "almost everything") and characterizes the advent of a new mode of being in the world and a new kind of epoch. It is this generality that has troubled me most in my exploration of discounting. How has discounting evolved from a *formula*, such as the Faustmann formula in forestry, to a *form*—a form of reasoning, a form of valuing, a form of relating to the future—that is ubiquitous enough to be described as "general"?

When I started writing this book,[9] I did not suspect that the exploration of discounting would lead me to so many different places and themes: from the biopharmaceutical industry and its uncertainty (Chapter 4), through forestry and sustainability (Chapter 2), and capital budgeting and financialization (Chapter 3), to mining and investor-state relations (Chapter 5). Nor did I suspect that all the moments that I was looking at as historical developments—in which discounting emerged, extended its territory, and triggered controversy—would resonate so vividly with moments in the present. At the core of the debates that the exploration of discounting made me traverse resides one fundamental question: the relationship between temporality and valuation. In this relationship is nested the key to the third trouble with discounting. To understand this, we need to move back to its original formulations.

The first formulations of discounting as a technique used to value nonfinancial assets date back to the nineteenth century, not just in forestry, but in the mining industry and the emergence of the railroads, among other places. Although during that period discounting had already been expressed in formulas and had been discussed in the literature, in particular, as to its mathematical specification, for example, the use of simple or compounded rate of interest, its use remained specific to a few niches in the economy and their problems. It was only at the beginning of the twentieth century, in the work of North American economist Irving Fisher, that discounting was formalized as a universal definition of the value of capital, and capital itself was redefined as anything that could engage in a particular relationship with time, oriented toward the future. I will analyze in further detail Fisher's theory in Chapter 1 and present it only briefly here in relation with the problem of discounting as a general form.

In *The Nature of Capital and Income*, first published in 1906, Fisher proposed to define capital in a way that departed from previous debates among economists. These debates, Fisher argued, had never reached consensus on what capital is because they assumed that capital is "a particular kind or species of wealth" (p. 53). What is particular about capital, he proposed instead, is not its nature, but its relationship with time: capital is "wealth in a particular aspect with reference to time" (p. 53). Capital is a "fund" that produces "income," that is, a "stream" or a "flow of services through a period of time" (p. 52). Anything, then, could be capital: a dwelling house, which produces flows of services under the form of shelter or rent, a piano, which produces flows of music, and even bread, which produces flows of nourishment. The relationship between capital and income is the reverse of the relationship between the value of capital and the value of income: physically, it is capital that produces income, but it is the value of income that produces the value of capital. For example, it is the orchard that produces the apples, but it is the value of the apples that produces the value of the orchard (Fisher 1907).

Fisher considers this reverse relationship between capital and income, when envisaged through their value, as a "fundamental principle" commanding that "the value of capital at any instant is derived from the value of the future income which that capital is expected to yield" (p. 188). This principle, he affirms, is "of fundamental importance for the theory of value and prices" for "it means that the value of any article of wealth or property is dependent alone on the future, not the past" (p. 188). He thus generalizes one aspect of the second trouble with discounting, its futurism as it appears in specific instances, into a fundamental economic principle.

The "fundamental principle" formulated by Fisher, which he calls "the principle of present worth" (p. 188) or "the principle of capitalization" (p. 205), entails a rupture with any temporality other than the future, that is, with the past and the present.[10] This radical orientation toward the future is entangled with a relationship to things through their value: capital is defined not through its physical properties, but through its valuation, which is entirely dependent on the future flows that it produces. That is why *anything* becomes capital as soon as it is projected in the future as a stream of flows. The discounting of these flows produces the value of the thing and indicates what should be done with it in a repertoire of actions that includes a range of options such as investing in it or abandoning it, selecting among competing proposals for investment, and shaping such flows to maximize value. It is this singular combination of temporality and valuation that produces the universalizing ambition of discounting as a way to describe all things.

What this does is sublate all particulars into that generalization, literally "discounting" them: not counting them as credible contributions to a thing's value. Thus, when Fisher writes that "the value of any article of wealth or property is dependent alone on the future, not the past" (p. 188), he gives the example of the Panama Canal, whose value "is dependent upon the future expected services, taken in connection with the expected cost of completion" and not upon the past cost of building the canal (p. 188). When Fisher was writing these lines, the United States was taking over the project of the construction of the canal after a complex engineering, political, and military history of construction involving Colombia, France, and the newly independent country of Panama itself (fig. I.3).[11] In 1902, the United States had acquired the option to purchase for $40 million the assets of the French company that had started the construction works; then, in January 1903, it signed a treaty with Colombia that projected a $10 million payment up front and an annual payment to the country in perpetuity, but it was not ratified by the senate of Colombia. The United States then supported the separation of Panama from Colombia and signed a new treaty with Panama as soon as it became independent in November 1903. In 1904, the United States finally purchased the French equipment and paid Panama $10 million up front and an annual payment of $250,000 in exchange of the right to build and indefinitely administer the Panama Canal Zone. But in Fisher's principle of capitalization, the value of the Panama Canal had no longer to do with France, Colombia, or even Panama—it had to do only with the investors—in this case, the United States—who controlled its future.

SPECIFIC CASES

What engages me in this book is this literal discounting of other aspects of valuation by what Fisher called the "fundamental principle," "the principle of present worth," and the ways in which the twinned troubles of the devaluation of the future by the present and the colonization of the present by the future operate within it. Against the grain of the universalization of what Fisher terms "the principle of capitalization," analyzing discounting requires us to attend to specific cases

Figure I.3. W. A. Rogers, "The News Reaches Bogota," *New York Herald* (1903), depicts President Theodore Roosevelt building the Panama Canal while shoveling dirt on Colombia (Everett Collection Historical/Alamy Stock Photo).

in which discounting is put forward as a solution to a problem or is criticized and contested and transformed. Whether the future is worth less than the present, whether instead it is the future that matters, and whether discounting is a general form of relating to the future is an empirical question whose answers emerge in particular situations. Examining some of those situations is the task of the chapters that follow.

Chapter 1 presents a theoretical and methodological approach to discounting, treating it as a situated practice that takes place in particular moments in history and in particular situations in which it is put forward as a solution to problems whose formulations it contributes to shaping. The study of discounting needs to expose the assumptions that underpin it, for it carries both a theory of value, characterized by its radically future-oriented temporality, and a theory of action, insofar as the value statements that it produces matter not so much as truth statements, but as action triggers. Approached in this way, discounting becomes a political technology, and analyzing discounting means dissecting its political qualities: how it dictates what is deemed valuable and hence worth existing, how it guides the allocation of resources, how it governs behaviors, and how it enables or constrains acting on the future.

Chapter 2 analyzes in further detail how the orientation to the future and the weight given to the present produced effects of exclusion and acceleration when, in Europe during the eighteenth and nineteenth centuries, forests started to be valued through the flows of the discounted expenses and revenues that they were likely to yield in the future. It attempts to denaturalize the reasoning that underpinned the development of discounting by highlighting the contradictions that its promoters faced. It further illuminates the troubles with discounting that I have begun to discuss above. The turn to the future raised the question of who is able to embrace the long temporality of the forest; at the same time, the view that time has a cost transfigured the forest into a capital whose value needs to be maximized and whose rotation durations need to be shortened. It examines, as all the subsequent chapters also do, what kind of imprint discounting leaves on some of the natural and technical objects that compose our world—here, not just forests, but factories (Chapter 3) and drugs (Chapter 4).

Chapter 3 follows the spread of discounting in US firms' investment practices since the 1950s and the controversies it triggered in the 1980s, pointing in particular to the role played by management consultants and strategy and finance scholars. It develops what Peter Miller and Christopher Napier (1993) call "genealogies of calculation," which, like all the chapters here, pay attention to the local conditions in which particular technologies of calculation emerge, the discourses with which these technologies are intertwined, the particular characters and problems involved, and the ensembles of practices and rationales of which they become part.

Discounting was mobilized in the pursuit of rationality in management. Among the principles invoked to achieve rationality in management, theorized as the capacity to make decisions that are in the interest of the company's shareholders, two were the constitutive principles of discounting: the orientation toward the future as a source of value and the need to discount that future in comparison with the present. However, when it moved into firms' practices, discounting changed: the redefinition of the discount rate from the rate of interest to the "cost of capital," that is, the reward required by investors, resulted in the disappearance of the future as a matter of concern, that is, as something that counts, because when redefined as the cost of capital, discount rates markedly increased—the worth of the future decreased. This change did not go unnoticed; finance and strategy clashed in a battle over discounting that was a crucial prelude to the advent of financialization.

Chapter 4 takes us, a few decades later, to the thriving period of financialization and examines the contemporary use of discounting in the biopharmaceutical industry, focusing on the intricacies of the estimation of future cash flows and the determination of discount rates for drug development projects. It shows how the critique of discounting has altered: it no longer has to do with whether managers take the future into account in their investment decisions nor with the extent to which they espouse investors' expectations, but with the ways in which they treat the uncertainty of the future. The future is often characterized by its inherent uncertainty, but this uncertainty comes in two different versions—uncertainty as lack of knowledge and uncertainty as the investor's concern. Uncertainty as lack of knowledge is at first glance blatant in the biopharmaceutical industry, but a closer examination reveals how the use of discounting formulas and the metrological infrastructure on which they rely transforms uncertain futures into certain futures. Uncertainty as lack of knowledge seems to vanish, but uncertainty reappears as the investor's concern, materialized in increased discount rates required by investors to shoulder the burden of uncertainty. Thus, once again, in the biopharmaceutical industry, if one judges by the level of the discount rates practiced by the companies operating there, the future appears to be worth much less than the present. But at the same time, the future is the temporality that drives this industry, characterized by its promissory dynamics and the role granted to biotechnology start-ups and venture capital in the development of drugs. The contradictory logic of discounting, simultaneously valuing and devaluing the future, permeates the biopharmaceutical industry. The contradiction resolves when the future is conceived not only as a temporal order, but as a political domain over which investors take control.

One of the most illuminating examples of the ways in which the question of the relevance of the future as the locus of valuation is entangled with the issue of control over the future as a political domain is the object of Chapter 5, which focuses on the nationalization of Chilean copper mines and the calculation of the right price to be paid to investors as a compensation in the event of expropriation by the state. Salvador Allende, who nationalized copper mines in 1971, held the view that the price of the mines should reflect the past: the book value of the investment made by the companies that acquired the mines, minus the "excess profits" that they had generated through their operations. José Piñera Echenique, minister of mines in the government of Augusto Pinochet, introduced discounting in the Chilean mining law of 1981 as a response to Allende's calculation and an attempt to attract investors. In Piñera's view, the price of the mines should reflect the future. The price that investors should be paid if ever the mines were expropriated, Piñera's mining law guaranteed, would be equal to the flows of discounted future costs and revenues that they would have experienced if the mines had not been expropriated.

Inscribing in law that in the event of expropriation, the compensation of investors should be calculated as the net present value of the costs and revenues that investors would have experienced had they not been expropriated produced a curious effect. It produced a new kind of future: a certain (that is, not uncertain) future entirely dominated by investors' expectations, which were granted the rare privilege to be met, no matter what the future might turn out to be.

In all of these cases, the book will argue, discounting—as a valuation device that considers things through the flows that they are likely to yield in the future and that simultaneously translates the value of these future flows in the present by means of the discount rate—has played a central role. It is through this device that forests, corporate projects, drugs, and natural resources have been *capitalized.* In light of the troubling effects of this process, in the conclusion of the book, I turn to the hopes that changing the discount rate or including social and environmental concerns into the cash flows to be discounted could reverse the process or at least "civilize" capitalization, as Michel Callon (2009) has argued for markets. As Jonathan Levy writes, "under capitalism, the process of capitalization has become so economically prevalent that it has become conceivable as a general form of strategic action and valuation" (Levy 2017, p. 501). To denaturalize discounting as a general form and free up other ways of acting on the future in response to the crises of the present, we require "prospective histories that explain how capitalization ever became a plausible way of relating the future to the present in the first instance," as he argues (p. 504). The chapters that follow are one attempt to examine how that happened and to begin to think otherwise about this practice, at once technical and mundane, that has so much influence on the world in which we live and in which we will live in the future.

CHAPTER ONE

What Is Discounting
and How to Study It?

Imagine the following situation. A government wants to purchase forest land or a copper mine from a private owner who may be an individual or a multinational corporation. How should the price to be paid for this forest land or copper mine be calculated? Discounting is a way of determining the value of something in order to set its price. To do so, discounting looks at the future: it contemplates the flows of costs and revenues that the thing being valued is likely to generate over its lifetime and translates the value of these future costs and revenues in the present by applying to them a "discount rate": a number that is supposed to reflect the idea that "a euro tomorrow is worth less than a euro today" and that gets all the more important as the euro in question is distant in time. A just price for this forest land or copper mine, some would say, is a price that corresponds to the "present value" of such discounted future flows.

Now imagine a different situation. At a pharmaceutical company, a decision is to be made between two drug development projects proposed by the Research and Development department. Both look promising, but resources are limited, and the company has to decide which one to pursue and which one to abandon. Discounting is a way of making this decision by considering the drug development project as an investment and determining its value. The decision is supposed to be made rationally, rather than in managers' guts or heads, scarred with their feelings and subjectivities. Value, again, is calculated by projecting the future flows of costs and revenues that the drug is likely to generate (the expenses incurred as the drug candidate moves along the successive phases of clinical development and then the sales that it will bring to the company once it reaches the market), each flow being reduced by a discount rate in order to be brought into the present—and all the more reduced as the flow is distant in time. The sum of these discounted future flows indicates the "present value" of the drug development project and provides our pharmaceutical company with a simple decision-making criterion: if the value of the project is positive, it is worth investing in, and if its value is negative, it should be abandoned. If two projects have positive values, the one to be selected is the one whose value is highest.

This fictional situation is certainly less complex than what a real situation would look like. Many projects would be competing, resources may not be so scarce, and decisions hardly rely on economic calculations alone. Still, discounting techniques are the most widespread tool that firms use to assess projects. The tool has a name: DCF, which stands for "discounted cash flow" analysis. To give one real-life example: in a survey on the valuation practices of US companies operating in different industries, 70 percent of the respondents (chief financial officers) declared they used DCF "always or almost always" to decide which projects to finance (Graham and Harvey 2001).

Another way to look at this is to open a corporate finance textbook. Such a textbook teaches aspiring managers the answer to the two basic problems that they will face: what a firm should invest in, including how much they should invest, and how the cash required for the investment should be raised (Brealey and Myers 1988). Present value is the unequivocal answer to the first problem. One-third of this particular textbook that I opened—which is known as the most authoritative reference in the field of corporate finance—is devoted to the exposition of the principles of discounting and the subtleties of its application and calculation. The study guide to the textbook rubs it in:

This [second] chapter introduces the single most important idea in finance: *present value*. Most investments produce revenues at some later date. Present value tells you how much the prospect of future income is worth today after taking account of the time value of money.... By accepting positive present value projects and rejecting negative present value decisions, financial managers will increase the value of the company. Such increases always serve the best interests of shareholders as long as they can buy and sell shares...in an efficient capital market such as we have in the United States. (D'Ambrosio and Hodges 1988, p. 6, italics in the original)

Imagine now a situation in which policy makers ponder a decision related to environmental policy, for example, whether asbestos should be banned. Like the corporate managers above, policy makers want to be rational and to make the right decision, rather than let either industry lobbyists or environmental activists carry them away. So they will proceed to a similar calculation: look ahead and compare the costs that regulation would incur for industry in the shorter term with the benefits that it will bring for society in the longer term, for example, the value of the human lives that it will allow saving. This calculation has a name, too: CBA, which stands for "cost-benefit analysis" (or sometimes BCA, which stands for "benefit-cost analysis"). Once again, because costs and benefits occur at different points in time, they need to be discounted in order to be made temporally commensurable and brought back to their values in the present.

In his seminal book *Trust in Numbers*, historian of science Theodore Porter (1995) traces the origins of CBA back to the economists-engineers of the French Corps des Ingénieurs des Ponts et Chaussées in the nineteenth century and then the US Army Corps of Engineers at the beginning of the twentieth century. A landmark in the history of CBA in the United States was the 1936 Flood Control Act, which stated that Congress could not authorize projects unless they had been examined by the US Army Corps of Engineers and that this examination should include CBA: "the federal government should improve or participate in the improvement of navigable waters or their tributaries, including watersheds thereof, for flood control purposes if the benefits to whomsoever they accrue are in excess of the estimated costs, and if the lives and social security of people are otherwise adversely affected."[1]

Porter recounts the dubious calculations to which the early estimations of costs and benefits gave way, with dazzling assortments of benefits being proposed by project proponents in order to push the ratio of benefits to costs above 1. Since the 1950s, CBA has been standardized and spread to all kinds of government expenditures and regulatory activities. Executive Order 12866, issued by President Bill Clinton in 1993, provided that "significant regulatory actions" be submitted to CBA and selected if they "maximize net benefits": "In deciding whether and how to regulate, [federal] agencies should assess all costs and benefits of available regulatory alternatives.... Costs and benefits shall be understood to include both quantifiable measures...and qualitative measures.... Further, in choosing among alternative regulatory approaches, agencies should select those approaches that maximize net benefits" (Executive Order 12866 of September 30, 1993, section 1[a]).

Porter's analysis is concerned with the reasons related to political and bureaucratic culture, rather than to economic expertise, that explain the transformation of CBA into "a universal standard of rationality, backed up by thousands of pages of rules" and animated by the "ideal of mechanical objectivity" (Porter 1995, p. 189). He examines CBA through the lens of quantification: the translation of costs and benefits into monetary terms. He is less interested in the other kind of translation that CBA operates, the translation that interests us here: the temporal translation of future costs and benefits when they are brought back to their NPV by means of a discount rate.

This second, temporal translation has tended to disturb the mechanical objectivity of CBA that Porter assumes to have been internalized by its practitioners. The disturbance has been caused by statements produced through CBA such as the following: the value of a human life saved by banning asbestos is $1 million, but if the cancer provoked by asbestos remains latent and causes death 40 years later, this value should be reduced to $22,000 because an event that occurs in 40 years is worth less than an event that occurs today. This statement, as bizarre as it may sound, was inserted by the Office of Management and Budget (OMB) in the policy decision-making process on whether asbestos should be banned that took place in the early 1980s in the United States. It led the Environmental Protection Agency (EPA) to withdraw the proposals that it had drafted. But it also triggered the attention of the House of Representatives Energy Committee, which commissioned a report. The issue leaked in the public sphere: an article in *The New York Times* described the clash between the view of the OMB for which "the practice of discounting reflects the amount of time it takes to get a return for money spent now to protect lives" and "allows available resources to be used more rationally to save more lives" and the view of the congressional committee, for which discounting was not only "morally repugnant," but also dangerous because, if widely adopted, it could "thwart regulation of many toxic substances through the application of cost-benefit criteria" and expose the nation to the risk of "fail[ing] to protect future generations from many serious chemical hazards" (Shabecoff 1985).[2]

Let us imagine one final situation. A household somewhere in the northwestern Ethiopian highlands is offered the following option: receive either an amount of cash, wheat, or salt equal to 13 Ethiopian birr now or a larger amount of cash, wheat, or salt equal to 17 Ethiopian birr one month later (Klemick and Yesuf 2008). The amounts seem derisory if translated in global currency (respectively, US $1.50 and $2.00 at the time of writing); they correspond, however, to at least two days of wages in the area where the respondents lived when the study was conducted and to the World Bank's international poverty line (US $1.25 at that time).

This situation is called a discounting experiment. Economists carry out that kind of experiment on populations that often consist of the nearby reservoir of university students (see, for example, the early study by Richard Thaler [1981]) or, farther away, of households in poor countries. They do this to search for evidence for the presence of discounting in individual decision-making. The common finding is that individuals do indeed discount: they find something now more worthy than the same something later, thereby giving empirical and quantified consistency to the financial principle that "one euro today is worth more than one euro tomorrow" or to the saying that "a bird in the hand is worth two in the bush." They also generally find that the poorer the individuals, the higher their discount rates, thereby opening new avenues for poverty-alleviation programs with ambitions to intervene in the psychology of poor individuals to make their future count more than it does through education or "commitment devices" such as special savings products (Ashraf et al. 2006; Bryan et al. 2010).

STUDYING DISCOUNTING AS PRACTICE, FORMULA, AND THEORY

Governments and just prices, finance and firm investments, policy makers and objective decisions, individuals and behavioral patterns: the kinds of situations in which discounting can be found have little in common except for discounting itself. Here, I study discounting through such situations. This book is not much interested in the links between these situations; it does not account for what and who brought discounting into them so that the analyst can find it there now. Rather, it is interested in the situations themselves: in which ways they are hospitable to the reasoning of discounting, how the issues at stake in them mingle with the statements and the numbers that discounting can produce, and ultimately, what happens when discounting starts being done somewhere. Addressing these questions means approaching discounting as a *situated practice*, instead of a variable that can be readily observed in markets or a natural disposition of individuals or organizations. The practices in which discounting intervenes are equipped with tools such as DCF or CBA. In what follows, I focus on

DCF and delve into the writings of one of its principal designers, US economist Irving Fisher, in order to characterize the peculiar theory of value that it carries. I then explore the different formulas in which this theory of value has been inscribed: DCF as formulated by Fisher, then NPV in corporate finance, and CBA in public policy. To make sense of these formulas, I draw on the literature on performativity and show that discounting is inseparably a theory of value and a theory of action.

A SITUATED PRACTICE

The four situations that I evoked above illustrate how discounting operates: look to the future, make the future commensurate with the present by reducing its value, following the assumption that what is distant in time is worth less than what is proximate. They also illustrate where discounting operates: in the practice of public and private actors, firms and policy makers, economists and managers, organizations and individuals. And they illustrate why it operates: because it serves as a solution to several kinds of problems, such as determining a fair price, making the right decisions by choosing the worthiest investments (be they corporate projects or public policies—the two being more and more akin today), and inducing individuals to care about their future, behave entrepreneurially, and get themselves out of poverty.

While attempting to solve such problems, discounting has given rise to new kinds of problems. Why should prices be based on value derived from the future? Could not the past or the present be more relevant places to look when searching for value, through the costs recorded in accounting systems or the prices observed on the market? Aren't the prices based on valuation through discounting artificially high? And aren't the values produced by discounting too fragile and volatile because they are based on the projection of future flows of costs and revenues, which by definition are uncertain? Doesn't discounting then lend itself to manipulation, serving to confer calculative legitimacy on the most powerful? Aren't the values produced by discounting too low when it comes to long-term and/or risky invest-ments? And aren't discount rates too high, for example in industries such as biopharma? Has discounting become a threat to innovation, productivity, and ultimately growth in industry? And has it become a threat for long-term policy making? Does it deprive policy makers from any objective reason to implement environmental policy, build infrastructure, fight against climate change, and more—all those policies whose benefits are so distant in time that, when discounted, they weigh little against the costs that their implementation would incur in the short term? Isn't it a form of discrimination against the "future generations" to which governments are supposed to be accountable, too? Doesn't discounting lead governments and firms to the same kind of "myopia" that experimental economists observe when they study how individuals make decisions, and that they crit-icize by relating high individual discount rates to poverty? Doesn't this myopia produce effects that are economically or politically harm-ful? And can it be alleviated by acting on discount rates? Can dis-count rates at all be decreased? Is it possible to govern through the discount rate?

These are the kinds of questions that discounting has raised while gradually spreading into firms' and governments' practices since its first appearances in the nineteenth century. It is through such ques-tions that discounting is explored in this book. Addressing them by approaching discounting as a situated practice differs from approaches epitomized by economists' attempts at measuring and altering indi-vidual discount rates. In the perspective of behavioral economics, dis-counting is to be found in people's heads, expressed through their preferences as revealed in economic experiments and prone to mea-surement and comparison, as with the comparison between the dis-count rates of more or less poor individuals. Its effects are to be found in individual behaviors, characterized by trade-offs between con-sumption in the present and savings for the future, and can be miti-gated through interventions such as nudges or commitment devices that more or less delicately force individuals to take the future into account.[3] The questions that economists in this field are interested in, for example, are whether discount rates vary across time (a problem analyzed in the terms of "dynamic inconsistency" and "hyperbolic discounting"), across people (depending on how poor they are, to what extent they are exposed to stress, etc.) and across experimental protocols. Such questions are not part of the scope of this book.

Instead, rather than assuming discounting is simply something that people do, this book looks at when, where, how, and why they do it in observable instances where it has been implemented. Treating it not as a natural disposition located in all individuals, but as a situated practice entails, first, attending to its history, for unlike natural dispositions, practices come into being and change in response to contingent circumstances. The premises of a history of discounting have been sketched by a few studies that have identified its origins in economic thought and its first appearances in economic practices and have shed light on some key moments in its gradual spread in the economy (Brackenborough et al. 2001; Deringer 2018; Faulhaber and Baumol 1988; Pezet 1997; Rubinstein 2003; Scorgie 1996). This book contributes to a historical analysis of discounting, but its objective is not to build a comprehensive history of the tool. Its objective is closer to what is accomplished by genealogies of calculation, which are interested in the local conditions in which particular technologies of calculation emerge, the discourses with which these technologies are intertwined, and the ensembles of practices and rationales, featuring particular characters[4] and problems, of which they become part (Miller and Napier 1993). As the works of Peter Miller (1991), focusing on the DCF formula, and of Frédéric Lordon (2000), on a competing formula known as economic value added (EVA) show, the extension of calculation techniques beyond the academic literature and into firm practices cannot be understood without delving into their interlinkages with certain kinds of actors and certain kinds of macroeconomic imperatives, notably, "growth" and "value creation."

Approaching discounting as a situated practice also means being attentive to situations in which discounting is devised as a solution to a particular problem, embedded in specific narratives, implemented with specialized calculative tools, and applied to specific objects—here, forests, mines, drugs, and public policies. The goal is to understand how actors make sense of discounting, how they translate it into everyday operations, how they calculate with it, what issues they face as they proceed, and how they attempt to solve them and with what consequences—in a nutshell, how discounting matters to its promoters, users, and opponents and what effects it produces on the objects that it encounters. This research design makes the book necessarily incomplete historically and geographically. The kind of completeness it aims at is not related to the uses of discounting or the moments and places in which it appears. Instead, it aims to show the ways in which discounting comes as a solution to problems that it also helps formulate and bring into existence and to illuminate the problems to which the acceptance of discounting as a general practice gives rise in turn.

A THEORY OF VALUE

Discounting practices are instrumented practices. When managers and policy makers engage in discounting, they are equipped with calculative devices[5] that are provided by economists, finance scholars, and consultants and that are formalized in textbooks, policy guidelines and circulars, and best practices. In the four situations I evoked above, these devices already have appeared under the names of DCF and CBA. To put it simply, DCF is what firms call discounting, and CBA is what policy makers call it. They look pretty much the same; however, CBA uses a so-called "social" discount rate, can take the form of a ratio, and has been the object of much less attention from academics and consultants.[6]

If someone were tasked with assigning DCF a date and place of birth, they certainly would be likely to choose 1906 and the publication of Fisher's *Nature of Capital and Income*. As I noted in the Introduction, in this book, Fisher grounds the distinction between capital and income in their relationship to time (Fisher 1906). Capital, he argues, is not "a particular kind or species of wealth," as many authors had tried to define it without reaching consensus, but "wealth in a particular aspect with reference to time" (p. 53). Capital is a "fund," a *"stock of wealth* existing at an *instant* of time"; by contrast, income is a "stream," a *"flow of services* through a *period* of time" (p. 52, italics in the original). For example, "a dwelling house now existing is capital; the shelter it affords or the bringing in of a money-rent is its income" (p. 52). The example is well chosen: a dwelling house is certainly not the first type of capital one would think of; it becomes capital not because it is a particular kind of wealth, but because it engages in a particular relationship with time. Other examples abound in the book: "Is that cigar in your mouth capital?" asks someone, and after some hesitation, the answer ends up being positive (p. 64); the wealth of a private family is capital if the family has decided to "call itself a joint stock company and draw up a balance sheet" (p. 64); a piano and even bread are capital because they produce services, respectively, music and nourishment (p. 106). They are all "instruments" that render "services"; this flow of services forms the "income" yielded by an instrument (p. 101). Income thus consists of "services rendered by capital" (p. 118).

With this definition of capital and income in hand, Fisher goes on to examine the relationship between the value of capital and the value of income. This relationship forms the theoretical backbone of discounting: the value of capital stems from the value of the income that it will—or rather, that it is expected to—produce in the future:

> The fundamental principle which applies here is that the value of capital at any instant is derived from the value of the future income which that capital is expected to yield. The expected services may, of course, not be the actual services. In our ignorance of the future we fix our present valuations on the basis of what we expect the future to be.
>
> The principle of present worth is of fundamental importance for the theory of value and prices. It means that the value of any article of wealth or property is dependent alone on the future, not the past. (Fisher 1906, p. 188)

That value is to be derived solely from the future, and not from the past, is counterintuitive. It means, for example, that costs of production are not taken into account in the determination of value if they belong to the past. Thus, Fisher declares that the value of the Panama Canal "is dependent upon the future expected services, taken in connection with the expected cost of completion," and not upon the past cost of building the canal (p. 188). In *The Rate of Interest* (1907), Fisher further develops this counterintuitive idea through the example of an orchard (Fischer 1907). Imagine an orchard of ten acres that yields 100 barrels of apples a year. What does this tell us about the value of the orchard? Nothing. How can we "pass from quantities to values" and "translate the ten acres of orchard and the 100 barrels of apples into dollars" (p. 13)? For Fisher, "this apparently simple step begs the whole question" of the value of the orchard because "the physical-productivity" of the orchard "does not of itself give any clew [*sic*] to what rate of return on its *value* the orchard yields" (p. 13). If the orchard is valued at $20,000, it is because of what it will return in the future. Passing from physical quantities to values requires reversing the arrow of time and imagining that while it is the orchard that will give birth to the apples, it is these future apples that give value to the present orchard:

> The statement that "capital produces income" is true only in the physical sense; it is not true in the value sense. That is to say, *capital-value does not produce income-value.* On the contrary, income-value produces capital-value. It is not because the orchard is worth $20,000 that the annual crop will be worth $1000, but it is because the annual crop is worth $1000 that the orchard will be worth $20,000. The $20,000 is the discounted value of the expected income of $1000 per annum; and in the process of discounting, a rate of interest of 5 per cent is implied. (Fisher 1907, p. 13, italics in the original)

The rate of interest, as Fisher famously defined it in the opening sentence of that book, is "an index of the preference, in [a] community, for a dollar of present over a dollar of future income" (Fisher 1907, p. 3).

This lies at the heart of discounting: a theory of value that simultaneously and paradoxically both values and devalues the future. It both claims that the future is the source of value (rather than the past, which is the temporality of production) and that the future is less valuable (than the present, which is "preferred" by the community).

Like sociologists who have analyzed money as a commensuration tool that transforms different qualities into a common metric (Espeland and Stevens 1998; Zelizer 1994), we can analyze discounting as a commensuration tool that transforms different temporalities into a common moment—the so-called "present value"—and thus constructs equivalences between the present and the future. These equivalences, however, are grounded in inequalities of worth. They are captured by the rate of interest and the so-called "preference" that it is supposed to express: a kind of "discount," in the most common sense of the term, that is to be applied to the future to make it commensurate with the present.

The rate of interest that translates the future in the present, Fisher notes, is not the "explicit" rate of interest indicated by the bank and written in a contract. It is an "implicit" or "natural" interest rate that is inherent in capital, that is, according to his definition of capital, in anything. This rate is "difficult to work out...definitely...but it has an existence in all capital," writes Fisher (1907, p. 11). In contrast, this book considers questions such as how the discount rate is "worked out" in discounting calculations today, how it has been brought into existence and become "natural," and how its definition and measurement have evolved over time.

A FORMULA

In Fisher's theory, the rate of interest is the link between the value of capital and the value of income. It is the operator that makes it possible to "'capitalize' income" (p. 202), that is, to derive the value of capital from the value of the income that it yields (or, in other words, from the flow of services that it renders): "If, for instance, one holds a property right by virtue of which he will receive, at the end of one year, the sum of $104, the present value of this right, if the rate of interest is 4 per cent, will be $100. If the property is the right to $1 one year hence, its present value is evidently 1/1.04 or $0.962" (Fisher 1906, pp. 202–203). Fisher continues this kind of reasoning with a series of examples of increasingly complex income stream profiles and of goods to which the "principles of capitalization" (p. 205) apply, among which are financial products such as loans and bills of exchange, but also "wealth [that] is in the course of production," goods in transit, wine, and young forests:

> For instance, the maker of an automobile will appraise it, at any of its stages in course of construction, as worth the discounted value of its probable return when subsequently finished and sold, less the discounted value of the costs of construction and selling which still remain.... A cargo leaving Sydney for Liverpool is worth the discounted value of what it will fetch in Liverpool, less the discounted value of the cost of carrying it there. Other classical examples are wine, the value of which is the present worth of what it will be when "mellow" and ready for consumption; and young forests, which are worth the discounted value of the timber they will ultimately form. In Germany and some other countries, such appraisement of forests is now worked out with considerable precision. (Fisher 1906, p. 205)

All these examples are brought into a "mathematical formula for the capital-value of any series of income installments" (p. 219), which states that the present value (V) of successive installments of income $(a_1, a_2, \text{etc.})$ accruing at various times distant from the present instant by the intervals $t_1, t_2,$ etc. is equal to the sum of these installments, reduced by the rate of interest i, to the power of time $t_1, t_2,$ etc.

$$V = \Sigma \frac{a}{(1+i)^t}$$

Figure 1.1. Fisher's formula for the value of capital (1906, p. 383)

Someone looking for the birth of discounting could have stopped here, but she would have missed a lot. A statement such as "Irving Fisher invented DCF in 1906" would be empirically wrong. As Fisher notes himself, this calculation was already present among German foresters: the so-called Faustmann formula for the valuation of forests (Faustmann 1968) to which I have devoted Chapter 2, preceded Fisher's formula by more than fifty years. It also took another fifty years for Fisher's formula for the value of capital to move into the practices of firms, evolving from a mathematical formula into the product called DCF and sold by consultants to managers in corporations who had started to worry about knowing the value of capital and making rational decisions, as we will see in Chapter 3.

In the process, the formula itself has changed and has multiplied. Actually, we should not talk about the DCF *formula*, but about the DCF *formulas*, in the plural. Today, DCF formulas can be found in places as distinct as corporate finance and public policy. Let us take a quick look at both. Here is what DCF looks like in a textbook on corporate finance (Brealey and Myers 1988, p. 30): a formula stating that the NPV of an asset that produces cash flows each year is equal to the sum of these cash flows (C_t), reduced by a discount rate (r_t), minus the initial cash flow (C_0):

$$NPV = C_0 + \sum \frac{C_t}{(1 + r_t)^t}$$

Figure 1.2. DCF in a corporate finance textbook (Brealey and Myers 1988, p. 30)

The change that is worth noticing concerns the definition of the discount rate. The textbook explains that "the present value of a delayed payoff may be found by multiplying the payoff by a discount factor," which is "expressed as the reciprocal of 1 plus a *rate of return*" (Brealey and Myers 1988, p. 12, italics in the original).

$$Discount\ factor = \frac{1}{1+r}$$

Figure 1.3. The discount factor in corporate finance (Brealey and Myers 1988, p. 12).

The rate of return is defined as "the rate that investors demand for accepting delayed payment" (p. 12), also referred to as the "hurdle rate" or the "opportunity cost of capital" (p. 13) — "hurdle rate," because it operates as a threshold that investment projects must overcome in order to be deemed valuable, and "opportunity cost," because it is "the return forgone by investing in the project rather than investing in securities" (p. 13), a kind of sacrifice made by the investor in compensation for which she claims a reward, as I will discuss in particular in Chapter 4. While referring to Fisher's "the pioneering work," the corporate finance textbook complicates the justification of discounting by adding to the idea of the preference of the present over the future, which economists view as something inherent in people's thinking, the idea of risk and return, which characterizes the figure of the investor:

> Cash flows are discounted for two simple reasons: first, because a dollar today is worth more than a dollar tomorrow, and second, because a risky dollar is worth less than a safe one. Formulas for PV and NPV are numerical expressions of these ideas. We look for rates of return prevailing in capital markets to determine how much to discount for time and for risk. By calculating the present value of an asset, we are in effect estimating how much people will pay for it if they have the alternative of investing in the capital markets. (Brealey and Myers 1988, p. 24)

The supremacy of the notion of risk and return in the definition of the discount rate is clearly visible in the study guide to this textbook, where the argument relating to the preference for the present is elided:

Suppose you have an investment which is expected to pay $100 in 1 year. How much is it worth to you today? Well, it all depends. On what? On the return you expect to make on other investments of comparable risk. If comparable-risk investments offer a return of 10 percent, an investment of $90.91 (=$100/1.1) today also is expected to produce $100 in 1 year. Your original investment has a *present value* of $90.91. If it costs only $80, it has a *net present value* of $10.91 (=$90.91–$80). It makes you better off by $10.91 relative to the alternative investments. (D'Ambrosio and Hodges 1988, p. 6)

Chapter 3 will argue that this seemingly innocuous change in the definition of the discount rate, from the cost of time (related to a supposedly human preference for the present or to the presence of a bank that offers a rate of interest) to the cost of capital (defined as the return required by investors who seek for investments that will make them "better off … relative to alternative investments") has been a key driver in what is commonly referred to as the "financialization" of the economy. Embedding the notions of uncertainty, opportunity, and risk and reward in the calculative devices that managers use to value the projects subjected to their assessment, this change instills the view of the "investor" in firms' everyday decision-making practices.

Some may find the link from a (small) formula to the (big) firm, and even to the economy, somehow far-fetched; however, it is not only acknowledged but also positively emphasized in the literature in corporate finance. For instance, the textbook examined above links the concept of net present value to the principle agent and shareholder value theories that are commonly associated with financialization: "The concept of net present value allows efficient separation of ownership and management of the corporation. A manager who invests only in assets with positive present values serves the best interests of each one of the firm's owners—regardless of differences in their wealth and tastes" (Brealey and Myers 1988, p. 24).

Let us now turn to DCF formulas in public policy, using as an example a report on environmental cost-benefit analysis (CBA) published by the Organisation for Economic Co-operation and Development (OECD 2018). CBA serves as a decision rule in public policy, stating that a policy should be accepted if its benefits outweigh its costs, with benefits and costs being measured as increases and decreases in individuals' well-being, translated in monetary terms. Although the notion of present value (PV) or NPV is absent here, CBA espouses Fisher's theory of value: the value of a policy is equal to the sum of the discounted costs and benefits that it will generate in the future. If this value is positive, the policy is worth implementing. In other words, policy is capital that produces income. The report justifies the use of discounting by the need to account for time:

> CBA is explicit that time needs to be accounted for in a rigorous way. This is done through the process of discounting. This rightly remains controversial, but it is impossible not to discount—or to (in one way or another) decide how impacts in the future, including the very distant future, should be regarded compared to present impacts. Note that the treatment of time in other decision-making guidance is far from clear. But failing to discount means using a discount rate of 0% which means that USD 1 of gain 100 years from now is treated as being of equal value to USD 1 of gain now. (OECD 2018, pp. 32–33)

The discount factor, which the corporate finance textbook above defined on the basis of the rate of return demanded by investors, is qualified here in the terms of a "temporal weight," which determines that "a unit of benefit or cost in the future has a lower weight than the same unit of benefit or cost now" (pp. 35–36).

$$DF_t = \frac{1}{(1+r)^t}$$

Figure 1.4. The discount factor in public policy (OECD 2018, p. 36)

This directly leads to a DCF formula identical to the one we saw in the corporate finance textbook, except the term "NPV" is missing,[7] and cash flows are replaced by "the flow of benefits and costs" (p. 36):

$$\sum\nolimits_{i,t} \frac{B_{i,t} - C_{i,t}}{(1+r)^t}$$

Figure 1.5. DCF in public policy (OECD 2018, p. 36)

There are two notable differences between DCF formulas in corporate finance and public policy, though. The first one concerns the treatment of risk: while in corporate finance risk is integrated in the discount rate and intertwined with the idea of reward, in public policy, the problem of risk is acknowledged, but dealt with outside the discount rate, through the use of expected values (multiplying future benefits and costs by the likelihood that they will occur) and sensitivity analysis ("using different values of the parameters about which there is uncertainty" [p. 36], for example, the discount rate).[8] The second difference, relatedly, concerns the definition of the discount rate. In public policy DCF formulas, the discount rate is called a "social discount rate." How is this social discount rate to be calculated? The report discusses various "candidates for the social discount rate," namely, the social rate of time preference and the social opportunity cost of capital (p. 201), which, as their designations show, vary according to whether they emphasize the argument of the preference for the present or the argument of the rate of return in the justification of discounting. The social opportunity cost of capital bears a striking resemblance with the cost of capital in corporate finance: it is defined as "the alternative rate of return that a government could obtain by investing public funds elsewhere in the economy, or, the cost of financing a public project from the capital markets" (p. 204). When government acts as an investor, the differences between DCF formulas in places as distinct as corporate finance and public policy easily blur.

With these DCF formulas in mind, let us now return to Fisher's formula for the value of capital with which we started (fig. 1.1). I contend that Fisher's contribution to the history of discounting is not to be understood as a "great moment" of invention (Rubinstein 2003), but as a forceful attempt at formulating in both literary and mathematical terms a theory of value that seemed to be at odds with common sense. The idea that the value of capital (let us repeat again: that is, according to Fisher's definition, the value of anything as soon as it is involved in a particular relationship with time) is to be derived from the future was not, and for many is still not, straightforward. Why does the value of the Panama Canal have nothing to do with what it has cost to construct it? The use of peculiar examples—an automobile, wine, forests, a dwelling house, bread—and their gradual integration into a mathematical formula that could be applied to any piece of capital (i.e., to anything) is an indication of both Fisher's *coup de maître* and of the effort required to espouse the form of reasoning inherent in his theory of value.

Fisher formulated discounting and its "principle of capitalization" as a universal theory of value by detaching it from the case of peculiar goods such as forests and expressing it in a formula that had the capacity to embrace any kind of object and transform it into capital. The proposition that anything is capital as soon as it engages in a particular future-oriented relationship with time actually means that anything can become capital as soon as it lends itself to the reasoning and formulas of discounting. What it means for something to become capital and how discounting intervenes in this process of capitalization is one of the central issues explored in this book.

A THEORY OF ACTION

Discounting is a theory of value expressed in a mathematical formula that links, by means of the discount rate, the value of capital with the value of the income that it is expected to generate, or, in other words, the value of anything in the present with the value of the services that it is likely to render in the future. Fisher's formula, which was known earlier as the Faustmann formula in forestry and later as the DCF formula in the evaluation of investments more broadly, is used in this book as a way to trace discounting. While the book is mainly interested in the historical sociology of discounting as a situated practice, rather than in the history of ideas and economic theories such as Fisher's, it uses the discounting formula as an entry point for accessing discounting practices. At this point, we need to ask what a sociological analysis of an economic formula may consist of and how it can be carried out.

Performativity is the short answer to this question (MacKenzie et al. 2007). Performativity is the characteristic of a statement that helps bring into existence the reality that it purports to describe. In his theory of speech acts, philosopher of language John Austin (1962) singles out performative utterances (e.g., "I declare you husband and wife") as distinct from constative utterances (e.g., "the book is on the table"). Unlike constative statements, he observes, performative statements cannot be true or false, but they can succeed or fail, according to whether the "felicity conditions" that they require are met in a given situation. Performatives "do things," perform an action that is not only the act of saying something. They do not refer to a world that is supposed to be external to them and that they describe more or less truthfully; rather, they intervene in a world that they thereby alter.

A statement such as "the value of capital at any instant is derived from the value of the future income which that capital is expected to yield" can be analyzed as either constative or performative. In the first case, it is its degree of truthfulness that matters. A critique of Fisher's theory of value would then consist of finding a better, truer, theory of value—a path that has been taken by Marxists in their critique of "fundamental value" and that, as some authors argue, has led them out of phase with the empirical transformations of categories of value in financial practices (Bryan and Rafferty 2013). In the second case, it is its degree of felicity that matters. A critique of Fisher's theory of value would then consist of observing what are the felicity conditions that it requires and how it has intervened in the world, what alterations it has produced, and what effects it has generated in the situations in which it has been mobilized. Of course, it is hardly likely to find situations in which someone pronounces a statement such as "the value of capital at any instant is derived from the value of the future income which that capital is expected to yield." What one easily finds, however, is a myriad of situations in which people make discounting calculations and "use" the DCF formula.

Probably the best-known performative formula is the Black-Scholes equation analyzed by Donald MacKenzie (MacKenzie 2003, 2006; MacKenzie and Millo 2003). The Black-Scholes formula allows estimating the price of an option.[9] Tracing back the history of this formula, its "invention" and use, MacKenzie arrives at the conclusion "that the world came to embrace the Black-Scholes equation was in part because the world was changing...and in part because the equation...changed the world" (MacKenzie 2003, p. 851). The world in which the formula was born in the 1970s was certainly hospitable: the derivatives market had gained in legitimacy, and financial models had started to acquire an important cultural role. But most importantly for the performativity argument, the formula altered the world in which it was inserted, and interestingly, it altered it in such a way that the world started resembling more and more to the formula's hypotheses and results. Because market participants were using the formula (for example, the sheets of theoretical option prices that the "spin-off" firm founded by Black was selling), theoretical and observed prices started converging. The availability of the formula fostered exchanges; one of the consequences of the increased volume of transactions in the market was to bring the hypotheses on which the formula was built (such as the absence of transaction costs), which were "wildly unrealistic" (p. 852) at the time when Black and Sholes's article on options pricing was published, much closer to reality—a reality that had been altered by the use of the formula.

The performativity described by MacKenzie for the Black-Sholes formula is a specific type of performativity in which the practical adoption of a theory or a model has an effect on its verisimilitude. MacKenzie calls this "Austinian performativity," in comparison with "generic performativity," which refers to the idea that the economy is performed by economic practices (marketing, accountancy, etc.) and by practices of metrology (MacKenzie 2004). However, Austinian performativity is not what we will be looking for in our analysis of the DCF formula for several reasons: First, because this definition of performativity remains trapped in the "truth" question, the question from which Austin tried to escape by focusing on performative utterances; second, because it inevitably leads to a proliferation of examples in which there is or there is not performativity. MacKenzie and Spears (2014b) have coined the term "counter-performativity" for the cases in which the adoption of a theory or model reduces its verisimilitude. They have also argued that the performativity of financial models is contingent upon the "evaluative cultures" in which they are embedded (MacKenzie and Spears 2014a). Ekaterina Svetlova (2012) has developed this latter argument in the case of the DCF formula specifically. In her study of investment practices in asset management companies and banks, she shows that "models are not performative *per se*" and that their "performative power...depends on the way they are used" (p. 421), in particular, on the extent to which the users of models apply their judgment and on the institutionalized investment process in which the use of models occurs.

The type of performativity that I will be looking for in my analysis of the DCF formula is closer to what MacKenzie calls "generic performativity" and ultimately refers to the perspective opened by Michel Callon in his introduction to *The Laws of the Markets* (Callon 1998a), in which he argues for the "the embeddedness of economic markets in economics" and identifies "the essential contribution of economics in performing the economy." Reflecting on the case of the Black-Scholes formula, Callon writes:

A formula that previously functioned in a paper world…subsequently functions, after many investments, in a world of computers and silicon, algorithms, professional skills, and cleverly adjusted institutions. We could say that the formula has become true, but it is preferable to say that the world it supposed has become actual. The supposed world has gained in precision, weight, robustness, and extension, through the intense work of articulating, experimenting, and observing that has been required to produce the gradual, mutual adjustment of socio-technical *agencements* and formulas. (Callon 2007, p. 320)

Economics, like all the natural and social sciences, are performative insofar as they "contribute toward enacting the realities that they describe" (Callon 2007, p. 315). The conditions of felicity of a statement (a theory, a formula) produced by economics depend on the mutual "adjustment" of this statement and "the world in which it functions" (p. 321). Callon calls this adjustment, which is "never given in advance and always requires specific investments" (p. 321), a process of "performation."

The theory of performativity that informs the analysis of the DCF formula in this book is certainly closer to Callon's definition of performativity as a process of performation than to a definition of performativity as a characteristic that certain types of statements would possess while others would not, either inherently or because of the "evaluative" or "calculative" cultures in which they are put (MacKenzie and Spears 2014a; Svetlova 2012). Here, it is not a question of whether discounting is performative, counterperformative, or not performative at all. In fact, "is discounting performative?" may well not be the right question. Asking it anyway, however, and answering it is one way to clarify how performativity functions as a critical concept in this book.

Is discounting performative? The answer is no, if performativity is envisaged as a linear theory of innovation in which something produced by economists (such as Fisher) moves more or less smoothly into the hands of practitioners. As we have seen and will see again at length, discounting was born in, before, and after Fisher's theory of capital, and its births and movements have been accompanied by the astonishment provoked by the counterintuitive reasoning it required and the controversies triggered by the effects it engendered. The answer is no again if performativity is envisaged as a variant of technological determinism in which artifacts (in this case, theoretical statements or formulas) impose behaviors. As we will see, the effects of discounting are ambiguous and emergent, and its users are cautious and reflexive.

The answer is yes, however, if performativity is envisaged as an invitation to look into the theories that calculative devices embed. As I have been emphasizing, discounting embeds a peculiar theory of value, but also a peculiar theory of time that, when translated into practice, has produced significant consequences. The answer thus is yes again, if performativity is envisaged as an invitation to examine those consequences, to search for the effects that calculative devices produce on the objects with which they come to be entangled.

This latter dimension of what could be called the performativity of discounting, focusing on the effects that it produces, is of particular importance here. As we have seen in the discussion of Fisher's theory above, discounting is involved in the process through which things become capital as they are conceived and valued as sources of future income. Symmetrically, discounting also is involved in the process through which things do not become capital because they are not deemed valuable enough as sources of future income, and not becoming capital, in this case, means simply not coming into existence. In other words, discounting is an instrument for making decisions about what will occur and what will not occur; an instrument for allocating resources among alternative destinations. Fisher gives the example of land and the choice between the different purposes for which it can be used:

> Land may be used for grazing, agriculture, building, or recreation purposes. Tools may be employed in a variety of ways, and the same is true of innumerable articles of wealth, particularly when taken in combination.

What determines the choice of the series of uses to which any given instrument may be put? Evidently that series of uses or income stream will be selected which yields the maximum present value. Thus, if land used for grazing purposes will yield a net service of $1000 a year forever, and interest is taken at four per cent, its value for grazing purposes is evidently $25,000. If, in like manner, the capital-value for some other use, say for growing wheat, is $20,000, it is clear that the land will be employed for grazing rather than for growing wheat. (Fisher 1906, p. 221)

The crucial link that Fisher highlights here is between valuing things through discounting and making decisions about them. In the quote above, the justification of this link lies in one word: "evidently"—it is taken to be self-evident. Since then, corporate finance theory has elaborated on the link between discounting and decision-making: when managers make investment decisions with discounting, they are making the right decisions because they serve the interest of their shareholders. The study guide to the corporate finance textbook that I examined above explains clearly how managerial work is to be understood as the work of making decisions whose ultimate criterion is shareholder value and whose key instrument is DCF and the NPVs that it calculates:

In order to carry on business, companies spend money to purchase various real assets such as factories, plants, and machinery. Decisions regarding which specific assets to purchase (or invest in) are the company's investment decisions.... What criterion is to be applied to select the best decisions? Remember, legally the shareholders are the ultimate owners of the firm and the role of the manager is that of an agent acting on behalf of the owners. Therefore, the financial manager's duty is to make decisions that will benefit shareholders, that is, will increase the value of their stake in the firm. (D'Ambrosio and Hodges 1988, p. 1)

How can the managers of a large company make decisions that will win the approval of all their stakeholders (who may number thousands)? The answer is by using present value. When managers make an investment with a positive net present value, they can be certain that they are making every stakeholder better off.... Managers don't need to keep asking owners, "Would you like me to do this?" Instead they can ask themselves, "Does this investment offer more than the capital market rate?" (D'Ambrosio and Hodges 1988, p. 6)

Thus, discounting is not only a tool for determining the value of things and transforming them into capital, but also a tool for deciding which things and activities should be brought into existence (such as grazing or growing wheat, in the example above) and how they should be managed, that is, what should be done with them, how they should be taken care of, and what they should look like (for example, how long the trees in a forest should be left standing until they are finally cut in order to be exploited). In other words, discounting is not only the literary and mathematical formulation of a theory of value; it also forms the basis for a theory of action.

To formulate this argument more clearly, we will need to leave the theoretical terrain of performativity while keeping in mind the key insights that we have drawn from it: abandon the question of the truthfulness (or "verisimilitude") of the values produced by calculative devices and conceive these devices in relation to the "worlds" that they suppose and in which they function; follow the process through which devices and their worlds are mutually altered (and sometimes adjusted to each other); seek for the effects that devices produce in their worlds without assuming that these effects will either go along with or counter any preexisting assumptions or intentions.

THE POLITICAL QUALITIES OF DISCOUNTING

The first part of this chapter argued that methodologically, discounting should be studied simultaneously as a situated practice and as a formula that carries a theory of value and a theory of action. The second part of this chapter provides a complementary, conceptual, answer to this question, arguing that discounting is a political technology (Doganova 2021). That technologies of calculation are political technologies has been demonstrated in the literature, for example with regard to insurance (Collier 2014; Knights and Vurdubakis 1993). More specifically, studying discounting as a political technology requires characterizing its "political qualities."[10] Four such qualities will be made visible throughout the chapters that follow. They relate to the contribution of discounting to making things by making them valuable, allocating resources, governing behavior, and acting on the future.

MAKING THINGS (VALUABLE)

The first political quality of discounting, making things valuable, is related to its performativity: in the understanding of performativity I outlined above, the effects that discounting generates as it is being thought and used, the ways in which it alters its "worlds" and hence our world, the imprint that it leaves on the objects that it encounters, and the shape that it gives to the entities that surround us. Discounting is a valuation device (Doganova 2019); like other valuation devices, it is an instrument for "making things valuable" but also for "making things" (Doganova and Muniesa 2015, p. 122). In other words, valuation is a process that not only transforms the "value" of things, by, say, increasing their economic value or transforming their environmental value into economic value, as in the case of clean technologies or carbon markets (Doganova and Karnoe 2015; Doganova and Laurent 2019), but that transforms the things being valued themselves.

This transformation can be more or less radical. It can touch upon the very existence of things, as I will discuss below when developing the second political quality of discounting, because things to which resources are allocated have higher chances to come into existence than things to which resources are not allocated. It can touch upon the form of things when they are configured so as to maximize their value. As I will discuss in detail in Chapter 2, a forest valued through discounting is not the same forest as a forest valued through annual yields; for example, its trees are felled at an earlier age. But the ways in which discounting "touches" upon the form of things are not predictable; in other words, the effects produced by the valuation device are not contained in the device or determined by it.

Science and technology studies (STS) provide helpful resources to think about the effects of discounting. Elaborating on Langdon Winner's famous question "Do artifacts have politics?" (1980), we could ask whether valuation devices such as discounting have politics and, more importantly, how these politics should be analyzed. Winner's argument starts with a problem of height, too—not the height of trees standing in a forest, but the height of bridges over the parkways on Long Island, New York. These overpasses, observes Winner, are surprisingly low. While many would see this "detail of form as innocuous" (p. 123), Winner spots in it the effect produced by a technology, a technology "deliberately designed to achieve a particular social effect": keep "poor people and [B]lacks, who normally use public transit...off the road because the twelve-foot tall buses could not get through the overpasses" (p. 124). This example serves to illustrate one of the ways in which "artifacts can contain political properties" (p. 123) or have "political qualities" (p. 121), as Winner puts it. For him, bridges are not political technologies per se, but they can become so in particular settings such as this one. Winner calls such technologies "flexible": the same artifact, in a different setting, may have very different political consequences. Other technologies, such as nuclear and solar energy, are, by contrast, "inherently political": "to choose them is to choose a particular form of political life" (p. 128).

Like the bridges that impede the poor from living in the suburbs, discounting impedes certain entities from being counted: it literally *dis-counts* them. The entities dis-counted by discounting are characterized by their temporality: they belong to the past or to the distant future. The past is simply not counted in the valuations produced through discounting. As we saw above, the cost of production of the

Panama Canal is irrelevant to its "present value." The distant future counts less than the near future: the value of something occurring in one year (for example, the cost of a drug development project or an environmental policy) is reduced by the discount rate at the power of 1 (e.g., 1.05, if the discount rate is 5 percent); the value of something occurring in 10 years (for example, the revenues that a firm pockets from a new drug that has reached the market) is reduced by the discount rate at the power of 10 (e.g., 1.6, if the discount rate is 5 percent); the value of something occurring in 100 years (for example, the damages provoked by climate change) is reduced by the discount rate at the power of 100 (e.g., 131.5, if the discount rate is 5 percent). The effect of discounting on the future generations affected by climate change is akin to the effect of Winner's bridges on the poor: they are partitioned off from the present, just as the poor are partitioned off from the suburbs.

However, the analogy stops here. Albeit discounted and counting for less, future generations unquestionably are taken into account in the present. They have featured in government decisions to decrease social discount rates: "the concern for future generations," for example, was one of the reasons justifying the revision of the French discount rate from 8 percent to 4 percent in 2005 (Lebègue 2005, p. 5). Albeit discriminated against by the mechanics of discounting, (at least some) long-term innovation projects such as drug development are carried out, and (at least some) environmental policies are implemented. We thus could say, like Winner, that discounting is a "flexible" political technology that sometimes does certain things and sometimes does not. Or we could say, as other theories in STS have done in the wake of Winner's analysis, that the distinction between the inherent characteristics of a technology and the settings in which it is used has to be suspended for the analysis of its political qualities to proceed.

Suspending the a priori distinction between technology and what is typically referred to as its context, its use, or, more broadly, society was the premise of actor-network theory (ANT). Madeleine Akrich's

(1992) proposals on how to "de-scribe" technical artifacts are particularly insightful for the analysis of the politics of a valuation device such as discounting. Against technological determinism and social constructivism, Akrich argues that "technical objects participate in heterogeneous networks that bring together actants of all types and sizes" (p. 206). Studying technical objects means studying these heterogeneous networks and hence moving constantly "between the technical and the social…between the inside and the outside of technical objects" (p. 206). Akrich uses the notion of a "script" to refer to the "vision of…the world" that innovators "inscribe in the technical content of [a] new object" (p. 208): the users to which the object is addressed, with their competences and desires, and the other objects with which the new object will cohabit through the process of its production and consumption. This script, however, is not defined once and for all. Unlike Winner's bridges, the script is challenged through the "negotiations between the innovator and the potential users" (p. 208) as the projected users gradually transform into real users or, sometimes, into no users at all. For the analyst who engages in the "description" of a technology, this means going "back and forth continually…between *the world inscribed in the object* and *the world described by its displacement*" (pp. 208–209, italics in the original).

It is to precisely this kind of "back and forth" that the history of discounting will lead us. "The world inscribed" in discounting is the theory of value and action that I started discussing above through the writings of Fisher. I will pursue this discussion throughout the book. To the inequalities of worth derived from inequalities in time (the past versus the future, the near future versus the distant future), I will add another type of inequality, an inequality that stems from the distinctions drawn between the actors who are supposed to have or who are granted the capacity to act over different temporal domains (poor or local populations, states, investors).

However, the world inscribed in discounting is not realized without trouble as the device expands in the worlds of its users. Unlike the entities discriminated against by the bridges in Winner's account, the entities discriminated against by discounting protest. The effects produced by discounting have been noticed and debated: among others, by the foresters who "discovered" discounting in the nineteenth century and worried about the acceleration in rotation lengths that such calculations recommended and by practitioners and academics who have worried, since the 1980s, about the short-termism induced by DCF and CBA in, respectively, corporate strategy and public policy. "The world described by [the] displacement of discounting" is thus a world in which the device undergoes transformation (in particular, the definition and the level of the discount rate) concomitantly with its users and observers, who not only change what they do once they encounter discounting (think in a different way about value, make certain decisions, engage into certain activities...) but also reflect about this device, tinker with it, alter its contents, analyze and criticize its effects, and contest them. In other words, discounting matters, but not in a kind of automatic, unquestioned way, merely discharging its theory of value and action over an inert world. It matters because it has become part and parcel of our world, and the entities that it encounters have to deal with it. Analyzing the politics of discounting thus means exploring from scratch what happens in particular situations of encounters with discounting.

ALLOCATING RESOURCES

One of the most troubling effects of discounting has to do with decisions about the allocation of resources. Herein lies its second political quality.[11] This political quality directly follows from the question raised by Fisher in the quote I discussed above: "What determines the choice of the series of uses to which any given instrument may be put?" And it follows from the answer that discounting provides to this question: "Evidently that series of uses or income stream will be selected which yields the maximum present value" (Fisher 1906, p. 221). There is of course nothing "evident" about the choice of land

being used for "grazing, agriculture, building, or recreation purposes." Controversies on the use of land in saturated urban areas, for
example, which bring to bear concerns for the environment against
concerns for the lack of housing and the skyrocketing prices of real
estate, are a clear indication of the political charge of such choices.
The "evidence" in question is part and parcel of the political effect
of discounting: political decisions instrumented with discounting,
either in the shape of DCF calculations in firms or CBA calculations
in government agencies, become "rational" decisions, and hence the
"right" decisions.

Such decisions about the allocation of resources echo the problem of the distribution of wealth in political economy and at the same
time redirect the focus from the social groups who benefit or lose from
distribution to the entities who come into existence or are forsaken
because resources are allocated or not to their development or maintenance. Of course, these entities do not exist independently from social
groups. The case of drug development discussed in Chapter 4 perfectly illustrates this point: decisions about which drug development
projects are to be initiated or pursued and which ones are to be put
on hold are ultimately decisions about which diseases stand a chance
to be treated and which ones run the risk of being "neglected." Current controversies over the high prices of drugs for orphan diseases,
such as the new "most expensive ever drug" Zolgensma (Stein 2019),
are another instantiation of this problem: Can millions of dollars be
devoted to diseases that affect only "rare" patients, while millions of
patients are suffering from other uncured diseases (Doganova and
Rabeharisoa 2022)? Older controversies on the use of forests, discussed in Chapter 2, point to the same problem: If maintaining forests for the long term, in an effort of rationalization supported by the
state's concern for the public interest, entails detaching them from the
short-term needs of the rural populations who live nearby, how can
we justify the transformation of forests into old-growth timber highly
valued for market and military purposes, rather than into wood with

low economic but high substantial value, used for immediate and local purposes such as warming? These are the kinds of "worlds" in which discounting performs.

Discounting frames responses to such questions in terms of rationality and truth. The high prices of drugs are justified as the result of discounting calculations, featuring estimations of the value that they will bring to "society,"[12] and high discount rates are justified by high levels of uncertainty. The right moment when trees should be felled—neither too early, nor too late—is explained as the result of discounting calculations in which rotation length is set so as to maximize the present value of the forest. Rational decision-making, equipped with discounting calculations, is akin to the search for the "true value" of listed companies in financial markets. As Horacio Ortiz (2014b, p. 42) argues, financial value is characterized in terms of its truth: the "true value" of a company is seen as its so-called "fundamental" or "intrinsic" value," equal to the sum of its future cash flows discounted at the rate of the cost of capital. Beyond financial markets, the prices and values calculated with discounting are supposed to express a certain truth, too: "the fundamental principle," as Fisher called it, "that the value of capital at any instant is derived from the value of the future income which that capital is expected to yield" (p. 188).

In *The Birth of Biopolitics*, Michel Foucault (2008) argues that one of the specific features of the liberal art of government is the constitution of the market as a site of the formation of truth. With liberalism, the market turns from a "site of jurisdiction" into a "site of veridiction": while the prices fixed in the market used to be the expression of some kind of justice—they were "just" in the sense that they had "a certain relationship with work performed, with the needs of the merchants, and, of course, with the consumers' needs and possibilities" (p. 30)—from the middle of the eighteenth century on, they became the expression of some kind of truth. Foucault describes the liberal idea of the "true price" in the following terms: "When you allow the market to function by itself according to its nature, according to its natural truth, if you like, it permits the formation of a certain price which will be called, metaphorically, the true price, and which will still sometimes be called the just price, but which no longer has any connotations of justice. It is a certain price that fluctuates around the value of the product" (Foucault 2008, p. 31).

The history of discounting reveals another shift, beginning in the middle of the nineteenth century and evident in Fischer's writings at the beginning of the twentieth: the site of veridiction moves from the market to economic calculation. The "true" price is one that still "fluctuates around the value of the product," but it is precisely this "value" that becomes the center of the problem. A price becomes "just" if it expresses the "true value" of the thing being priced. And this "true value" lies in the flows of revenues that this thing, as capital, is likely to generate in the future, corrected by a discount rate.

GOVERNING BEHAVIOR

One of the rare sociological analyses of discounting is Miller's account of the spread of DCF in the United Kingdom in the 1960s (Miller 1991). Miller's interest lies in discounting as a case of innovation in accounting; the question he asks is how DCF has moved from an initially controversial proposition that made accountants raise an eyebrow to an established method in corporate practice. His answer highlights the role of a particular actor—government bodies—that saw in discounting an instrument to "act at a distance" on firms' decisions by imposing a method of calculation and setting the discount rate, and the operation of a particular process—"problematization"—through which discounting appeared as a solution to the problem of economic growth with which government was concerned and for the sake of which it sought to ensure the quality of investment decisions of managers within firms. "Action at a distance," as he defined it,

> refers to the possibility of a particular point becoming a centre with the capacity to influence other points that are distant, yet without resorting to

direct intervention. The points in question can be government agencies, individual enterprises or even individual managers, and the distance that separates them can be either geographical or administrative. In the context of this paper the notion of action at a distance refers to the attempts by government and other agencies to exert influence over the investment decisions of both private enterprises and nationalized industries through the use of a particular calculative technology. (Miller 1991, pp. 738-39)

This form of action at a distance lies at the heart of the third political quality of discounting. Discounting is a political technology insofar as it is a "technology of government" in the definition given to this term by works in the social studies of accounting that draw on Foucault's conception of "governmentality." In a programmatic article that sets out to renew the analysis of the exercise of political power in liberal democratic societies, Miller and Nicholas Rose (1990) identify different mechanisms for "governing economic life," from centralized economic planning to calculative procedures and management techniques within firms. "Technologies of government" consist in "the actual mechanisms through which authorities of various sorts have sought to shape, normalize and instrumentalize the conduct, thought, decisions and aspirations of others in order to achieve the objectives they consider desirable" (p. 8). Miller and Rose argue that the analysis of such technologies of government, among which are mundane calculative devices, is crucial to understanding modern forms of rule:

> To understand modern forms of rule, we suggest, requires an investigation not merely of grand political schema, or economic ambitions, nor even of general slogans such as "state control," nationalization, the free market and the like, but of apparently humble and mundane mechanisms which appear to make it possible to govern: techniques of notation, computation and calculation; procedures of examination and assessment; the invention of devices such as surveys and presentational forms such as tables; the standardization of systems for training and the inculcation

of habits; the inauguration of professional specialisms and vocabularies; building design and architectural forms—the list is heterogeneous and is, in principle, unlimited. (Miller and Rose 1990, p. 8)

Discounting is one of the examples that Miller and Rose develop in their discussion of technologies of government. In its aspiration for "economic growth," the UK government could create plans and agencies, but it could not intervene "directly within the 'private' enterprise and at the micro-level of individual decision" (p. 16). Discounting provided a solution to this puzzle: "Whilst politicians and their economic advisers could not themselves control the decisions of individual enterprises, whether private or nationalized, persuading managers of the advantages of the technique of discounted cash flow analysis (DCF) held out the promise of delivering economic growth" (Miller and Rose 1990, p. 16).

The broader history of discounting developed in this book reveals that a configuration in which discounting helps government to govern other entities is only one of the configurations in which discounting has acted. Indeed, although economic planning bodies that used to determine national discount rates, such as the National Economic Development Council in the UK and the Commissariat Général au Plan in France, no longer exist, governmental and intergovernmental agencies and organizations are still concerned with setting the "social" discount rate at which projects pertaining to public policy should be evaluated—projects such as building infrastructure, reimbursing drugs, or implementing environmental regulations.

Ironically, we could say, discounting has become a technology for government to govern itself rather than to govern private enterprise. Discounting can be analyzed as an instrument of liberalism, in Foucault's definition, insofar as it conditions decisions on the allocation of resources on the calculation of the "true" value of the things worthy enough to deserve these resources, but it also can be analyzed as an instrument of neoliberalism, again in Foucault's definition, insofar as it has become a lens through which the action of government is conceived and assessed. Foucault describes neoliberal governmentality as both an extension and a transformation of liberal governmentality. It's an extension because neoliberalism "demands even more from the economy": "let's ask the market economy itself," says neoliberalism, "to be the principle, not of the state's limitation, but of its internal regulation from start to finish of its existence and action" (Foucault 2008, p. 116). It's a transformation because as the principle of the market becomes a principle of government, its definition shifts from exchange to competition, that is, competition between enterprises and entrepreneurs. It is American neoliberalism that pushes "the generalization of the economic form of the market" to its most encompassing degree, "including the whole of the social system not usually conducted through or sanctioned by monetary exchanges" (p. 243).

And the two illustrations that Foucault discusses in his analysis of American neoliberalism—CBA and human capital—are both related to discounting. Foucault describes CBA as an "economic grid" used to "test governmental action, gauge its validity, and to object to activities of the public authorities on the grounds of their abuses, excesses, futility, and wasteful expenditure" (p. 246):

> In short, it involves criticism of the governmentality actually exercised which is not just a political or juridical criticism; it is a market criticism, the cynicism of a market criticism opposed to the action of public authorities. This is not just an empty project or a theorist's idea. In the United States a permanent exercise of this type of criticism has developed especially in...the American Enterprise Institute whose essential function, now, is to measure all public activities in cost-benefit terms, whether these activities be the famous big social programs concerning, for example, education, health, and racial segregation developed by the Kennedy and Johnson administrations in the decade 1960-1970.... It is criticism in the form of what could be called an "economic positivism"; a permanent criticism of governmental policy. (Foucault 2008, pp. 246-47)

This form of permanent critique, which submits public action to the scrutiny of CBA, is not limited to the domain of institutions such as the American Enterprise Institute that are external to public authorities. It also is integrated into the routine practices of government agencies and intergovernmental organizations themselves through the standardization of CBA and social discount rates. It has been the object of battles between different agencies, such as the Office of Management and Budget (OMB) and the Environmental Protection Agency (EPA)—the battle over banning asbestos in the 1980s, for example and, more recently, the battle over raising discount rates under the Trump administration (Grab 2017). Its presence spills over administrative or geographical boundaries and certainly precedes the era of neoliberalism because the birth of CBA can be traced as far back as the economic calculations performed by French and US engineers in the nineteenth century and the beginning of the twentieth (Porter 1995).

As the Stern/Nordhaus controversy over the discount rate to be applied when dealing with climate change shows, this form of permanent critique has been entrenched. From the observation that CBA leaves public action powerless in front of what appears to be the major threat that our world is facing today, because the "present value" of such action is null or even negative, follows the proposition to reduce discount rates in order to give more value to the future, which is in turn countered as a transgression of the naturality of discount rates (supposed to be observed in the market rather than decided collectively). This certainly exemplifies "the cynicism of a market criticism opposed to the action of public authorities" to which Foucault refers in the quote above.

So if discounting is a technology of government, it not only helps government govern other entities such as private enterprise, it also helps government govern itself in the spirit of neoliberalism. But discounting also intervenes in other configurations in which some entities "act at a distance" on other entities. In the discounting experiments I briefly described at the beginning of this chapter, the behavior of poor individuals, deemed insufficiently future-oriented, is being governed through the manipulation of the discount rates supposed to be somewhere there in their heads. The redefinition of the discount rate from the cost of time to the cost of capital since the 1950s, as I argue in Chapter 3, has repositioned the investment behavior of managers within firms from contributing to national economic growth to maximizing investors' returns—and this happened more than a decade before the doctrine of shareholder value and agency theory made explicit the relationship between managers and investors that is integral to what is commonly referred to as "financialization." Likewise, the introduction of discounting as the legitimate (and sometimes legally prescribed) method for calculating the compensation that governments owe to investors in the case they harm their interests (such as in cases of nationalization or expropriation) since the 1980s has operated a similar transformation on the behavior of not just managers, but government itself.

ACTING ON THE FUTURE

This latter example brings us to the fourth political quality of discounting: the extent to which it makes possible or inhibits acting on the future. The analysis of this political quality requires us to conceptualize the future not only as a temporal, but also as a political domain. Until now, I have used the notions of "the present" and "the future" as if they were self-evident. In doing so, I have followed common sense, as well the bulk of the literature in the social sciences that has taken "the future" as an object of analysis. In both, the future simply is treated a temporal domain that is distinct from the past or the present. Its distinctiveness is first of all cognitive: the future is analyzed in terms of its lesser ability to lend itself to attempts to know it. It is what we do not yet know, because it has not yet occurred, and what we aim at knowing through technologies such as prediction, forecasts, scenarios, planning, and so on,[13] which inevitably fail in the face of uncertainty. The distinctiveness of the future is also normative: the future is analyzed as something that we should care for, even though we tend to neglect it, trapped in the webs of myopia and short-termism—the "we" in question spanning from poor individuals subjected to discounting experiments to rich nations struggling with the issue of climate change and its effects on future generations. The future instinctively appears as something inherently good that we stand the risk of losing as we advance in the epoch of the Anthropocene and of pandemics.

Probably the most intriguing aspect of the analysis of discounting as a political technology is that it leads us to questioning this cognitive and normative separation between the present and the future. Each of the chapters of this book works toward shifting our understanding of the future from a temporal domain defined by its unknowability and its desirability to a political domain in which some entities have the capacity to act, while others do not. Chapter 2 associates three temporal domains—the present, the short-term future, and the long-term future—with three types of forest stakeholders: local populations, whose precarious subsistence depends on the fruits and woods that the forest readily procures; private owners, who act as investors and experience time as a cost, seeking quick returns; and the imperishable state, which appears as the only entity that has the ability to plan for the long-term future and to keep forests intact for the sake of economic and military strategy, as well as for future generations. Chapter 3 positions discounting as an obstacle to the capacity of managers to act "as if tomorrow mattered" (Hayes and Garvin 1982) and hence a threat to the future of nations and their industries, defined as the prospect of growth or decline. Chapter 4 shows how, in the calculations of discounting and the narratives in which they are grounded, the uncertainty of the future shifts from a problem of knowledge to a problem of reward that investors claim to deserve precisely because they take charge of the uncertainty of the future. Finally, Chapter 5 examines how discounting has served to displace problems for those who live in the present, namely, the problem of the public or private ownership of natural resources, into problems for those who will gain control over the future, namely, the valuation of the streams of revenues into which these resources are transformed.

The peculiar ways in which discounting both describes and produces the future become more readily apparent when integrated in a broader history of the future. The episodes discussed in this book can be read as a continuation of the process of "temporalization" analyzed by Reinhart Koselleck, a process that occurred between the fifteenth and the eighteenth centuries and resulted in the peculiar form of "acceleration" which characterizes modernity (Koselleck 1985). This process has put on center stage the "opposition between the past and the future, thereby sending away the opposition between here below and hereafter [*ici-bas et au-delà*]" (Koselleck 2016, p. 32). Koselleck's perspective allows envisaging the past, present, and future not as preexistent partitions of time, akin to the geographical distribution of more or less distant territories, but as the outcome of a process of temporalization in which these different temporal domains become amenable to action.

What is at stake here is the analysis of the actors who have the capacity to act within the domain of the future delineated through the process of temporalization. As Koselleck (2016, p. 47) puts it, "from a political point of view, the issue is to know who accelerates—or slows down—and whom or what, where, and why." Discounting is part of the answer to this question.

Koselleck's argument is that the autonomization of the experience of the acceleration of time, set free from its theological premises and Christianity's expectation of salvation and driven by technological progress and the philosophies of history, has provoked an "opening of the future" (*ouverture de l'avenir*) since the eighteenth century (Koselleck 2016, p. 42). This notion of the "open future" has been mobilized in recent sociologies of the future. Notably, Jens Beckert argues that a future that is "open, containing opportunities to be seized and risks to be calculated" is characteristic of the temporal order of capitalism (Beckert 2016, p. 22). In his account, the future of capitalist societies is contrasted with the future of traditional societies, a future viewed as part of a circular repetition of events. One illustration of this contrast can be found in Pierre Bourdieu's study of the transition from traditional Kabyle society to a capitalist economy in Algeria. This transition, Bourdieu argues, was accompanied by a change in the "attitude toward time" and more precisely in the attitude toward the future: from a future that society "attempts to shape by the means available to it, to the image of the past, by trying to reduce the countless possibles, which bear all the unknown and foreseen threats, to the past, reassuring because it is over and exemplary," to a future defined as "the lieu of an infinity of possibles" (Bourdieu 1963, p. 41). In a similar vein, Elena Esposito characterizes today's "risk society" as "a society no longer defined by its past or its traditions, but turned to the future," a society that no longer "defines the present by looking backwards, but "by looking forward" and "seeing the present as a preparation for an unknown future" (Esposito 2011, pp. 3-4).

Such transformations from more or less closed to more or less open futures occur because the definition of the future is subject to being contested. Koselleck highlights the role of different actors struggling for the control of the future. While the church was the master of the "closed future," marked by the awaiting of the last judgment and an apocalyptic end, it is the state that has served as the instigator of the "open future"—first transformed into a "domain of finite possibilities arranged according to degrees of higher or lesser probability" (Koselleck 1985, p. 13) through the art of prognosis and then transformed into a radically new future, characterized by "the acceleration with which it approaches us, and…its unknown quality" (Koselleck 1985, p. 17). And they both struggled to maintain control over "their" futures, by means of monitoring, marginalizing, or absorbing competing visions of the future:

> A ruling principle *(Herrschaftsprinzip)* of the Roman Church was that all visionaries had to be brought under its control. Proclaiming a vision of the future presupposed that it had first received the authorization of

the Church.... Correspondingly, the future of the world and its end were made part of the history of the Church; newly inflamed prophets necessarily exposed themselves to verdicts of heresy. (Koselleck 1985, p. 7)

The genesis of the absolutist state is accompanied by a sporadic struggle against all manner of religious and political predictions. The state enforced a monopoly on the control of the future by suppressing apocalyptic and astrological readings of the future.... The course of the seventeenth century is characterized by the destruction of interpretations of the future, however motivated. Where it had the power, the state persecuted their utterance...ultimately driving them into private, local, folkloric circles or secret associations. (Koselleck 1985, pp. 10–11)

If we focus on how different types of actors are associated with different types of futures, rather than on the difference between more or less open futures and their characterization in the terms of cyclicity or the drift to the unknown, it becomes apparent how it's possible to approach the future not as a temporal, but as a contested political domain and discounting as a political technology. In the chapters that follow, actors who have the capacity to act within the domain of the future delineated through the process of temporalization struggle over the control of the future. We witness, for example, local populations, private owners and the state struggling over forests, governments and foreign investors struggling over copper mines, present and future generations struggling over the world we live in. These struggles may be more or less embodied, more or less violent, more or less consequential. What they have in common is the involvement of discounting as an instrument for the description and production of the future and thus for control over what it will be.

The future constructed by discounting thus bears limited resemblance with the "open" future that sociologists have associated with capitalism. It does indeed contain "opportunities to be seized and risks to be calculated," as Beckert puts it, but the description of the openness of the future in terms of opportunities and risks reveals a very peculiar form of future, one that is trapped in the singular perspective of the investor. The investor appears as the entity that has the capacity to look to the future and to attempt to control it. The investor's experience of the future does not lie in the expectation of an apocalyptic end or in the definition of strategies within a finite number of possibilities; it lies in the generation of streams of revenues.

Because we are interested here in the relationship between types of actors and types of futures, we need to ask what actors see the future from this particular perspective. The investor whose gaze dominates the future is not limited to the proverbial "shareholder" whom, according to the theory of shareholder value, firms should serve. It is not the "venture capitalist" to whom, in an economy that dedicates its energy to innovation, has been granted the role of selecting the technologies and business models that are worth bringing into existence (Doganova 2013). It is not even the "financial system" that, as Lawrence Summers[14] put it in a speech he delivered to the banking community, has been given the task "to make the most important decisions that society makes," namely, "Where is its capital going to be allocated in the future? How is the use of that capital going to be monitored when it is entrusted to particular individuals and particular institutions? How much of society's resources are going to be allocated to the present and how much are going to be oriented to the future?" (Summers, in a lecture given for the bicentennial celebration of the London Stock Exchange, 2001, quoted in Buchanan, Chai, and Deakin 2012, p. 47)."

Instead, the investor who acts by discounting the future is rather a form of subjectivity, a way of seeing the world and a way of being and acting in the world that sometimes materializes in a professional occupation but most often materializes as a function in normative discourses and as an operation, an act of investing, equipped with this peculiar device. Sabine Montagne and Ortiz (2013, p. 7) argue that "the figure of the investor is central in the representation of financial flows proposed by regulation and law, financial theory, and an important part of media and political discourse"; it is "the central notion from which the world of finance describes itself and is described." The implications of this argument become clear when the definition of the "world of finance" is expanded from more or less exotic places such as the London Stock Exchange, whose bicentennial Summers was celebrating in the quote above, to banks giving (or not giving) credit to particular individuals or firms and governments deciding whether to issue more debt and whether to repay it now or later—and then expanded more to the formulation of corporate strategies and public policies, which have been gradually penetrated by the narrative and calculative technologies of finance, namely, discounting, a movement that Eve Chiapello (2015) has aptly described as the "financialisation of valuation." As we have argued elsewhere (Muniesa and Doganova 2020), the "world of finance" is not limited to financial markets and the actors that gravitate to and orbit around them (traders, analysists, economists, etc.); instead, it is defined by the circulation of a peculiar form of valuation, which this book captures as discounting. The notion of "capitalization" serves to describe this generalization of financialization because it decenters the study of finance from financial markets and helps observe the transformation of objects such as entrepreneurial projects, scientific outputs, or hospital beds into objects of investment, prone to producing returns in the future (Doganova and Muniesa 2015; Muniesa et al. 2017).

The notion of capitalization brings us back to the notion of capital with which we started our exploration of discounting in Fischer's writings. Recall his argument: capital is anything that can engage with a specific temporality, the production of future streams of revenues. It is anything that can lend itself to the mechanics of discounting. This generalized definition of capital served as the foundation for later theories of human capital, whose most prominent proponent was American economist and Nobel Prize winner Gary Becker. It is precisely the theory of human capital, which Foucault discusses extensively as an example of American neoliberalism, that leads him to his famous description of the neoliberal *homo oeconomicus* as "an entrepreneur of himself being for himself his own capital, being for himself his own producer, being for himself the source of [his] earnings" (Foucault 2008, p. 226).

This formulation has provided inspiration for a countless number of studies of neoliberalism, but the term "capital" in it has generally been taken metaphorically. Foucault's understanding of capital was not metaphoric, though:

> People like Schultz and Becker say: Why, in the end, do people work? They work, of course, to earn a wage. What is a wage? A wage is quite simply an income. From the point of view of the worker, the wage is an income, not the price at which he sells his labor power. Here, the American neo-liberals refer to the old definition, which goes right back to the start of the twentieth century, of Irving Fisher, who said: What is an income?... An income is quite simply the product or return on a capital. Conversely, we will call "capital" everything that in one way or can be a source of future income. Consequently, if we accept on this basis that the wage is an income, then the wage is therefore the income of a capital. Now what is the capital of which the wage is the income? Well, it is the set of all those physical and psychological factors which make someone able to earn this or that wage, so that, seen from the side of the worker, labor is not a commodity reduced by abstraction to labor power and the time [during] which it is used. Broken down in economic terms, from the worker's point of view labor comprises a capital, that is to say, it as an ability, a skill; as they say: it is a "machine." And on the other side it is an income, a wage, or rather, a set of wages; as they say: an earning stream. (Foucault 2008, pp. 223–24)

What does it mean for an individual to be "an entrepreneur of himself being for himself his own capital"? As in the discounting experiments to which I referred at the beginning of this chapter, becoming capital means letting a desirable future invade the present and directing this present entirely to the realization of future "earning streams." In the language of discounting, this entails decreasing one's discount rate. At the same time, capitalizing means claiming reward for taking charge of the future—a reward that materializes in a higher discount rate, justified by the idea of the risk or uncertainty that the future entails because of its unknowability. More than the notion of the entrepreneur, the notion of the investor, and its correlated notion of the "investee" (Feher 2018), allow employing these two moves—relating the present to a desirable future and claiming a reward for taking charge of the future—as ways of acting to produce that future. They appear to be contradictory at a first glance, but the contradiction dissolves if they are both considered as a means to collapse the distinction between the present and the future and to contest what the future will be and to whom it belongs.

CHAPTER TWO

The Origins of Discounting in Forestry:
Valuing and Managing Futures in the Woods

This chapter explores the origins of discounting. As often happens, origins are multiple and dispersed, and one can hardy find a single point in history to which the birth of an innovation can be precisely and firmly attached. Historical analyses of discounting indicate a few moments and places in which discounting made its first appearances.[1] At the roots of discounting, one finds the "present values" of life annuities that were developed by actuaries in the seventeenth century (Rubinstein 2003), the "discounts" that already in the fourteenth century Italian merchants provided to customers who paid their bills before their due date (Faulhaber and Baumol 1988), and the compound interest tables that supported their calculations (Smith 1967). Evidence for the application of discounting to "semi-monetary resources," namely, land, can be found as early as the sixteenth century and even before; and evidence for the application of discounting to "non-monetary resources," such as trees, can be found in the eighteenth century (Scorgie 1996). However, the extension of discounting beyond finance is generally located in the nineteenth century, with three often-cited examples: coal mines in the United Kingdom (Brackenborough et al. 2001), railroads in the United States (Faulhaber and Baumol 1988), and forestry in Germany. This latter case is the object of this chapter.

Forests are a perfect starting point for a journey into the history and the logics of discounting. They served as a laboratory for several problems whose intersections lie at the heart of discounting: sustainability and the future, economics and the public interest, and science and the state. I will briefly consider each of them in turn.

Forests were the birthplace of the notion of sustainability and of a concern for the longer future (Hölzl 2010; Warde 2011). Like discounting, sustainability is a way of relating the present to the future. For instance, sustainable development was defined as "development that meets the needs of the present without compromising the ability of future generations to meet their own needs" (World Commission on Environment and Development, 1987, ch, 2, sec. 3, ph. 27). In the debates on forests in the eighteenth and nineteenth centuries in Europe featured prominently figures of "future generations," such as "posterity" and "offspring" (Hölzl 2010, p. 439), with whom forests were to be shared and for whom they had to be preserved. The history of forest management thus can be read as a history of the long term and its varying conceptions (Nordblad 2016)—as a history of the future and its construction as an object of knowledge, of government, and of time (Mårald and Westholm 2016).[2]

Forests are also an object that economists have liked to think with, and as such, they have been central to the development of economic theory. Economists have seen forests as a textbook case insofar as they are a form of "pure capital": a model of production without labor, production "whose unique factor is time" (Vatin 2013, p. 238). Economists have also seen forests as a challenge insofar as they provide manifold and easily observable examples of the discrepancy between the public and the private interest, with the former tending to preserve the forest and let trees grow and the latter urging the felling of trees and the release of the pecuniary value that they carry.

The invention of marginal analysis by eighteenth-century economists has been described as a response to this problem and as a way to reconcile the public and the private interest by scientifically determining the optimum or the right moment when a tree should be felled (Vatin 2008). Two centuries later, Paul Samuelson, recipient of the Nobel Prize in Economics and father of the theory of public goods, introduced the modern concept of externalities in an attempt to settle the debate still raging between "forestry experts and the general public on the one side and professional economists and profit-conscious businessmen on the other" (Samuelson 1976, p. 466). "Everybody loves a tree and hates a businessmen," he wrote, and probably in a few centuries, "the human race will be as conditioned to abhor economists as it has become to abhor snakes" (p. 467). He wished the debate opposing cherished forests to loathed businessmen and economists would be brought to an imaginary court. On each side would sit PhDs in economics who would describe, "carefully and objectively," the activity of forestry and the externalities it generates. He argued that "if the externalities involved could be shown to be sufficiently important, I am naïve enough to believe that all economists would be found on the side of the angels, sitting thigh next to thigh with the foresters" (pp. 467–68). More concretely, he argued that reconciliation between economists and foresters required correcting the errors that authors in economics and forestry alike had made in attempting to determine a forest's optimal rotation period. For Samuelson, the author who had come closest to a correct solution to the problem of when a tree should be cut was Martin Faustmann. I will revert to Faustmann's formula below.

Economists were not the only ones to dream of forests and science. James Scott's *Seeing Like a State* opens with the example of forests and their encounter with "the abstracting, utilitarian logic of the state" (Scott 1998, p. 13). The result of this encounter was the "normal forest"—monocultural, even-aged, easy to measure, liable to control, prone to revenue maximization—imagined and created by German scientific forestry in the eighteenth century. Scott recounts the short-lived success and resounding failure of this "utopian dream of scientific forestry" (p. 19), pointing to the discrepancy between "the administrators' forest" and "the naturalists' forest" (p. 22) and to the impossibility of reducing the ecological and social complexity of the forest to the simplifying gaze of a state serving its fiscal, managerial, and commercial ambitions.

Beyond this episode, historians of the environment have shown the role of forests in the formation of early modern states (Radkau 2008; Warde 2006). For the state, forests were a source of wealth, and some of the resources that they provided—fiscal revenues and timber for ship building—were closely linked to the exercise of its sovereign power. Forests were also a laboratory for the modern art of government in which knowledge and power are inextricably linked (Foucault 2004). In the eighteenth century in Germany, forestry became part of the so-called "cameral sciences," the sciences of public administration in which state administrators were trained, and mathematics became part of the curricula in forestry schools (Lowood 1991). The cameral sciences subjected different aspects of state administration to scientific scrutiny, and "scientific forestry" used mathematics to address the problem of the deterioration of woodlands and mounting worries about a possible shortage of wood and timber. Whether these worries were justified or not has been debated by historians. In any case, they drove a move toward the rationalization of the management and use of forests as a natural resource. Rationalization meant "entrusting the forests to the hands of state-based scientific forestry" (Hölzl 2010, p. 436) by detaching them both from routines based on empirical observation and rules of thumb and from rural populations and pastoral practices.

These kinds of problems—sustainability and the future, economics and the public interest, science and the state—underpinned two questions that concerned European foresters in the eighteenth and the nineteenth centuries: "What is a forest worth?" and "When should a tree be felled?" These apparently simple questions gave rise to increasingly sophisticated analyses ripe with philosophical elaborations and mathematical subtleties. It is to these two questions that discounting came as an answer. To understand the kind of answer it provided, we need to delve into the reasoning of its proponents.

My entry point for doing so is the Faustmann formula, which, as we've seen, is often described as the first application of discounting to forestry.[3] It was born in an article published by Faustmann on December 15, 1849, in the German *Journal of Forests and Hunting* (*Allgemeine Forst- und Jagd-Zeitung*). The article, entitled "Calculation of the Value which Forest Land and Immature Stands Possess for Forestry," demonstrated that the value of a forest can be expressed as the sum of the future costs and revenues that the exploitation of this forest will generate, discounted at the interest rate. According to some authors, the Faustmann formula is "the earliest known application of the principle of discounted cash flow (or DCF as it is now popularly known)" (Gane 1968, p. 5).

Faustmann's demonstration was a direct response to an article entitled "On the Determination of the Money Value of Bare Forest Land" that had been published two months earlier in the same journal by head forester (*Oberförster*) and forest mathematician Edmund von Gehren. More broadly, it was the culmination of a more than century-long conversation that developed among German and European foresters. Faustmann was a student of Carl Gustav Heyer, who was himself a student of Heinrich Cotta (Peyron and Maheut 1999, p. 681). In 1804, Cotta published a widely read book entitled *Systematic Instructions for the Assessment of Woods* in which he presented new mathematics-based methods for the quantification of forests. These methods allowed, for example, transforming a forest into a quantity of wood mass, thereby completing "the chain of conversions from wood to numbers to units of currency" that could be used "to predict income, calculate taxes, assess the worth of the forest, or determine damage to it resulting from a natural disaster" (Lowood 1991, p. 330).

Cotta's tables on the growth of trees and on tariffs for the calculation of the value of forests were translated into French by Dagobert de Salomon and included in his *Traité de l'aménagement des forêts, enseigné à l'École royale forestière* (de Salomon and Cotta 1837).[4] They had an important effect in France, where the question of the right moment to fell a tree was debated. This debate has been analyzed with great detail and finesse by sociologist François Vatin (2005, 2008, 2012, 2013), who brought to light several important works: Georges-Louis

Leclerc Buffon's *Mémoire sur la conservation et le rétablissement des forêts* (Buffon 1739), Philibert-Charles-Marie Varenne de Fenille's *Observations sur l'aménagement des forêts, et particulièrement des forêts nationales* (Varenne de Fenille 1791), and Louis Noirot-Bonnet's *Théorie de l'aménagement des forêts* (Noirot-Bonnet 1842). Their help in understanding the politics of the discount rate—a problem that we will encounter all along this book—is inestimable.

The authors mentioned above are the protagonists of this chapter. The first two sections shed light on two antithetical images of discounting in its early manifestations: a trying reasoning ripe with contradictions, as it appears in von Gehren's "On the Determination of the Money Value of Bare Forest Land," and a general form of valuation composed of a principle and a formula, as it appears in Faustmann's response. The value of a forest, Faustmann contended, is its "economic value," derived from the future of projected flows of costs and revenues, and not its "market value," derived from the present of observable prices. Discounting thus replaced the present with the future as the relevant temporality of valuation.

Examinations of the implications of this orientation toward the future then follow. First, I argue that the present and the future are not only alternative temporalities of valuation, but also conflicting political domains. The urge to look to the future in order to value raises the question of who can afford to look to the future. The answers given to this question in the debates on forestry in the eighteenth and the nineteenth century pointed to the state, whose capacity to look to the future was distinguished from poor populations' enmeshment in the present, on the one hand, and from private forest owners' limitation to investing in a short future, on the other hand. Albeit both oriented toward the future, the temporalities of the state and of private owners diverged as soon as the forest was considered as capital. It is at this moment, when time came to be seen as a cost and the forest owner came to be seen an investor for whom waiting for the trees to grow further meant losing money, that discounting the future came to be seen as necessary.

Valuing forests by discounting their future produced two views of the forest, which I then examine—the forest as wood and the forest as capital. I discuss their relationship by addressing three questions in turn. What does it mean to say that the forest is capital? How does the forest become capital? And how does the forest as capital translate into the forest as wood? The answers to these questions lead me to examining the limits of the analogy between the forest and capital, the intricacies of the determination of the discount rate at which forests should be capitalized, and the effects that discounting produces on the forest when it operates simultaneously as a principle of valuation and a principle of management. The analysis shows the contradictions of discounting as revealed by its origins in scientific forestry and actualized in contemporary debates on the environment.

DISCOUNTING AS REASONING WITH CONTRADICTIONS

> Due to legal prescriptions envisaged in Kurhessen for the extinction of grazing rights by the surrender of bare forest land, and the handing over of forest land for clearing, at a purchase price to be ascertained, instead of the concession system used hitherto, the question of determining the money value of bare forest land is being discussed more than ever before. As this question is of general interest, it is very desirable that it should be examined from different aspects and be satisfactorily settled. In the following pages, I will attempt an answer, which I hope will be thoroughly tested and corrected. (von Gehren 1968, p. 19)

Thus begins the article by von Gehren to which Faustmann responded and, in doing so, "invented" discounting. I begin my exploration of discounting with this first article because it provides an easy introduction to what I call *the reasoning of discounting*: the kinds of problems to which it came as a solution, the logical process that it built, and the difficulties that it faced. As the above quote explains, legislation required that forest land should be converted to agriculture, and the question arose of how to determine the amount of compensation that the owners of that land should receive. So this is the problem to which discounting came as a solution: how to "determine the money value" and ascertain a "purchase price" for forest land. It is a problem of valuation, to which, as we will see in the next sections, was coupled a problem of management. For the moment, let us delve into the reasoning of discounting, bearing in mind the following questions: How does discounting proceed in valuing the forest? What kind of difficulties does it raise, and how does it cope with them?

VALUING WITH DISCOUNTING

To address the question of "the money value of bare forest land," von Gehren proposed the following example.[5] Consider bare land suitable for Scots pine grown on a rotation of eighty years. The land will produce a series of yields, with thinnings occurring every ten years (starting from the twentieth year) and the final felling occurring in the eightieth year. Plantation costs per acre are given; administration and protection costs and taxes are ignored. The rate of interest is 4 percent. What is the value of an acre of this land?

Before we enter into the calculation, let us pause for a moment and reflect on the direction in which this way of formulating the forest takes us. We might think of forests as spaces of wilderness and imagination (Harrison 1992). We might also think of them, or rather let them think, as spaces of living and representation (Kohn 2013). And we might think of forests, or rather "be forests," as spaces of struggle and conflict (Vidalou 2017). This is not what we will be led to do here. We will think of forests as spaces of production. We will see forests "like a state" (Scott 1998)—through the lens of measurement and standardization—but more importantly like an entity that is interested in their produce, be it wood and timber, or financial revenues. More specifically—and this is precisely where the effect of discounting is to be found—we will see them "like an investor," for whom the forest is a capital capable of producing revenues in the future. This figure of the investor can be espoused by different entities, public and private alike. A state can see (does see in fact) like an investor. What makes it different is the kind of future that it can claim.

What does von Gehren see when he looks at the forest? First of all, he sees Scots pines. A common example in the writings of German foresters in the nineteenth century, the Scots pine is still popular today and was even elected "tree of the year 2007." An article written on this occasion explains what Scots pine mean "from an economic point of view":

> The Scots pine is a much sought after tree from an economic point of view. They make up around 24% of forest cover in Germany...making it the second most common tree after the Norwegian spruce. After the last ice age pine trees together with birch trees took over most of central Europe.... Towards the end of the middle ages the pine started to be planted artificially over large areas.... Most of the areas covered by pine trees are not natural forests but have been planted.... Due to its tolerance of drought and high temperatures the pine will most likely increase in importance in view of the climate change. (Karopka and Milad 2007, unpaginated)

To know about the value of Scots pines, planted and grown so as to become forest, envisaged "from an economic point of view," one certainly needs to know about the kind of things that von Gehren gave as input parameters in his example: plantation costs, rotation length, and probably more surprisingly, the rate of interest. To these parameters von Gehren added the volumes of different types of wood produced by the forest in each tenth year (from the twentieth to the eightieth year), obtained from available normal yield tables.[6] Volumes of wood were translated into amounts of money using local prices (fig. 2.1). For example, in the sixtieth year thinnings, the extraction of 25 cubic feet of timber, 75 cubic feet of cordwood, 150 cubic feet of billets and faggotwood, and 12 cubic feet of stumpwood, valued at their respective local prices, would produce an amount of 1955 pfennigs (Pf.).

Each of these amounts of money expected in the future was then reduced to its "present value" by means of a discount rate equal to the rate of interest (fig. 2.2). For example, the 1955 Pf. produced by the six-tieth year thinnings would be equal to 327 Pf. in present value. And the 42,379 Pf. produced by the thinnings and the final felling after eighty years and recurring every eighty years (for von Gehren imagined the same scenario repeating all over again) would be equal to 4,794 Pf. in present value.

Adding the present values of all the future revenues and deducing the plantation costs, von Gehren arrived at the following conclusion: "the value of an acre of good land = 19 Rthlr. 10 Sgr. 8 Pf." (p. 22). What did this mean?

MAKING SENSE OF VALUE

What does it mean to say that the value of land is equal to 19 Rthlr.? Is this number correct, true, or at least credible? Let us try to make sense of this number by comparison with three other numbers present in von Gehren's article.

The first number is 22 Rthlr., the value of an acre calculated by adopting a shorter rotation length: sixty years instead of eighty years. Hence value increases (by 3 Rthlr.) as rotation length decreases (by twenty years). This is the effect of acceleration that discounting produces.

The second number is 9 Rthlr. How does one move from a value of 19 to a value of 9? By changing the calculation method: compound interest, instead of geometric-mean interest. Hence value varies significantly (from 19 to 9) as apparently minor technical details in the method of calculation are altered. These "fluctuations in value" (p. 26), affected by "influences" such as the method of calculation, but also many others, troubled von Gehren so much that he warned the reader from the very beginning of his article about the impossibility to produce "reliable" numbers:

im 20ſten Jahre	Durchforſtungsholz =	200 Kubikfuß	Prügel - u. Reisholz à 5 Pf.	= 1000 Pf.
„ 30ſten „	„ =	20 „ 280 „	Nutzholz . . . . à 24 „ Prügel - u. Reisholz à 5 „	= 1880 v
„ 40ſten „	„ =	20 „ 180 „	Nutzholz . . . . à 24 „ Prügel - u. Reisholz à 5 „	= 1380 „
„ 50ſten „	„ =	15 „ 160 „	Nutzholz . . . . à 24 „ Prügel - u. Reisholz à 5 „	= 1160 „
„ 60ſten „	„ =	25 „ 75 „ 150 „ 12 „	Nutzholz . . . . à 24 „ Scheitholz . . . à 7½ „ Prügel - u. Reisholz à 5 „ Erbſtockholz . . . à 3¼ „	= 1955 „
„ 70ſten „	„ =	30 „ 120 „ 150 „ 18 „	Nutzholz . . . . à 24 „ Scheitholz . . . à 7½ „ Prügel - u. Reisholz à 5 „ Erbſtockholz . . . à 3¼ „	= 2433 „
„ 80ſten „	Durchforſtungsholz = Hauptnutzung =	32 „ 128 „ 160 „ 20 „ 490 „ 1960 „ 2450 „ 306 „	Nutzholz . . . . à 24 „ Scheitholz . . . à 7½ „ Prügel - u. Reisholz à 5 „ Erbſtockholz . . . à 3¼ „ Nutzholz . . . . à 24 „ Scheitholz . . . à 7½ „ Prügel - u. Reisholz à 5 „ Erbſtockholz . . . à 3¼ „	= 42379 „

Figure 2.1. Von Gehren's method of calculation: from wood to money
(von Gehren 1849, p. 362).

The forester should…know what the forest land to be given up would be worth if it remained part of the forest area. This is a matter of determining the value of the bare (timberless) land from the timber yields that could be produced on it; this value depends, however, on the species and type of management, whether the system is intermittent or sustained, on the length of the rotation, especially on the ratio of the wood assortments (timber, cordwood, etc.) and the money obtained from them, and finally on the method of calculating the interest. The effect of these factors is so great that small changes in the assumptions, which are quite in the bounds of possibility, may make the land value either excessive or insignificant or even negative; such large fluctuations may arise that it is not possible to find even a mean figure which is reliable. (von Gehren 1968, p. 19)

Demnach erfolgen:

nach 20 Jahren 1000 Pf. = 1000 × 0,50354 . . . . = 504 Pf. jetziger Werth,
vom 20sten Jahr an alle 80 Jahre wiederkehrend = 1000 × 0,50354 × 0,11313 = 57 „ „ „
nach 30 Jahren 1880 Pf. = 1880 × 0,37493 . . . . = 705 „ „ „
vom 30sten Jahr an alle 80 Jahre wiederkehrend = 1880 × 0,37493 × 0,11313 = 80 „ „ „
nach 40 Jahren 1380 Pf. = 1380 × 0,28239 . . . . = 390 „ „ „
vom 40sten Jahr an alle 80 Jahre wiederkehrend = 1380 × 0,28239 × 0,11313 = 44 „ „ „
nach 50 Jahren 1160 Pf. = 1160 × 0,21657 . . . . = 251 „ „ „
vom 50sten Jahr an alle 80 Jahre wiederkehrend = 1160 × 0,21657 × 0,11313 = 28 „ „ „
nach 60 Jahren 1955 Pf. = 1955 × 0,16721 . . . . = 327 „ „ „
vom 60sten Jahr an alle 80 Jahre wiederkehrend = 1955 × 0,16721 × 0,11313 = 37 „ „ „
nach 70 Jahren 2433 Pf. = 2433 × 0,13000 . . . . = 316 „ „ „
vom 70sten Jahr an alle 80 Jahre wiederkehrend = 2433 × 0,13000 × 0,11313 = 36 „ „ „
nach 80 Jahren und alle 80 Jahre wiederkehrend = 42379 fl. × 0,11313 . . . = 4794 „ „ „

Zusammen = 7569 Pf. jetziger Werth,
oder = 21 Rthlr. — Sgr. 9 Pf.

Hiervon gehen ab:
die jetzigen Culturkosten . . . . = 1 Rthlr. 15 Sgr. — Pf. ⎫
dieselben alle 80 Jahre wiederkehrend = 1,5 Rthlr.   ⎬ = 1 „ 20 „ 1 „
× 0,11313 . . . . = — „ 5 „ 1 „   ⎭

Also ist vom guten Boden der Werth eines Ackers = 19 Rthlr. 10 Sgr. 8 Pf.

Figure 2.2. Von Genhren's method of calculation: from future flows to present value
(von Gehren 1849, p. 363).

As he progressed with his calculations, von Gehren struggled with these "fluctuations," which faced him with values such as 6 Rthlr., a number that struck him as "certainly a long way from the true value of good land" (p. 23), or with "even greater uncertainties and absurdities" (p. 19), such as a negative number as a measure of the value of land.

The third number is a range: between 6 and 48 Rthlr. How does one move from a single value of 19 to a value range of 6 to 48? By changing the principle of valuation and considering that value is to be found not in the calculation of uncertain future flows, but in the observation of present market prices. According to farmers, von Gehren observes, purchase price per acre of bare forest land varies between a maximum of 48 Rthlr., for meadow land of higher quality, and a minimum of 6 Rthlr., for pasture land of lower quality. Quite surprisingly, after all his discounting calculations, von Gehren concludes his article with a scale of local prices for different qualities of land, a scale that "can be used as a guide for appraising the (agricultural) value of forest land to be surrendered" (p. 26).

Notice the discrepancy between the discounting calculations developed in von Gehren's article and the final proposal to use a scale of local prices as a guide. The scale indicates current market prices, not value derived from future yields, and it refers to agriculture, not forestry. Even if von Gehren contended that land *should* be valued for the future yields that it is likely to produce, which depend on the type of use to which it is put (forestry or agriculture), he acknowledged that it is "much more suitable to determine the value of the land according to its agricultural quality, e.g. as meadow-, wheat-, rye-, oats-, and pasture-land...because it is then easier to determine the annual revenue and (by deducing expenditures) to arrive at the annual net yield, for capitalization" (p. 26). In other words, while the article starts by affirming the principle of discounting, it ends by retreating in front of the difficulties of its execution, stepping back to the present-driven principles of valuation, precisely the principles to which discounting came as a critique.

Such a conclusion could have banned discounting from the valuation of any activity that does not benefit from regularity and certainty—or just from any activity, for certainty should be forsaken as soon as one looks to the future. However, it did not. In the next section, I will examine how Faustmann, who may be said to have "invented" discounting, dealt with this problem. But let us already note that the problem has never been solved: because discounting looks to the future to value the present, it is inevitably subject to uncertainty, fluctuations, and sometimes "absurdities," the most striking example of which is the negative value assigned to entities that no one would dare describe as not valuable—entities such as land, as we have seen above, or drugs, as we will see in Chapter 4. This is why discounting means reasoning with contradictions.

Discounting is a form of reasoning that is trying, difficult, and at odds with itself. Mastering this reasoning requires learning competences that are not just technical, but ideological. It requires mathematical skills, but also a certain worldview, that is, a theory of the sources of value that grants the ability to discriminate between what is of value and what is not. It also requires assuredness, the ability to stay on the road, even though the road is a succession of bumps and potholes. I would wish that any author who takes her reader into the terrain of discounting would start the journey as von Gehren did, with a warning that this will be a journey through fluctuations, uncertainties, and absurdities whose proposed destination will not be reached, but is nevertheless worth imagining and playing with. Not all authors do this, of course. Faustmann's article, to which I will turn next, excludes the rhetoric of doubt. And so do contemporary economists, most of whom have espoused Irving Fisher's view of discounting as a universal theory of value.

Contradiction is inherent in discounting. It is intimately linked to the way in which discounting relates to the future by both valuing and devaluing it. Most discussions of discounting inevitably lead to some form of conundrum. The approach proposed here is to use these conundrums not as evidence that "discounting does not work" or that "an error has occurred and should be corrected," but as invitations to reflect upon the complicated ways in which we and our tools think of the future. I will therefore be careful to attend to how these conundrums emerge and how they are dealt with: what kind of reactions they arouse and what kind of solutions they call for.

Von Gehren's retreat from the forester's to the farmer's standpoint is one solution that is often encountered.[7] It consists of delimiting domains of applicability: claiming that certain kinds of objects or activities fit discounting, while others do not; that certain kinds of actors can discount, while others cannot; that certain things should be discounted more, while others should be discounted less. The relevance of discounting per se is barely questioned. In other words, the conundrums discounting faces do not seem to shake its foundations; rather, they expand or refine its territory.[8] This observation works toward understanding the third trouble that I discussed in the Introduction: the capacity of discounting to become a general form.

THE PRESENT AND THE FUTURE
AS ALTERNATIVE TEMPORALITIES OF VALUATION

Faustmann's article, which gave birth to the now-famous Faustmann formula, is a direct reply to von Gehren's article. So how did Faustmann deal with the conundrums of discounting? From the very beginning, he expressed his intention to avoid von Gehren's retreat to the farmer's standpoint and to "consider the subject from the forester's standpoint" (Faustmann 1968, p. 27). In order to do so, he built what can be read as a genuine (and probably the first) *theory* of discounting. I examine two of its components, the expression of discounting in a mathematical formula that could be applied not only to land, but also to the trees standing on it, and the association of this formula with a principle that is assumed to be "correct": the principle of "economic value," calculated by discounting the future, as opposed to that of "market value," indicated by the observation of prices in the market. These two principles of valuation involve divergent temporalities, that is, the future of discounting versus the present of the market.

A FORMULA AND A PRINCIPLE OF VALUATION

While von Gehren reasoned through an example, Faustmann sought to express the value of land "generally in a formula" in order to set valuation free from the peculiarities of the objects being valued (in this case, the type of land): "We express [the land value] generally in a formula, and thus remove one difference between forest land and agricultural land (viz. the timing of their yields and expenditures) which, according to Herr von Gehren, makes the value calculation of the former more difficult than that of the latter" (Faustmann 1968, p. 28). Like von Gehren, Faustmann started by considering the value of bare forest land under intermittent yield management. His demonstration resulted in the following formula (fig. 2.3):[9]

Nun ist es leicht, den Werth des holzleeren Waldbodens oder **B** zu finden; es geschieht durch einfache Kapitalisirung der jährlichen Waldbodenrente. Also ist

$$B = \frac{R}{0{,}0p} = \frac{E + rD - C\,(1{,}0p)^u}{(1{,}0p)^u - 1} - \frac{A}{0{,}0p}\,.$$

Figure 2.3. Faustmann's formula for the value of bare forest land (Faustmann 1849, p. 443).

Where B is the value of the bare forest land; E is the cash value of the final yield; D is the value of yields from thinnings during the rotation and rD the value of the latter compounded to the end of the rotation; C is the size of the plantation costs necessary at the start of the rotation; A is the total annual expenditures for administration, protection, etc.; u is the rotation length; and p is the interest rate percent. To put it simply, the formula states that the value of land is equal to the sum of its yields (the thinning and the final felling), minus expenditures, divided by the interest rate p to the power of the rotation length u.

Interestingly, when Faustmann applied his formula to von Gehren's example, the result he obtained was much lower: 5 Thlr., instead of 19 Thlr. But to him, this was not a conundrum. Where von Gehren would have seen another frustrating "fluctuation" of value, Faustmann saw the result of a series of calculation decisions—the use of compound interest and the inclusion of administrative costs. Most importantly, whether this value was low or high was not a concern for Faustmann. Here, as he put it, he was "only concerned with principles": "In this article we do not wish to investigate whether this small value is caused by estimates of yields and timber prices which are too low, or by an incorrect ratio of assortments, because here we are only concerned with principles. If it is assumed that they are correct, then this low result indicates that the rotation chosen was too long" (Faustmann 1968, p. 32).

Faustmann thus made the rather audacious proposition that once the "principles" of valuation are assumed to be "correct," situations in which they lead to unlikely results should be taken as evidence not against the coherence of these principles, but against the coherence of that to which they are applied. In other words, if the values produced by discounting are too low, it is because the objects being valued are not made valuable enough. As a consequence, the mismatch between the formula and its object is resolved by the transformation of the object so that it fits the formula that values it. As we will see later, the formula, when used as a management device, leads to the recommendation to fell trees at an earlier age. If trees are felled at an earlier age, the values produced by the formula become adequate, and its "principles" can be confirmed to be "correct." This is certainly the most vivid illustration of the performativity of discounting. This type of performativity, however, should be treated cautiously, as I will suggest in the last section of this chapter.

Another important feature of Faustmann's formula is its generality. As Faustmann noted himself, expressing discounting "generally in a formula" allowed him to "remove one difference between forest land and agricultural land" (p. 28). It did even more: it allowed him to extend the principle of discounting to other objects beyond land. To him, the formula should be able to express not only the value of bare land, but also the value of land that carries a stand of trees and therefore the value of the trees themselves. The value of immature stands, he argued, is not accurately captured by the sale price of their present timber content, which he called their "market value." Instead, it stems from the value that they will achieve in the future, when mature, which he called their "economic value":

> Before maturity, the stands (if they already possess a market value) should be regarded as a product of the land which is not fully ripe, the harvesting

of which causes loss to the forest owner in the same way as cutting wheat before time does to the farmer. Just think of a Scots pine stand say 10 years old, whose present market value is indisputably smaller than that which it possesses as the bearer of a future final yield. The latter is the economic value of the stand which we can express by a money capital, just like the economic value of the land. (Faustmann 1968, p. 32)

This argument led Faustmann to positioning the valuation principle of discounting against another, probably more intuitive, valuation principle: that of market prices. The former derives the value of things from the future—their value, as Faustmann put it, "as the bearer of a future final yield." The latter derives the value of things from the present. While economic value is indicated by discounting future yields, market value is indicated by the current price at which wood and land can be sold. In another article published a few months earlier in the same journal,[10] Faustmann explicitly compared these two principles of valuation and associated them with different courses of action. He took the example of a forest comprising six pine stands in different site classes and imagined two scenarios. In the first ("liquidation"), the forest was immediately clear-cut and sold on the market with the bare land. This scenario realized its market value (in this case, 26,935 Florins). In the second scenario, the forest was converted to sustained management and kept in forestry use to infinity. This scenario realized its economic value (in this case, 14,095 Florins).

THE FUTURE OF DISCOUNTING VS. THE PRESENT OF THE MARKET

The two valuation principles that Faustmann opposed diverge in their temporal orientations. According to valuation at market value, the price at which a forest can be sold *now* exhausts its value now and in the future. Sociologist François Vatin (2005, p. 62) refers to this principle as the market's "principle of instantness [*principe d'instantanéité*]," which was celebrated by liberal thinkers in the eighteenth century. Revisiting the critique of the "foundation" (an organization based on money assigned in perpetuity to fulfil a purpose envisaged by the founder) that French economist and politician Anne Robert Turgot wrote in Denis Diderot and Jean le Rond d'Alembert's *Encyclopédie*, Vatin observes:

> The foundation imposes for the present and to those who live, rules that have been produced for the past and by those who are dead.... It subjugates the present to the past. It creates a diachronic reason. For the liberals, the great virtue of the market by contrast is its essentially synchronic nature. It is this principle of instantness, rather than the idea of the pursuit of the individual interest, that profoundly characterizes the moral traits of this social form. (Vatin 2005, p. 62)

Economic valuation, too, creates a diachronic reason, but in a different hierarchy of temporalities: it subjugates the present to the future, instead of the past. Turgot criticized the "foundation" and its illusory and dangerous ambition to realize the will of an individual beyond the scope of her individual existence.[11] Vatin imagines the same argument transposed to the act of planting a tree. He insightfully reminds us of the question that three young men asked an octogenarian who was planting a tree in one Jean de La Fontaine's fable "The Old Man and the Three Young Ones" (fig. 2.4). Why should an old man burden himself with care for a future that is not made for him?

> What fruit can he expect to gather
> Of all this labour and expense?
> ... What use for thee, grey-headed man,
> To load the remnant of thy span
> With care for days that never can be thine?
> (La Fontaine 1882, p. 193)

Seen through Turgot's lens, the answer that the old man gave to the three young ones—"my descendants, whosoe'er they be, shall owe these cooling fruits and shades to me"—reveals the questionable pretention to act on the future and impose his own will to those who will come after him. If the act of planting a tree is motivated by a concern for the future, how can we be assured that the future generations will actually need this tree and the services it provides?

Building on Antoine Augustin Cournot, a French mathematician and philosopher famous for introducing mathematical analysis in economics in the nineteenth century, Vatin then extends the problem of intertemporality to embrace not only the existence of the individual, but also that of society or humanity. Reflecting on the possibility of exhausting resources through exploitation, Cournot showed that intertemporality disarms economic analysis, for it raises a number of "transcendent problems" that the "philosophers" will never be able to solve:

> One would need to know the exact destiny of living species, and the destiny of human kind; if it is preferable that the fire of civilization burns longer, or that it burns faster and with greater ardor...that a longer series of generations find more or less warmth and light in its beams, or that its action focuses on a few privileged generations: all these are questions that everyone can, and even must, take as she wishes...by taking into consideration the present and the special interests in her care, and also, a little, by taking into consideration the future and a broader philanthropy, in such a way as to avoid any extreme consequences that practical common sense would reject, but without any precise rules, such as those that would require the rigor of a scientific construction. (Cournot 1863, quoted in Vatin 2005, p. 66)

Cournot's argument can be read as a fundamental critique of the ambition of discounting to value the future. The future, as von Gehren discovered, is fraught with uncertainties that hinder calculation and lead to "absurdities." The future, Faustmann affirmed, indicates the value of trees and land and the treatment to which they should be submitted. The future, Turgot argued, is something that does not belong to us, but to those after us, upon whom our wills should not be projected (Cournot 1863, quoted in Vatin 2005, p. 66). The future,

Figure 2.4. La Fontaine, "The Old Man and the Three Young Ones,"
G. Doré; Pannemaker-Doms, 1868 (Bibliothèque nationale de France).

Cournot claimed, is the realm of "transcendent problems" that can be addressed only at the individual level, through "common sense" and with no "precise rules."

These different views serve to relocate Faustmann's affirmation back into the debates that aroused his contemporaries. In this perspective, discounting poses the following question: If the future is the relevant temporality for valuing and managing forests, who has the right and the capacity to look to the future and to act on it? The next section turns to this question.

THE PRESENT AND THE FUTURE AS CONFLICTING POLITICAL DOMAINS

In his *Théorie de l'aménagement des forêts*, published in France a few years before the articles by von Gehren and Faustmann, the forest surveyor Noirot-Bonnet (1842) imagined what forests looked like "in the ancient times" (p. 162). Land served for grazing and hunting; trees, whose growth was then unhindered, provided fruits that fed wild animals and men. These were, according to Noirot-Bonnet, the "unique foundations of the pecuniary value of forests." Wood was collected by "the first to come [*le premier occupant*]"; its value was uniquely made of labor value: the labor necessary to fetch dead trees and the bits lying on the ground. Such forests still existed, in certain cantons in Southern France, where "oaks are only valued for the product of their nuts; pines are sold for only 2 francs per unit when they are felled. There are other forests that are even less productive; they barely return what is necessary to pay the fee for the guards and the taxes: the only reason they subsist is that no one takes the trouble to destroy them" (Noirot-Bonnet 1842, p. 163).

Noirot-Bonnet referred to the Burgundians' Code, which granted to all those who did not possess a forest the right to take dead wood and to fell the trees that did not bear fruits, even in privately owned forests, without paying any indemnity. He used this example to show that forest trees were valued only for the utility taken from their fruits. However, the possibility of exchanging wood on the market led people to "attack standing trees" (p. 164): first the biggest and hence the oldest, but then, as prices gradually went up, needs incessantly expanded, and the stock of old trees came to an end, younger trees were chopped down and grew again from their stumps. This, for Noirot-Bonnet, marked the advent of coppice forests, forests regenerated from shoots formed on the stumps of the previous crop trees, and the disappearance of high-forest massifs, forests of large, tall, mature trees with a closed canopy.

WHO CAN AFFORD TO LOOK TO THE FUTURE?

What may sound today as a tragic description of the first steps in a long process of environmental destruction was for Noirot-Bonnet "the formidable effect of the progress of civilization and the multiplication of wealth: a benefit, not a disaster" (p. 165). His objective was not to lament the degradation of forests, as many of his contemporaries did, but to establish the difference between two modes of forest management (*aménagement*):[12] coppice (*taillis*) and high forest (*futaies*). The difference between coppice and high forests resided in the age of trees and, hence, in the actors able to *manage* them.[13] Coppice forests, whose rotation lengths range from ten to forty years, can be managed by private owners, that is, as Noirot-Bonnet puts it, by "owners with limited existence" (p. 169). By contrast, high forests, whose rotation lengths range from 80 to 300 years, can be managed only by public owners, the state or the municipality, that is, "owners with unlimited existence." The temporalities of high forests, he affirmed, can be borne only by "an imperishable being" (p. 169) and a being that is "rich enough" so it "does not feel any real loss…does not experience any damage in his fortune" (p. 248) while waiting for the future.

In other words, the issue of the management of forests is inseparable from the issues of inequality in time and inequality of wealth. The inequality in time at stake here is not the one that separates present generations from future generations, as with the three young men and the octogenarian planting a tree for his "descendants" in La Fontaine's fable. It is an inequality between different groups of actors all present in the present who are assumed to vary in their capacities to look to the future because they vary in the amount of wealth that they possess. In his interpretation of Noiret-Bonnot's argument, Vatin makes a direct link between notions of the poor and the rich, the short term and the long term, high and low discount rates, in dealing with the issue of the management and ownership of forests: "The poorest, who can only reason in the short term, have a high discount rate. The richest, who can reason in the long term, have a low discount rate. They do not give the same value to time. According to Noirot-Bonnet, the ownership of forests should therefore be reserved to the richest, and namely, to the state" (Vatin 2013, p. 242).

Noirot-Bonnet's argument sheds light on the kinds of demarcations and exclusions to which the question of the future gives rise. There are not many actors—temporally "unlimited," "imperishable," and "rich enough"—who can afford to look to the future, especially the longer future. One such actor, as Noirot-Bonnet suggests, is the state. Thus, from the problem of forest management emerged a vision of the state as the guardian of the future and the keeper of the long term, in opposition with two other types of actors—on the one hand, "local" or "rural" populations, chiefly defined by their poverty and their entrapment in the present, with their valuation of the forest limited to the fruits and the remains that they could collect, and on the other, private forest owners, who could value the forest for its future yields, and therefore *manage* it, but whose sight was shortened by their "limited existence." As we will see, keeping trees for the future meant extracting them from the present of poor populations and triggered social conflict. The future of discounting is thus to be analyzed in contrast not only to the instantness of the market, as I did above, but also to the instantness of poverty. And as we will see as well, the reason why private owners' future is shorter than that of the state not only has to do with their limited life span as human beings, but with their acting as investors, for whom waiting for the future entails a loss and deserves reward. This idea, which converts an understanding of time as duration into an understanding of time as cost, grounds the notion of the discount rate.

THE STATE'S FUTURE VS. THE POOR'S PRESENT

Environmental historian Richard Hölzl (2010) has described how the implementation of scientific forestry in the region of Spessart in Germany in the early nineteenth century affected local populations and triggered social conflict. Keeping trees for the future meant extracting them from the present and from the current needs of those who lived beside them and, to a certain extent, from them. People were denied access to areas that they used for pasture, cutting grass, and collecting litter; this resulted in an increasing number of forest offenses in the 1830s and 1840s, threats against forest personnel, and violent clashes between forest personnel and rural populations during the 1848-49 revolution. Hölzl quotes an excerpt from a letter of complaint by the community administration of Laufach, dated March 28, 1848, that illustrates the villagers' claims to "collect dead wood, fallen branches and windfall as fuel for the hearths...then to receive litter/foliage outside clear-cut areas as well as timber for maintenance and new buildings, each according to our needs, and to have cattle, pigs, etc. graze outside clear-cut areas" (Hölzl 2010, p. 448).

Quoting a report from local authorities to the Munich government, he also describes the foresters' dismay, their call for the protection of the (scientifically managed) forest against "gangs of poachers," their fear of both the "devastation of the forests" and "anarchy among the mainly poor local populations" (Hölzl 2010, p. 448). Keeping the trees for the future required judicial and military intervention. In the Spessart region, one out of every ten inhabitants stood trial every year for committing a forest offense, and military troops invaded the region three times during the 1848-49 revolution, occupying villages and patrolling the forest.

Commenting on a series of articles that Karl Marx published in 1842 as an editor of the *Rheinische Zeitung* on the debates on the law on the theft of wood that were then taking place at the Rhine Province Assembly, Marxist historian Peter Linebaugh (1976) describes a similar situation. In 1836, three out of four prosecutions brought in Prussia were against "wood pilfering and other forest offenses"; the same year in Baden, one out of every six inhabitants had been convicted of stealing wood, and the proportion rose to one out of four in 1842 (p. 13). Following the Forestal Theft Act of 1837, which regulated Prussian forests, several German states revised their codes. The law on the theft of wood debated in the Rhineland was one example. Other examples included the codes of Thuringia and Saxe-Meiningen, according to which

> Written permits were required for berry and mushroom gathering. Dead leaves and forest litter could be gathered for fodder only "in extreme cases of need." The topping of trees for May poles, Christmas trees, rake handles, wagon tongues, etc., was punishable by fine and prison. (Linebaugh 1976, p. 13)

Linebaugh's analysis inscribes these events as part of a longer trend that gradually eroded a tissue of customary rights that was seen as standing in opposition to intensive sylviculture. The first decades of the nineteenth century were marked by an appreciation of the value of timber, driven by the growing needs of construction, machinery, and fuel consumption. (For example, Linebaugh reports, between 1830 and 1841, the price of beech doubled, while that of construction timber rose by 20 percent.) "Anxious to socialize the capital locked up in private forest acres" (p. 12), the Prussian state expanded the proportion of the forests that it owned and reduced their clear-cutting. It fostered the development of scientific forestry under the lead of figures such as Georg Ludwig Hartig and Johann Heinrich Cotta. The plans developed by "these specialists in sustained yield and capital turnover" clashed with the practices of "a working population increasingly ready to thwart them" and their enforcement required "the cadres of the police and the instruments of law" (p. 13).

As we've seen, it was the debates on the law of the theft of wood in the Rhine Province Assembly that gave Marx "the first impulse to take up the study of economic questions" (Marx 1904, p. 10). He cast his analysis of the situation in terms of the opposition between "the right of human beings" and that of trees; between the forest owner, supported by the state, and the "poor, politically and socially property-less," for whom Marx demanded the return of customary rights. (Marx 1842), but I will recast this opposition in a different light. This opposition involves the attempt to extract forests from the domain of the present and to reserve them for the domain of the future and hence for those who can afford to look to it.

There are different presents that stand in opposition to the future as seen in discounting. One is the present of the market, which I discussed in the previous section: the instantness of the market translates the complex question of value into the readily available signals of current prices. Another is the present of poor populations: the instantness of poverty, the start-and-stop temporality of precariousness, the haste of survival, the immediateness of the fruits on the trees and of the litter and grass on the ground. It is from that kind of present that discounting marks a departure. When looking to the future appeared to fall within the capacity of the state, it also appeared to fall beyond the capacity of the poor, attached to the necessity of the present (fig. 2.5).

THE STATE'S LONGER FUTURE VS.
PRIVATE OWNERS' SHORTER FUTURE

Debates on forests and their temporalities opposed the state not only to poor populations, but also to private forest owners. This opposition was expressed in the tension between the public and the private ownership of forests, or between the interests of the individual and the general interest. It, too, is beautifully illustrated by sociologist Vatin (2005, 2008, 2013) in his analysis of the debates on forests that took place in France in the eighteenth and nineteenth century.[14] A good entry point into these debates is the article "Forest" in Diderot and

Figure 2.5. Jean-François Millet, *Women Carrying Faggots*, ca. 1858.
(Metropolitan Museum of Art)

D'Alembert's *Encyclopédie*, attributed to Georges Le Roy: "The state needs wood of all kinds, and all of the time.... If wood is used for present needs, it also needs to be conserved and prepared well in advance for the next generations. By contrast, forest owners are in a hurry to enjoy, and sometimes their haste is understandable" (Le Roy 1757, p. 129).

The divergence between the interest of the state and the interest of the forest owners again stems from their temporalities. The state needs time to grow timber, for its "present needs" but also for those of the "next generations." By contrast, private owners are "in a hurry" to benefit from their forests. The divergence seems inherent in the very nature of these two types of beings: their limited or unlimited existence, to use again Noirot-Bonnet's terms. Can this gap be closed? Is it possible to reconcile the general interest and the interests of the individual? The answer requires understanding why forest owners are "in a hurry." The writings of two French forester-mathematicians, Buffon (more widely known for his work as a naturalist) and Varenne de Phenille, demonstrate that forest owners' "haste" is due not only to their "limited existence," but also to their acting as investors, solicitous of maximizing the value of their capital, that is, forests.

A few years before the publication of the *Encyclopédie*, in the midst of debates on the deplorable condition of French forests, Buffon proposed a solution that held the promise to align the interest of the state and the interest of forest owners with the help of economic calculation (Buffon 1739). The solution lay in the concept of the "optimum": the right moment—neither too early nor too late—when trees should be felled, defined as the age that maximizes the production of the forest. This moment, Buffon argued, can be determined scientifically, and mathematical analysis shows that it corresponds to the age when the growth of the tree starts to decline, that is, the moment when the growth of the tree (and not the size of the tree) reaches its maximum value.[15]

The possibility of aligning the individual and the general interest by scientifically determining the right moment when trees should be felled—"right" both for the forest owner and for the public—faced two obstacles. First, it did not solve the problem of the "limited existence" of private owners. As we have seen above, rotation lengths for high timber range between 80 and 300 years and hence exceed the span of human life: the temporalities of the individual and of the forest seemed to remain incommensurable. The temporality of the forest was embodied in the figure of "the public" and "future generations"—a figure readily embodied by the state.

While the first obstacle to the alignment of the individual and the general interest was related to time understood as duration (the span of an existence), the second one was related to time understood as cost. Forest owners are "in a hurry" not only because like all human beings they contemplate the end of their lives; they are in a hurry because they act as investors for whom, as everyone now knows, "time is money." Here appears the second facet of discounting, which looks to the future, but dis-counts that future.

The question of the discount rate surfaced half a century after Buffon's memoire, when Varenne de Fenille (1791) revisited the notion of the maximum—this moment when trees should be felled—by introducing the problem of capital in its definition. Varenne de Fenille wrote in the wake of the French Revolution. His *Observations sur l'aménagement des forêts…* was published in the same year as the law that liberalized the exploitation of forests in France. Varenne de Fenille distinguished two types of maximum relevant to two types of actors: the forest owner and "the Consumer, or the Public." The maximum relevant for the public, which he called "the simple maximum," was the one defined by Buffon: the maximum of the growth of trees. The maximum relevant for the forest owner, which he called "the compound maximum [*maximum compose*]," took into account not only the physical growth of the trees, but also the capital invested in the forest, or in Varenne's words, "the pecuniary interest that would have yielded the price of the coppice sold, and from which we are deprived if we postpone the sale" (p. 30).

The idea of a loss was central in Varenne's reasoning on the compound maximum. Counterintuitively, the growth of trees means a loss to the owner: "the loss of the interest on the price of the unsold thing" (p. 41). Each moment that the forest owner spends tending to his forest without exploiting it entails a loss: "an opportunity cost," as modern economics would put it. In Varenne's terms, if the forest owner postpones the felling, he loses the interest on the sale price, for which he needs to be compensated:

> An Owner does not always fell his trees to consume them; more usually, he fells his trees in order to sell them. If he postpones, he loses the interest on the sale price; if he postpones during several years, the interest accumulates and becomes significant. Therefore, it is a matter of ensuring, by means of calculation, that the added value [*mieux value*] that he will obtain by postponing the felling will compensate him overabundantly for the loss that he is making on his interests and of determining how he should act as a careful manager [*économe attentif*]. (Varenne de Fenille 1791, pp. 39-40)

Varenne's work included tables (illustrated in fig. 2.6) that compared, for each year, the value gained by coppice thanks to its growth and the value lost by not felling and selling this coppice, including the interest that the sale would have generated. As soon as the value gained becomes lower than the value lost, the coppice should be felled. In Varenne's tables (pp. 42-43), this occurs at the end of the twenty-first year.

Varenne satisfactorily observed that forest owners' habitual practice to fell their coppices at the age of twenty years was close to "what the theory of the compound maximum announces" (p. 46). When he compared the results obtained for the compound maximum, relevant for the private owner, with the results obtained for the simple maximum, relevant for "the Public," he observed a significant discrepancy: the simple maximum led to the recommendation to fell coppice at the age of thirty years, instead of twenty-one years. Based on "the very great

TABLE PREMIÈRE.

Age.	Diamètre.	Carré du diamètre.	Différence de l'accroissement d'une année quelconque fur la précédente.	Valeur en argent.	Valeur perdue par la non reproduction du terrain pendant l'année précédente.	Intérêts perdus par défaut de vente.		Total de la perte.		Excédent du gain fur la perte.	
	lignes.	lignes.	lignes.	liv.	livres.	liv.	f.	liv.	f.	liv.	f.
9	36	1296	....	1296							
10	40	1600	304	1600							
11	44	1936	336	1936	160	80		240		96	
12	48	2304	368	2304	176	96	16	272	16	95	4
13	52	2704	400	2704	192	115	4	307	4	93	4
14	56	3136	432	3136	208	135	4	343	4	88	16
15	60	3600	464	3600	224	156	16	380	16	83	4
16	64	4096	496	4096	240	180		420		76	
17	68	4624	528	4624	256	204	16	460	16	67	4
18	72	5184	560	5184	272	231	4	503	4	56	16
19	76	5776	592	5776	288	259	4	547	4	44	16
20	80	6400	624	6400	304	288	16	592	16	31	4
21	84	7056	656	7056	320	320		640		16	
22	88	7744	688	7744	336	352	16	688	16	perte 16	

Figure 2.6. An example of Varenne de Fenille's tables comparing the value gained and lost by not felling a coppice (Varenne de Fenille 1791, p. 42; Bibliothèque nationale de France).

difference between the INTEREST OF THE OWNER who cuts wood to sell it, and THE INTEREST OF THE CONSUMER, that is, of the Public" (p. 59), he argued that the coppice forests owned by the state should be subjected to longer rotation times (thirty years), which ignore the logic of capital and the calculations of the compound maximum: "It has thus been demonstrated, in the eyes of reason, the extreme importance, or rather the absolute necessity, to put off felling in national coppice forests to a much more remote period than common felling in forests owned by private individuals" (Varenne de Fenille 1791, p. 60).

The distinction between the simple and the compound maximum thus led Varenne to associate the distinction between the ways in which public and private forests should be managed in terms of rotation lengths with different types of actors, as Noirot-Bonnet was to do, basing this distinction on the difference between achieving "the simple maximum" and the "compound maximum," and with it, the concept of compensation for future losses. The longer future appeared to fall within the capacity of the state not only because of its unlimited existence, but also because of its vision of the forest, driven by the maximization of the growth of wood. It appeared to fall beyond the capacity of the private forest owner not only because of his limited existence as a human being, but also because of his impatience as an investor. Postponing the felling, sustaining the forest, drawing time out, enabling the future to proceed: all this involves a loss for which the forest owner should be compensated.

It is precisely this idea of a loss that grounds the concept of the discount rate. The discount rate captures the alternative scenario in which the investor is compensated for each moment she decides not to halt her investment: not to sell the trees' wood on the market and gain an interest rate on the money thus obtained, or, as we will see in Chapter 3, not to sell the shares of a company to buy the shares of another company that performs better. The discount rate is the reward that the investor constantly appears to be claiming for forsaking the present and acting on the future—albeit a shortened future.

THE FOREST AS WOOD AND THE FOREST AS CAPITAL

Writing half a century after Varenne, Noirot-Bonnet (1842) echoed the distinction between the simple and the compound maximum, but his analysis widened even further the gap between the state's longer future and the private owners' shorter future. Starkly put, in one view, the forest took the form of wood. In the other view, the forest took the form of value. Noirot-Bonnet, too, calculated the age at which a forest should be felled, espousing each view in turn and showed that they led to opposite results. If the product of the forest was envisioned as wood, the highest annual revenue was obtained when trees are felled at the age of 150 years. By contrast, if the product of the forest was envisioned as value, the highest annual revenue was obtained when trees are felled at the age of 1 year. The gap in these results was not only strikingly large, it was driven by "laws" that were opposed to each other, so that the growth of value (the forest's "monetary production") could be achieved only at the expense of the growth of wood (the forest's "material production"):

> We saw previously…that exploitation at the age of 150 years, approximately, brings to the highest degree the material production of forests of hard wood [*bois dur*], and we have just seen that, in the same forests, exploitation at the age of 1 year gives forest land the highest capital value and assures the owner the most significant annual revenue, or which maximizes the pecuniary production of the forest. Therefore these funds [*fonds*] provide two products of a distinct nature whose development is subject to dissimilar laws; there is even such a contrast between these laws that one of the products cannot grow without immediately entailing a decrease in the other product. In fact, material production, in annual average terms, goes incessantly increasing from 1 year until 150 years, while the annual monetary production goes incessantly decreasing from the first of these terms to the other. (Noirot-Bonnet 1842, p. 90)

ANTAGONISM AND ANALOGY:
WHAT DOES IT MEAN TO SAY THAT THE FOREST IS CAPITAL?

Noirot-Bonnet's analysis draws our attention to two alternative views of the forest, which I will call the *forest as wood* and the *forest as capital*. What is the nature of the relationship between them? According to Noirot-Bonnet, the "antagonism" (p. 98) between the forest's material and monetary production was founded on an "analogy" between the forest as wood and the forest as capital: "the material production of trees offers a perfect analogy with the interests of a capital that would be represented by forest land. From the point of view that we will take, the forest funds will be capital in our eyes, and their products will be interest" (Noirot-Bonnet 1842, pp. 77–78). Similarly, Cotta (1837) emphasized the equivalence between the revenues that forests and capital produce—equivalence insofar as the source of revenues is immaterial to their value: "A net annual revenue of 1,000 crowns, which one receives continually and has to settle for forever, without being able to attack the capital, has, considered as a revenue, only one value whatever the source it stems from, be it a forest that has more or less products or a large or small capital" (de Salomon and Cotta 1837, p. 239). For Cotta, the value of the forest is to be derived from the revenues it yields, just as for any capital that generates annual interest. For example, if a forest yields a net product of 5,000 francs per year, and the relevant interest rate is equal to 5 percent, then the value of this forest is equal to 100,000 francs, because if a capital of 100,000 was put in the bank at an interest rate of 5 percent, it would yield 5,000 francs per year (de Salomon and Cotta 1837, p. 244).

Noirot-Bonnet foresaw the following objection to the analogy between forests and capital: the point of view that sees the forest as capital has more to do with "financial operations" than with "the principal objective of forestry economy, which is to teach the conservation and the improvement of forests" (p. 78). His response to this objection was a mix of contemporary utilitarian ideology and modern theories of "natural capital": the demonstration of the economic value of nature is a necessary condition (or even an incentive) for its protection. He gave the example of the "splendid" high forests of the Alps or the Pyrenees, which can "arouse our curiosity," but "excite no interest," and as a result are "abandoned" to pasture and fires (p. 79). To put it simply, no one would care for nature if nature was not valuable. In Noirot-Bonnet's more elegant words: "An uncontested truth is that utility, the primordial basis of the value of things, is the principle and the mobile of the production and the conservation of wealth [*richesses*], as well. What attention, indeed, could we grant to what offers no utility and hence no value" (Noirot-Bonnet 1842, p. 78)?

Observe here, again, the contradictions to which discounting leads and the ways in which these contractions are dealt with. Noirot-Bonnet depicted the relationship between the forest as wood and the forest as capital both in the terms of analogy and antagonism: an antagonism so strong that it sent opposite signals to the forest owner: wait 150 years, or fell the forest as soon as it starts growing and put the money in the bank. Cotta looked at this alternative scenario of felling the forest and putting the money in the bank and wondered how realistic it was. In many countries, he noted, forests cannot be "exploited arbitrarily" but have to be "treated with economy [*management*]" (p. 236). In other words, cutting a whole forest in order to sell its timber would simply not be allowed. And even if that were allowed, it would not be possible to sell at once such a large quantity of timber on the market. The counterfactual—in the vocabulary of modern evaluation techniques—on which the theoretical apparatus of discounting rests turns out to be nonfactual. However, this does not appear to shake the foundations of discounting. Remember how Faustmann suggested that if the values produced by his formula are too low, it is not because the formula is wrong, but because the object being valued (forest land) was not made valuable enough (that is, rotation lengths were not short enough). We could imagine that Cotta's observation on the alternative scenario that discounting presupposes could lead, in a similar vein, to the proposition that regulations and markets should be redesigned so that this alternative scenario becomes possible. The idea that regulations could be changed in order to allow for this particular scenario of clear-cutting a forest after one year looks both absurd and scary, but it is reminiscent of manifold contemporary policy interventions meant to unleash value.

DISCOUNT RATES: HOW DOES THE FOREST BECOME CAPITAL?

The analogy suffices to say that the forest can be treated *as* capital. Nevertheless, it does not suffice to say how the forest *becomes* capital. The forest as capital and the forest as wood are not merely related conceptually by antagonism or analogy. The forest as wood becomes forest as capital when discounting intervenes in its valuation. To understand this, we need to look again into the process of capitalization and examine how the future flows that the forest is expected to yield are brought into the present, that is, capitalized by means of the discount rate.

Realistic or not, the alternative scenario to which growing the forest is compared in order to justify discounting consists of putting money in the bank and receiving interest on it. The return in this alternative scenario is represented by the rate of interest. It is this rate that the forest needs to outperform in order to be worth growing. Consequently, this is the rate at which its future yields are discounted in most of the foresters' writings. Most often, the discount rate was set at 4 percent, sometimes 3 percent. While the problem of the method of calculation of the interest rate (simple, compound, geometric mean…) was generally mentioned, the problem of the definition of the discount rate seldom appeared.

However, debates on the relevant discount rates[16] in forestry existed in the context of larger debates on interest and usury.[17] Martin Moog and Matthias Bösch (2013) provide a helpful review of the literature in Germany that addressed this problem in the early nineteenth century, before Faustmann's famous article. Two positions can be identified there: one held that forest discount rates should be higher than the market interest rate (that is, the prevailing interest rate offered by banks); the other held the reverse. They can be illustrated respectively with the arguments developed by Hartig and Cotta.

In a paper written in 1812 as a supplement to his 1795 textbook on forest management, Hartig argued that forest discount rates should be higher than the market interest rate because forestry is a risky activity and because capital "tied up in the forest" is not as easily available (Moog and Bösch 2013, p. 4). Moreover, he argued that rates should increase with distance in time because the further we move in the future, the higher the risk. He thus suggested to start with a discount rate of 6 percent and then increase it by half a percentage point for every age class (every twenty years).

In his textbook published in 1804, Cotta appealed to an argument related to the structure of capital markets, instead of to the degree of risk inherent in forestry. He argued that forest discount rates should be slightly below the market interest rate because capital markets are not perfect, and hence creditors cannot always receive their interest income on time or reinvest it immediately. But Cotta also found an ambiguity in the discount rate when viewed in terms of risk. He argued that the determination of the discount rate should take into account the "security [*sûreté*]" of the investment. However, the comparison between forest and financial investment was not conclusive. On the one hand, Cotta noted, it is usually admitted that buying land provides greater security than investing money; hence, the buyer should be content with lower interest rates. On the other hand, land, too, is subject to insecurity: "war, fire and water can cause great damage in the forests, wood prices can decrease, taxes can rise, etc." (de Salomon and Cotta 1837, p. 234). Therefore, the forestry discount rate could be both lower or higher than the market interest rate.

If there was no agreement on the right level of the discount rate among German foresters, how could we explain that the interest rate, usually equal to 4 percent, intervenes in a nonproblematic fashion in all the calculations that we have analyzed in this chapter, appearing without any discussion, as if it was a pregiven parameter? One clue can be found in the next step of Cotta's argument, which moves from the question of how the discount rate should be set to the question of who should calculate it. Interestingly, Cotta observed, while the law determines a maximum that the interest rate of investments in money cannot exceed, there is no such limit for investments in land. Unlike the interest rate, the discount rate has no real anchor. The "evaluator," to whom Cotta addresses his writings, should not consider this problem as part of her work. According to Cotta, discount rates should be determined by the contracting parties, in the case of voluntary sale, and by national laws or tribunals, in the case of legal assessments, then "indicated" (p. 243) to the evaluator, who will apply them in the calculation.

Cotta's observations resonate with the debates on descriptive versus prescriptive discount rates that I briefly examined in the Introduction. Like modern evaluators, Cotta's forest evaluator is not concerned with the determination of the relevant discount rate. It is "indicated" to him, just as it is indicated to managers by their financial departments and to policy makers by their authorities. Nevertheless, it is not observed in the market, as Nordhaus argued in his critique of the *Stern Review.* Cotta's proposal that discount rates should be determined collectively, by negotiation or law, appears closer to Stern's argument for prescriptive discount rates. Although discount rates were not problematized in the early writings of the scientific foresters who laid the foundations of discounting, they were still not conceptualized as given: they appeared as a matter of decision-making, rather than revelation.

MANAGING WITH DISCOUNTING: HOW DOES THE FOREST AS CAPITAL TRANSLATE INTO THE FOREST AS WOOD?

The forest as wood becomes forest as capital when discounting intervenes as a principle of valuation. And then the forest as capital becomes the forest as wood when discounting intervenes not only as a principle of valuation, but also as a principle of management. Faustmann clearly posited this twofold role of discounting when he presented his formula. He argued that it provided an answer to the two questions that had animated forestry for more than a century: "What is a forest worth?" and "When should a forest be felled?" Faustmann wrote: "The practical importance of this calculation is easy to see. From it we obtain the necessary information on the forest value in such cases as voluntary and enforced sales (expropriation), destruction of the forest by fire, insects, man, etc., and assessment of the most advantageous silvicultural system and length of rotation" (Faustmann 1968, p. 27).

Commentators in the field of forestry have described this link between the problem of forest valuation and the problem of forest management as Faustmann's greatest innovation and the reason why his "theory" could achieve an "incontestable generality":

> Faustmann seems to be the first to see so clearly that the two problems of the value of a forest and of the optimization of its management [*gestion*] had one and the same solution: the value of a forest depends on the net revenues that it has the capacity to generate in the future, and hence on its management [*aménagement*]; optimizing the management [*gestion*]

of a forest is simply a matter of choosing the treatment that maximizes its value. This unification of what had hitherto appeared as two different approaches gives Faustmann's theory incontestable generality as well as great coherence. (Peyron and Maheut 1999, p. 691)

I discussed above the contradictions to which the Faustmann formula gave rise as a valuation device, for it produced values that appeared too low. As a management device, the formula gave rise to contradictions, too, for it recommended rotation lengths that were shorter that the ones foresters habitually used. Like in the calculations of Varenne de Fenille and Noirot-Bonnet, Faustmann's formula induced an acceleration effect. Taking into account the "cost of time," or in Varenne's words, the "loss" provoked by waiting for the future instead of felling and selling in the present, discounting urges the forest owner to reason and behave as an investor and thus makes him impatient.

Discounting also gives rise to one final contradiction. It resides in the discrepancy between the recommendations of the formula as a management device and the changes that can be observed in the management of forests after the appearance of the formula. Can the effects attributed to the formula be traced to the translation of the forest as capital back into forest as wood? In other words, can the effects of discounting as a valuation device be related to the effects of discounting as a management device? This question deserves a nuanced answer.

The results to which the formula led triggered a "bitter controversy," such as the one that Paul Samuelson attempted to solve more than a century later with his concept of externality: a controversy that opposed "one side which advocated shorter *financial* rotation lengths" (obtained by maximizing the economic value of the forest) and another side that "supported the longer rotations which were usual in practice and sought to manage their forest lands to obtain the greatest annual income regardless of the amount in capital locked in them" (Gane 1968, p. 12). At the time when Faustmann wrote his article, rotation lengths were globally rising in Germany (Hölzl 2010,

p. 439; Radkau 2007, p. 168). Hölzl (2010, p. 444) gives the example of the Bavarian Forest Department, which in 1844 argued that all forms of forests should be transformed into timber forest and established "the highest possible rotation time" as a general policy. A report from 1849 entrusted the forest administration with the mission to produce "high quality products" such as oak, which enjoyed high demand on the west European market but also required rotation lengths of up to 400 years. Does this mean that Faustmann's formula was powerless in the face of the routines of foresters and the ambitions of the state, which converged on longer rotation lengths than those calculated with discounting?

The literature indicates that the Faustmann formula was at first barely used in Germany. It encountered greater success later in the twentieth century in France and in the United States. I had the opportunity to evoke this question with two forest economists who played a role in the promotion of economic analysis (and of discounting in particular) in forestry in France and in the United States. "The Faustmann formula was controversial because discounting accelerates rotation cycles," I suggested to both of them.

"Everything depends on how the discount rate is set," replied the French forest economist.[18] According to the "official methods," the discount rate is the one determined by the government (until recently, by the Commissariat Général au Plan). The "practical methods," by contrast, look at the average values of similar goods on the market and "adjust the formula so as to obtain values close to the market ones." Listening to my interviewee, I remembered all the efforts Faustmann had put in his article to distinguish the "market value" of the forest, signaled by the prices that can be observed in the present, from the "economic value" of the forest, which his formula proposed to calculate from the estimation of future flows. The important thing with the Faustmann criterion, my interviewee reassured me, is that "we can discuss the formula." It produces a "theoretical value" that is a "useful reference" in the negotiations.

But how the discount rate should be set, and even its relevance, remained in question. The North American forest economist recalled how in the 1960s, when he started his career as a professor of forest economics, discounting was already widespread, but the definition of the discount rate remained murky. He commented that

> every forestry company and even the United States Forest Service would do a discounted cash flow analysis to figure out if it was worthwhile planting trees or thinning trees or doing forestry operations. I think everyone was using that, but then they would come and ask me, "Well, Jim,[19] what rate of interest should we use or what?" ... I would have to come to the financial officer of the company and find out the interest rate that the company would pay to borrow money, and so I would say: "Just use that."[20]

So in this case, the Faustmann formula was applied as such, probably with discount rates determined by the company's cost of capital, as I will explain in the next chapter. But did this lead to shorter rotation lengths? My interviewee replied with an anecdote. He was on a visit in the southwest of Scotland, and the district forester took him out and showed him hemlock stands:

> I said to him: "What kind of rotation are you actually using? I have just done my calculations and I think it should be about 40 years, financially."
>
> And he said, "Right, but Jim, it has got nothing to do with finance; here in the southwest of Scotland, there are a lot of heavy winds, and as soon as your trees get higher than maybe sixty feet, you have the wind blowing them down. Then once trees are blown down, they fall crisscross, and it is very expensive to harvest them. There are physical rotations and there are financial rotations." ...
>
> I congratulated him. I said, "You have got it just about right financially." He said, "'Jim, it's got nothing to do with finance, it has all got to do with the wind."[21]

This anecdote serves as a caution when thinking about the effects of discounting. It urges us to look for the imprint that discounting leaves on the objects that it encounters. However, we should not expect that this imprint would be a kind of stamp that the use of discounting automatically imposes. We should not expect that the specter of the forest as capital would simply descend upon the forest as wood and model it to its image. As this chapter has shown, discounting is a reasoning that is rife with contradictions and requires the ability to embrace a certain worldview, then proceed with assuredness. Discounting is also a formula, a machine that produces statements not only about the value of things, but also about how these things should be managed, how they should be cared for, and what they should look like. These statements can be and have been, challenged, either because they appeared in conflict with incumbent practices or because the strings of calculations that produced them were deemed faulty or unreliable. The controversies over rotation lengths and modes of calculation that surrounded the use of discounting in forestry have halted its automatic application to forest management in spite of the aura of scientific forestry and the promise of rationality that the formula held.

OPEN QUESTIONS

By delving into its origins in European forestry in the eighteenth and nineteenth century, this chapter has shed light on the contradictions of discounting. Several questions remain open. That the answers to these questions will appear to be ambivalent teaches us that discounting should be treated with caution and analyzed through careful empirical scrutiny and an open normative stance.

As I have already suggested in the Introduction, the relationship of discounting to time is troubling because it simultaneously values and devalues the future. The innovation of the Faustmann formula resided in its turn toward the future as a principle of valuation, which was accompanied by the critique of an alternative principle of valuation that focused on the present. However, discounting required a form of reasoning that was difficult to apply consistently and often failed. It calculated values that appeared inappropriate and recommended management decisions that did not comply with established practices. The low values and short rotation lengths produced by the Faustmann formula were due to its assumption that time has a cost, that waiting for the future to occur entails a loss for which the forest owner, henceforth acting as an investor whose capital is locked in the forest, had to be compensated. The discount rate devalued the future to capture this idea of experienced loss and required compensation. As we will see in Chapters 3 and 4, it still does today, in an effort to capture the notion of risk and reward, intimately linked to the figure of the investor.

What happened with the lower values and shorter rotation lengths produced by discounting? What effects did they engender in forest valuation and management practices? How did the forest as capital model the forest as wood? In other words, as I already asked in Chapter 1, was discounting performative? The analysis of this early episode teaches us that history of discounting cannot be told in the terms of invention through formulas and principles, application to new objects, and diffusion in a world becoming increasingly hospitable to it and compatible with it. It is precisely because discounting was troubling to its contemporaries that it aroused controversies and progressed with difficulty. What spread with discounting was not a triumphant formula, but a certain way of looking at things—through the lens of their valuation in terms of future flows. As the French forest economist whom I interviewed explained to me, the Faustmann formula was heavily criticized initially and barely used in forestry practices for a long time. Today, he added, it is more and more often used beyond the strict scope of the valuation of forests: "we try to use the formula in climate change calculations...in order to find out what we should plant now."[22]

His assessment resonated with a video recording projected at the last Conference of the Parties (COP27) that took place in Sharm el-Sheikh, Egypt, in which Lee White, minister of water, forests, the sea, and environment of the Gabonese Republic, sang the praises of Gabon's REDD+ sovereign carbon credits in the following terms:[23]

> With living, breathing carbon credits, the carbon credits we create in the rainforest, it's a little bit like a fine Bordeaux wine. A Bordeaux wine produced in 2022 is not worth the same as a wine produced in 1990 because they mature over time. And these rainforest carbon credits, which are living, gradually accumulate biodiversity over time. So you have carbon credits that are actually maturing and becoming better value over time.[24]

The combination of forests and wine reminded me of the same two examples that Irving Fisher used to arrive at his formula that expressed the value of anything, as capital, by means of discounted future flows of costs and revenues. And the implication of forests in the fight against climate change struck me as an unexpected contemporary manifestation of the reasoning of discounting in a place where the issue at stake is precisely to make the future count, rather than discount it.

The important question, I am inclined to conclude, does not have to do with whether the Faustmann formula has actually been applied and has shortened rotation lengths. It rather has to do with how it has shaped our way of looking at forests, through the lens of their valuation as future flows. This way of looking at forests seems to have remained intact. Only the scope of future flows has expanded. The plantation costs and revenues from thinnings and the final cut that were included in the Faustmann formula have been joined by new flowing entities such as carbon credits, biodiversity, and ecosystem services.

As the definition of the flows that form forests' futures has expanded, the relationship between the actors who claim the right and the ability to act on these futures has gotten more complicated. As this chapter has shown, in forestry debates in the eighteenth and nineteenth centuries in Europe, discounting implicated the present and the future not only as alternative temporalities of valuation, but also as conflicting political domains. It led to demarcations between the immediate present of the poor, driven by necessity and survival; the short future of private forest owners, acting as investors for whom sustaining the forest entailed a loss to be compensated; and the long future of the state, enabled by its imperishability and its wealth. As forest futures are redesigned today to include carbon credits, biodiversity, and ecosystem services, the identities of the actors who claim the right and the ability to act on these futures are evolving to include local populations, multinational companies, different states, and multilateral organizations.[25]

The ways in which forests have come to feature prominently in what Asdal et al. (2023) call "the good economy" and in particular the fight against climate change and the search for sustainability leads us to one final contradiction of discounting. This chapter has shown that we should look for the effects of discounting on the objects that it encounters, but with caution and with the idea in mind that we might not find these effects, or at least not where we looked for them in the first place. The case of forests also illustrates that when looking for the effects of discounting, we should be prepared to revisit our normative stance. Are the effects of discounting good or bad? It is pretty clear by now that discounting devalues the future, creates haste and acceleration, shortens rotation lengths, urges the forest owner to behave as an investor, and lures him into felling and selling trees. What is less clear, however, is how bad this is. Or rather, how good is the opposite move, which is again instrumented by discounting: value the future, embrace the long term, extract trees from the present for the sake of sustainability and preservation.

For the North American forest economist whom I interviewed, the position of foresters and environmentalists was clear: as he explained to me, "many foresters didn't like [the results produced by the Faustmann formula] because they thought bigger trees are better and . . . now environmentalists hate to see . . . short rotations."[26] But are bigger trees better? Are the longer futures that they embody better? Think of the high hemlock stands that the Scottish wind blows down—a vulnerability that foresters already observed in the nineteenth century that led them to revisit the scientific foundations of forest management and redefine the concept of sustainability (Hölzl 2010; Lowood 1991; Scott 1998). And think of the four-hundred-year-old oaks, capable to provide the high-quality timber much demanded on the West European market, for the sake of which the Bavarian government barred the access of rural populations to the forest products that they used according to the present-trapped principle of "necessity" (Hölzl 2010, p. 445).

My objective here is not to say that tall trees are better or worse than shorter trees, that the longer future is better or worse than the shorter future, or that a concern with the future is better or worse than a concern with the present. My objective is merely to suggest that the future is not only a temporal domain that has certain specificities, usually discussed in terms of the degree to which it lends itself to knowing and caring, but also a political domain in which futures are contested. That is, my objective is to probe the implications of considering the future as a domain of which some actors become part while others do not, a domain over which some actors claim the right and the ability to act while other actors do not. It is mainly as such that the future is explored in this book by means of the analysis of discounting as a political technology.

How Did Discounting Conquer Firms' Practices? The DCF Tool, the Investing Manager, and the Disappearance of the Future

Imagine a company that has just gone public.[1] As it gets penetrated by capital markets, the behavior of its managers is gradually altered. Their temporalities shorten. The entities for which they care get focused on the figure of the "investor."[2] This figure is embodied in people with whom managers meet on a regular basis to present performance results. It is also instantiated in a permanent gaze—"the public eye"—that managers feel directed at them and that they attempt to please. Managers put their efforts into understanding how investors think and what they want. They try not to disappoint investors and to keep the promises they have made to them. The focus on the investor entails a temporality oriented toward the future, and this future is proximate, materialized in cash flows and quarterly results. "We think in quarters," managers say, and "this way of thinking in quarters is now part of everyday life" (Kraus and Strömsten 2012, p. 197).

This chapter argues that discounting has been central to the encounter between managers and investors and to the transformation that companies have undergone as part of what it is typically referred to as the *financialization* of the economy. Viewed in terms of discounting as a situated practice, in the scenario I've just described, this encounter is not the physical encounter between the managers of a company, on one side, and the fund managers and financial analysts who work for the company's investors, on the other. Neither is it the encounter between managers and the "public eye" whose imagined expectations they internalize.[3] The encounter configured by discounting is an everyday encounter that occurs repeatedly through the calculative tools that managers use to make decisions about the allocation of resources and the selection of projects that are to be initiated, continued, or closed down. If managers espouse the investor's point of view and ultimately act as investors, it is not only because they regularly meet with investors and orient their behavior in preparation for and as a result of these meetings (Roberts et al. 2006). It is also because the idea that managers should act as investors is inscribed in the most common tools with which they are equipped.

Chapter 2 showed how the early applications of discounting in the nineteenth century put the forest owner in the position of an investor, for whom the forest is capital and time is a cost. This chapter examines how, in the middle of the twentieth century, the perspective of the investor was further embedded in discounting through three major changes. First, discounting became a tool: standardized, packaged, and diffused under the name of DCF—discounted cash flow analysis. Second, it became a solution to the problem of determining "capital productivity" and ensuring "rationality" in investment decisions by maximizing stockholders' earning power. Third, its contents were altered: the definition of the discount rate shifted from the rate of interest to the "cost of capital," that is, the reward required by investors. As a result, a new figure of the manager has emerged since the 1950s, which I call "the investing manager" (Doganova 2014). It is characterized by its moral duty, its temporal orientation, and its toolbox. The moral duty of the investing manager is to act in the name of investors. Her temporal orientation is to look at the future as the source of value and to discount that future in order to reward investors. In her toolbox, there is DCF.

Viewing the financialization of the economy through the lens of the investing manager and her toolbox casts new light on the nature, the emergence, and the consequences of financialization. I will briefly discuss these three points in turn.

First, what does financialization consist of? The exploration of discounting proposed in this chapter aims at specifying what it means for a technique to be a financialized technique.[4] The story of discounting that I have told so far is that it is a technique that came from finance, insofar as it was used for the valuation of financial objects such as loans or annuities, and that encountered nonfinancial or "real" objects, in finance parlance, such as forests, mines, and railroads in the nineteenth century. The story of discounting continues in this chapter with the story of how it became a "financialized" technique: it entered textbooks in corporate finance and capital budgeting alike, it underpinned the practices of finance professionals and firm managers, and it caused the logic of financial markets to penetrate everyday decision-making when its relationship with the future was redefined through the cost of capital.

Second, when did financialization emerge? Following discounting as a tracker of financialization leads to locating the early stages of this broad process not in the 1970s and the 1980s, but in the 1950s. Managers started using DCF to make decisions about investments before they embraced doctrines such as shareholder value and witnessed their companies being thinned down, sliced, and merged. This chapter shows that the expansion of DCF started in the 1950s in the United States at the instigation of Joel Dean, a professor of economics at Columbia University. Dean was the author of *Capital Budgeting* (Dean 1951), a book concerned with, as he put it, "the kind of thinking that is necessary to design and carry through a systematic program for investing stockholders" money" (p. 1). He positioned discounting as one of the "principles" that should guide this "kind of thinking" and managers' investment decisions. The shape that Dean gave to discounting was different from the one we found in the calculations of German foresters in the nineteenth century and of Irving Fisher in the beginning of the twentieth century in one crucial aspect: the discount rate was no longer the rate of interest, but the cost of capital. Moreover, discounting was revamped from a mathematical formula (such as Faustmann's and Fisher's formulas) into a product offered to companies by the consultancy firm that Dean founded. The selling argument for DCF was that it ensured rationality in managerial decision-making, with rationality being defined as the capacity to make the decisions that were in the interest of the company's shareholders.

Third, what have been the consequences of financialization? As I mentioned above, one of them has been found in managers' short-termism, often equated with the pace of the quarterly presentations of companies' performance results (hence the notion of "quarterly capitalism"). The lens of discounting reveals a different kind of short-term temporality. As we have seen in Chapter 2, discounting induces an effect of acceleration that leaves an imprint on the entities that compose our world—visible, for example, in the height and age of trees. This chapter continues this line of analysis and describes the imprint left by DCF on entities such as factories and assembly lines, which, albeit far distant from forests, appear to undergo a similar kind of transformation when valued and managed through discounting calculations.

As was the case with forests, the consequences of discounting did not go unnoticed. The use of DCF as a tool for decision-making within US companies became the object of vivid controversies that implicated different academic disciplines and even reached the public sphere. These controversies erupted in the early 1980s, when strategy scholars at the Harvard Business School got worried by the consequences that the use of financial tools (and DCF in particular) produced in the companies that they were studying and in the statistics for the national economy that they were observing. By the end of the 1980s, these controversies were ended by the contribution of a powerful argument advanced by corporate finance scholars at the MIT. Their argument was not dissimilar to Faustmann's assertion that if the values calculated by his formula were too low, it was not because the formula was wrong, but because the objects to which it was applied were not managed well enough, were not made valuable enough. Finance scholars' argument posited that if DCF led managers to making wrong decisions, it was not because DCF was wrong, but because it was misapplied by these managers, who manifestly lacked solid competences in financial analysis. Ironically, the remedy to financialization was...more finance. The outcome of this controversy consecrated discounting and marked the victory of finance over other academic disciplines with which it competed for the control of the "real world" (in finance parlance again) of corporate activity. This battle was a crucial episode in the advent of financialization.

The chapter tells the story of financialization by discounting in three episodes. I start by examining the reinvention and expansion of discounting in the 1950s, drawing inspiration from Peter Miller's (1991) seminal analysis of discounting as an instrument for acting at a distance on managers' investment decisions. In the writings of Dean, I examine how discounting evolved as it was implicated in the relationship between managers and investors, and I follow out the implications of the seemingly innocuous shift in the technical contents of discounting, thereafter packaged as DCF. In the 1950s, discounting came as a solution to a problem (the estimation of "capital productivity") and as a tool for a user (the "investing manager") that emerged concomitantly with its reinvention. The definition of the discount rate as the cost of capital not only embedded the investor's perspective in the manager's tool, but also caused the future to disappear. I follow the gradual expansion of DCF through surveys of US firm' practices as it supplanted competing tools for the evaluation of investment projects in the 1970s, even before managers explicitly embraced shareholder value and the primacy of the investor. Thus, financialization progressed in disguise.

The expansion of discounting did not follow a smooth, linear trajectory. We did not become blind to the future blindly. We did so by shutting down the controversies that discounting triggered and by silencing the warnings voiced by many actors in many places. What we did with the future can be analyzed in the terms in which historian Jean-Baptiste Fressoz (2012) analyzed what we did with the environment: we consciously and repeatedly decided not to care about it. The history of discounting can be told in the terms of a series of "little disinhibitions," a term that, as Jean-Baptiste Fressoz (2012, p. 16) explains, "condenses the two moments of acting out: that of reflexivity and that of disregard, that of the acknowledgement of danger and that of its normalization."

I describe these two moments of disinhibition: the concerns that the expanding use of discounting in US companies raised and then the responses with which they were met and eventually silenced. Fressoz insists on the "littleness" and the "ad hoc nature" of disinhibitions, describing modernity as one "little *coup de force*" after another (p. 16). It is on the same kind of "little" events that I focus here, building on the bits of stories that some of the protagonists included in their writings or shared with me in interviews to sketch the tribulations of discounting in the 1980s. Littleness indeed characterizes the size of these events: a few articles published by management and finance scholars and a brief encounter in the cafeteria of Harvard Business School. Littleness also characterizes the scope of the claims that were put in play: we will not observe any far-reaching deliberations on the truthfulness of finance theory or on the purpose of the firm. While the opening scene of the debate on discounting in the 1980s was by no means little, for it put at stake the demise of US industry threatened by the rise of competing nations, its closing scene was sewn with remarks on misapplications that can be easily corrected and on the obviousness of valuation principles that do not require any further proof.

DISCOUNTING AS A PROMISE TO THE INVESTOR

In his brilliant analysis of the introduction and spread of discounting in the UK in the 1960s, Peter Miller (1991) demonstrates that this calculative technology emerged in relation to a specific problem: the "growth" of the British economy. The macroeconomic problem of growth was translated into the microeconomic problem of the quality of investment and firms' decision-making processes. The UK government searched for a way to "act at a distance" on firms' decisions in order to ensure their rationality, but without resorting to direct intervention, and Miller argues that discounting enabled it to do so. It was promoted for its theoretical superiority and associated with modern managerial expertise. It was recommended to the private industry and imposed on the nationalized industries. The 1967 *White Paper on the Financial and Economic Obligations of the Nationalised Industries* required that discounted cash flow analysis should be used for all important projects and that "projects submitted to the government for approval should be expressed in present value by the use of a specified discount rate" (Miller 1991, p. 756). The white paper recommended a test discount rate of 8 percent, which represented "the minimum rate of return to be expected on a marginal low-risk project undertaken for commercial reasons" (Cmnd. 3437 1967, p. 5, quoted in Miller 1991, p. 756).

GOVERNING WITH DISCOUNTING

Miller's demonstration sheds light on one of the political qualities of discounting that I outlined in Chapter 1: discounting is an instrument for governing. In the UK case analyzed by Miller, the entities that govern and are being governed are clear: managers' investment behavior is being acted upon, and it is the UK government that acts at a distance. A similar analysis can be made in the case of France (Pezet 1997). The Plan Commission (Commissariat Général au Plan) introduced its first discount rate with the Fourth Plan in 1962. The plan's rate [*taux du plan*] was set at 7 percent. The general commissioner of planning was then Pierre Massé, who had previously (1948 to 1957) served as the deputy general director at the French electric utility company Electicité de France (EDF), which made official the use of discounting for the comparison of alternative investment projects in a report from 1953 known as the "Blue Note."

In the case of the United States, which is analyzed in this chapter, discounting was an instrument for governing, too. However, the entities involved are less clear. As in France and the UK, what was acted upon was managers' investment behavior. And action at a distance was enabled by, on the one hand, the requirement, or at least expectation, to use DCF as a tool for decision-making and, on the other hand, by the definition of imposed, or at least recommended, discount rates. Yet the use of DCF and the definition of the discount rate were addressed to different problems. The problem that DCF simultaneously conceptualized and provided a solution to was not the quality of investment insofar as it enables economic growth, but insofar as it maximizes shareholders' earning power. The relationship that the discount rate operationalized was not between the present and the future, but between the money that investors put into a company and the rewards that they require in return. As a result, the entity that appears to be acting at a distance on managers' behavior by means of discounting consisted of investors, and more precisely, a company's shareholders. The channels through which investors' action proceeded also differed from those documented in France and the UK. Instead of guidelines, notes, and national plans, it is through textbooks and articles, through business education and management consulting, that discounting reached US managers.

CAPITAL RATIONALITY

The most impactful of these textbooks and articles were certainly Joel Dean's. Dean was a North American economist, professor, and consultant, known as one of the founders of business economics and the inventor of "capital budgeting" (Zeff 2008). Dean published his two most influential books in 1951. One was called *Managerial Economics* and aimed to show "how microeconomic theory could be used to make managerial decision making more rational" (Zeff 2008, p. 186). The other was called *Capital Budgeting* and applied the attempt to rationalize managerial decision-making to the problem of investment and the analysis of capital expenditures. The managers that Dean described in his book made arbitrary decisions based on subjective judgment, "determined by skill and persistence of persuasion rather than by objective indexes of company welfare" (p. 2). The remedy that he proposed was "a system for capital budgeting founded on economic analysis and designed to reduce the executive time and confusion involved in making decisions" (p. 2). This system was supposed to ensure that managers would make the right decisions, based on rational calculation.

The requirement of rationality was supported by moral and political arguments: money belongs to stockholders; it is to them that managers are accountable; it is in their name that they have to act, that is, to invest. The opening sentences of the book are illuminating as to the type of rationality that managers were invited to achieve:

> This book is concerned with the economics of capital budgeting—that is, the kind of thinking that is necessary to design and carry through a systematic program for *investing stockholders' money*. Planning and control of capital expenditures is the basic top-management function, since management is originally hired to take control of stockholders' funds and to maximize their earning power. In a broad sense, therefore, product-line policy, promotion, pricing, and labor relations can be viewed as subsidiary problems of administering management's trusteeship over capital. (Dean 1951, p. 1)

A novel conception of the manager emerges in these lines. For the manager who was concerned with balancing costs and revenues[5] is substituted a manager who is concerned with maximizing the value of the funds with which he has been entrusted. This new investing manager (Doganova 2014) has to choose the right investments so as to spend stockholders' money in the most profitable way. To make such choices, faced with the many investment proposals that are addressed to him, the investing manager is advised to rely on a number of "principles" for estimating "capital productivity" (p. 20). Dean's book lists eleven of them, two of which are constitutive of discounting.

Before we look at these principles, let us underline the novelty of the vision proposed by Dean. His proposition that managers should act on behalf of investors predates agency theory and its model of managers being "agents" acting on behalf of "principals" who are the firm's shareholders (Jensen and Meckling 1976). His notion of capital productivity—implying that capital has an idiosyncratic product and hence a price that can be different from the rate of interest—needs to be situated in its historical development, too. Illuminating in this respect is the contrast with accounting and management practices in the period of the Industrial Revolution in Great Britain. They were characterized by what would today be seen as two "heresies": first, "the treatment of capital as an auxiliary to entrepreneurship instead of the central motive force behind the firm," and second, "the confusion between capital and revenue" (Pollard 1965b, p. 233). According to economic historian Sidney Pollard, accounting practices were then driven by a "common, though unspoken assumption" that capital is not directly related to profits and therefore does not deserve a special reward, other than the rate of interest:

> the assumption that profits are not directly related to the quantity of capital, and therefore are not payment for capital or created by capital. Capital is adequately rewarded by interest at the current rate, at which, incidentally, the supply is clearly assumed to be highly elastic and limited by personal and specific shortages rather than by price. Profits are distinct and are rewards of entrepreneurship *per se*, depending on skill, the concrete business situation or sheer luck, the entrepreneur using capital merely as a tool for which he pays a market rate. (Pollard 1965b, p. 234)

So the "productivity of capital" for which discounting was mobilized in Dean's textbook emerged through the very process of its estimation through discounting. In other words, discounting came as a solution to a problem that it helped formulate. Asking how to measure the value of capital and choose the right investments or how to employ capital so as to maximize its value makes sense only if capital exists as a separate category and is thought to deserve a special treatment. It was only at the beginning of the twentieth century that investments were isolated from current expenditures and classified in a separate account; identifying investments as a specific category allowed for measuring the "return on investment," which compared the profits generated with the amount of capital employed (Haka 2006).[6] This, in turn, opened the way for rewarding capital with a specific price for its services.

When and where exactly that happened is difficult to determine, as such origins always are, but some authors seem to concur on the case of the Du Pont company in the first years of the twentieth century (Johnson and Kaplan 1987; Levy 2014). According to Johnson and Kaplan (1987, pp. 69 and 89), the DuPont de Nemours Powder Company inaugurated a system for accounting assets (plants and equipment) in 1903; a corporate document from 1911 described the measure of return on investment (ROI) as net earning divided by net asset. Johnson and Kaplan draw a contrast between the nineteenth century manager concerned with costs and revenues, and the rationality of the Du Pont managers in the early years of the twentieth century:

> Single-activity firms before 1900 assessed net earnings, if at all, in relation to costs of operations and not in relation to the firm's total investment in assets. The typical nineteenth-century entrepreneur, being chiefly concerned with controlling costs and raising efficiency in a single activity, had little reason to measure return on investment. The Powder Company's executives also recognized the importance of controlling day-to-day operations costs, but they perceived that "a commodity requiring an inexpensive plant might, when sold only ten percent above its cost, show a higher rate of return on the investment than another commodity sold at double its cost, but manufactured in an expensive plant." They concluded that "the true test of whether the profit is too great or too small is the rate of return on the money invested in the business and not the percent of profit on the cost." (Johnson and Kaplan 1987, p. 69)

Quoting a Du Pont executive (an accountant, actually), Levy (2014, p. 193) specifies that "money invested" meant "the capital embodied and used in physical structures." Levy argues that as a measure of profit, ROI "narrated a corporate history of the life cycle of fixed industrial capital" (p. 193), by contrast to its predecessors' histories of commerce and costs and its successor's history of financial markets and future valuations. In the history of capital budgeting, DCF thus stands somewhere in between ROI and its successor, ROE (return on equity, prevalent from the 1980s), in Levy's history of profit. The Du Pont managers, tooled up with ROI, prefigured the investing managers, tooled up with DCF, to whom Dean addressed his book. They shared a similar problem—how to measure return—but diverged in their views of investment and capital. For the former, investment was embodied in plants and equipment. For the latter, investment was an act that they performed on behalf of investors. It is precisely this act of investment that discounting came to equip.

THE INVENTION OF DCF, OR THE REINVENTION OF DISCOUNTING

In his book, Dean listed eleven "principles" for estimating the "capital productivity." The third and the sixth principles referred to the two essential ingredients of discounting: respectively, the orientation toward the future as a source of value and the need to discount the future with regard to the present: "3. It is future profit on additional investment that is relevant.... The record of the past is useful only as a guide to estimates of the future," and "6. Discounting the stream of capital earnings to take account of the diminishing value of distant earnings is an integral part of the theory of capital value" (Dean 1951, p. 22). Dean did not expand on the issue of the discount rate, but mentioned, with reference to the "complications of measurement" that discounting a firm's future income streams could introduce, that the discount rate is "logically the firm's cost of capital" (Dean 1951, p. 22).

As noted by Johnson and Kaplan (1987), Dean's book did not include a precise mention of "discounted cash flow analysis" as a method of capital budgeting. In the discounting calculations in the book, streams of earnings are discounted, instead of cash flows;

moreover, the complications induced by discounting and its inappropriateness for certain types of projects are clearly acknowledged. However, the technique of discounted cash flow analysis was popularized in the years that followed the publication of the book through the publication of an article in the *Harvard Business Review* (Dean 1954), the creation of an academic journal, *The Engineering Economist*, devoted to the dissemination of capital budgeting techniques, the publication of textbooks, and the development of present-value procedures by engineers, in particular in large oil companies, for some of which Dean worked as a consultant (Johnson and Kaplan 1987).

Consulting was crucial in the dissemination of discounting theory and the DCF tool. Insights into the role played by Dean's consulting firm are provided by Gordon Shillinglaw, a management accounting scholar who worked for Joel Dean Associates between 1951 and 1954 while completing his PhD in economics at Harvard and before joining MIT and later Columbia (Burrows 2013). In a personal communication to Zeff dated February 21, 2008, Shillinglaw claimed credit for coining the term "discounted cash flow" while he was with Dean's consulting firm (Zeff 2008, p. 187). He described how DCF was transformed from a tool that engineers were tinkering with into a "product" sold by the consultants to the companies they worked for:

> The first week I was on his payroll we journeyed to Philadelphia to talk to Horace Hill and John Schultz at Atlantic Refining Company. They were using what they called the Investors Method to analyze capital expenditure proposals. Schultz was the real brain behind all this, and a number of my better problems came from him. Anyway, he had prepared an extensive set of discount tables based on continuous compounding...[and] we decided to add this to the product line of Joel Dean Associates, but we adapted it for different clients. Our first major client was the Chesapeake and Ohio Railroad, where John Kusik was CFO. Because most of the people on his staff had engineering backgrounds, we called it the Engineers Method. It was only after that that we decided to call it what it was, discounted cash flow." (Shillinglaw, quoted in Burrows 2013, p. 648)

Note the early name of discounting among the companies that used it: "the Investors Method." Discounting embeds the investor's point of view and imprints it on the manager using the DCF tool to make decisions on the investments to be carried out by the firm.

In one of the first explicit formulations of the "Discounted Cash-Flow method," Dean opposed it to the "Accounting Method" of return on investment:

> There are several ways to calculate rate of return. These different methods are not equally good, and I should like to spend a few moments outlining what I think is the best method. I shall call this method the "Discounted Cash-Flow" method in contrast with what might be termed the "Accounting Method." The essence of the Accounting Method is to compute a ratio of net earnings to the amount invested. The Cash-Flow Method is far less commonly used for this purpose than the Accounting Method, and there are far fewer variations to it. The mechanics of the method consist essentially of finding the interest rate that discounts future earnings of a project down to a present value equal to the project cost. This interest rate is the rate of return on that investment. (Dean 1953, p. 121)

The above quote is taken from an article that Dean published in 1953 in the *Journal of Finance* and signed with affiliation to both Columbia University and Joel Dean Associates. It advocated the superiority of the rate of return as a measure of investment value compared with the methods that were widely used by companies at that time, such as the payback period.[7] The rate of return, Dean argued, was "the only economically valid index of investment value." It was the tool that the investing manager needed to perform her "function": "Such an index is an essential part of a good capital management program, since in the last analysis management's function is to invest the stockholder's money in ways that will maximize return on it" (Dean 1953, p. 120).

Both DCF, the discounted cash flow method, and the accounting method, measured return on investment, ROI, but they did so in different ways. In the DCF method, the rate of return is the "interest rate that discounts future earnings of a project down to a present value equal to the project cost" (pp. 121–22). This method has become known as the internal rate of return (IRR) and it has been criticized since then. The criticism, however, was not addressed at discounting per se, but at the idea that projects should be ranked by their rate of return. This led to the emergence of the alternative discounting method known as NPV or net present value.

In NPV and IRR alike, the valuation exercise consists of discounting and summing future cash flows. The difference between the two methods lies in the ways in which the discount rate is determined: in IRR, the discount rate is the result of the calculation (it is the rate at which NPV is equal to zero), while in NPV, the discount rate is an input to the calculation, and projects are ranked according to their NPV, which can be positive or negative. A question arises in both calculations: What is the criterion that allows assessing the rate of return? When NPV is calculated, a criterion is needed to set the rate at which future cash flows should be discounted. When IRR is calculated, again, a criterion is needed to decide, for example, whether a 15 percent return is "good enough" or whether only investments worth 30 percent or more should be made.[8] This criterion is the cost of capital as determined by investors' expectations and demands: "Ideally, the minimum acceptable rate of return should be determined on the basis of the company's cost of capital funds, that is, the rate-of-return which outside investors require before they will entrust their money to the management of the company" (Dean 1953, p. 126).

This seemingly innocuous shift is one of the key moments in the history of financialization. In the calculations of the German foresters, the discount rate was the rate of interest. When discounting became involved in the relationship between managers and investors, the meaning of the discount rate changed. Future cash flows were to be discounted using a different number: not the rate of interest, but the cost of capital. The cost of capital reflects the cost for the firm of the two types of capital that it uses (debt and equity); that is, the returns required by two types of stockholders (bondholders and shareholders). The justification for discounting was no longer that time had a cost or that the future was distant and uncertain, but that capital should be rewarded for the services it renders, for the profits it generates. The future disappeared. It disappeared as a focus of concern for managers, replaced by concern for the present interest of investors. It also disappeared materially because with high discount rates, flows that are distant in time barely matter. And discount rates increased indeed once they were redefined as the cost of capital: contrast the rate of 4 percent used by nineteenth century foresters with rates such as 15 percent or 30 percent that Dean used as examples in his writings.

THE EXPANSION OF DCF, OR FINANCIALIZATION IN DISGUISE

By the end of the 1950s, the principles of discounting had stabilized. We can see them brought to completion in an article published in 1959 in the journal *The Engineering Economist* by Shillinglaw, the Joel Dean Associates consultant who coined the term DCF and who by then had become a professor at MIT. First, he says, discounting is the tool that enables the investing manager to perform her duty, that is, select the investments that are "best" for investors: "The principal objective of capital expenditure management is to protect the investor's equity in the firm. Protection, however, is much more than a mere maintaining of the status quo. Rather, capital management protects by seeking to achieve the most favorable future profit position in relation to investment by selecting the best among investment alternatives currently available" (Shillinglaw 1959, p. 1). Second, the criterion that serves to assess the return on investments is the cost of capital. Shillinglaw refers more precisely to the "weighted cost of capital," determined by "weighting the capital costs of the various sources [retained earnings, debt, equity] in proportion to their respective roles in the company's long-range financing plan" (p. 9).[9] Third, rates of return should be determined by "some method that embodies the concept of discounting the after-tax cash flows of a project during its expected life" (p. 13).

Shillinglaw discusses three such methods, among which are NPV, with future cash flows being discounted at a pregiven rate corresponding to the company's cost of capital (10 percent, in his example), and IRR, "known variously as the investor's method or discounted cash flow method" (p. 14). The criticism addressed to the internal rate of return is discussed, but the paper concludes that the results to which NPV and IRR would lead will not differ significantly. The important message is that the method used should incorporate the principles of discounting, unlike alternative methods such as ROI or the payback period.

Albeit stabilized, the principles of discounting had not yet spread in firms' practices at the beginning of the 1960s. In a study based on interviews with top-ranking executives of forty-eight major companies, D. F. Istvan (1961) observed, in a highly critical tone, the insufficient use of discounting. His results showed that the majority of the firms (77 percent) used as an acceptability criterion the payback period or its reciprocal, the "simple rate of return," which corresponds to the rate of return in the accounting method discussed above. The author argued that that these two measures, which simply compare the initial investment with the earnings that it will generate, suffer from "fallacies" and "deficiencies," namely, their "failure to consider the time dimension" (p. 47). He recommended the use of "the time-adjusted rate of return: the 'discounted cash flow,' as it is termed by its leading proponent, Joel Dean" (p. 48). Observing that only 10 percent of the firms he interviewed used discounting as a measure for the acceptability of investments, the author lamented: "Businessmen overwhelmingly fail to have regard for a basic tenet of economic theory, namely, that time has economic value, or, stated in slightly different terms, that money has a time dimension" (Istvan 1961, p. 50).

Surveys of firms' practices a decade later reveal a completely different picture. In an article published in 1975, Eugene F. Brigham (1975) shows that the great majority (94 percent) of the thirty-three firms that he surveyed used "one or more of the DCF criteria" (IRR, NPV, and profitability index), and 70 percent used the NPV method (p. 18). More than half of them (61 percent) based their discount rates on their cost of capital, defined as "the weighted average of (their) cost of debt and equity" (p. 19). The only explicit alternative to the cost of capital mentioned in the survey are historic rates of return on investment, which turn out to be used by only 10 percent of the companies and are criticized by the author for "not maximizing stockholder wealth" (p. 19). The article celebrates these results, revealing the adequacy between firms' practices and theoretical statements that, as the author puts it, "most academicians would accept": that DCF techniques, and the NPV method in particular, "should be used to evaluate capital expenditure proposals" and that a firm's discount rates "should be based on its average cost of capital" (p. 17). No data are provided on the level of the discount rates observed, but the examples given use 15 percent as a discount rate.

Another survey conducted by Thomas Klammer (1972) and based on a larger sample (184 US companies in different industries) found that the majority of firms (57 percent) used discounting (NPV or IRR) as their primary standard for project evaluation (p. 393), leading the author to conclude that "the advanced theory of the 1950s has increasingly become the practice of the early 1970s" (Klammer 1972, p. 394). This survey is particularly interesting because it reveals how discounting gained popularity during the 1960s at the expense of other methods, such as payback or the accounting method rate of return. Surveyed companies were asked to compare their current and past practices: 57 percent of them declared that they used discounting techniques in 1970, against 38 percent in 1964 and 19 percent in 1959. Payback, which had appeared as the most popular method in previous studies, followed the opposite evolution: while 34 percent of companies declared that they used payback as their primary project evaluation technique in 1959, only 24 percent did so in 1964 and 12 percent in 1970.

However, while the use of discounting as a financial tool spread, those who embraced it did so without grasping its implications as serving the financial interest of the firms' investors. In a survey whose results were published in *The Engineering Economist* in 1975 (Petty et al. 1975), the "discounting techniques," described as the "evaluation methods generally thought to be 'theoretically correct'" (p. 163), were ranked first by more than half of the companies (50 percent ranked them first for projects dealing with existing product lines and 58 percent for projects dealing with new product lines), far ahead of other methods such as payback or the accounting rate of return. The majority of the responding firms (84 percent) reported that they set a minimum rate of return that projects should comply with. Most often (in 40 percent of the cases), this rate was determined by management; more rarely, but still quite often (30 percent), it was based on the "weighted cost of sources of funds"; and only a minority of responding firms (13 percent) used historical rates of return. The authors concluded, on a positive note:

> As contrasted with early studies, the current effort reveals that a surprisingly large number of major United States corporations are utilizing the preferable discounted cash flow techniques in project evaluation. In fact, in reply to a direct question, almost one-half of the respondents expressed that the firm has moved to more quantitative and formal analysis. This change in procedures represents the dominant improvement in their budgeting process. While the executives indicated that the maximization of common stock price is not the major financial objective of the firm, such a goal is implicit in the use of the theoretically correct evaluation techniques. (Petty et al. 1975, p. 170)

Notice the contradiction here. When US managers in the early 1970s were asked whether their objective was to maximize shareholder value, they answered no. When they were asked whether their tool for making decisions on investments was discounting, they answered yes. As Petty et al. (1975) suggest, the two answers are contradictory, because shareholder value is "implicit" in the use of discounting and the definition of the discount rate as the cost of capital. In other words, the threads of financialization penetrated firm practices earlier and in a subtler way than accounts focusing on the spread of the shareholder value rhetoric, agency theory, or particular consultancy products would indicate. The ideology of financialization arrived disguised as a "theoretically correct" tool of discounting.

DISCOUNTING AS A THREAT TO THE ECONOMY

In the beginning of the 1980s, the United States started worrying about the decline of its economic power. An article published on May 30, 1982, in the *New York Times* is exemplary of the debate that such worries triggered and the ways in which discounting and finance theory featured in it. It asked: "why the nation's bedrock industries, such as autos and steel, have withered in the face of foreign competition" (Wayne 1982).[10] To the usual suspects such as "heavy-handed regulation, the avarice of labor unions, the decline of the work ethic, the oil crisis or the Japanese," the article added a new culprit: US managers, thanks to the education that they receive at business schools and the incentives that they follow once they start their corporate careers, which all push them to care about "short-term profits" and neglect "the factory floor and the assembly line":

> These days corporate managers are taught, as the dominant approach, that big corporations, whatever their nature, whatever they produce, can and should be managed like an investment portfolio. Their numerous divisions should be seen mainly as so many possible investments competing for scarce funds. Some businesses are to be invested in, others harvested for their cash. All are held strictly accountable by the common yardstick of the return they earn from the resources they consume. (Wayne 1982)

"We have found the enemy, and it is us," the article concluded. This diagnosis aroused heated letters from managers who felt that the accusations addressed to them were harsh and wished to provide other explanations. Some attempted to redirect the blame on the general economic environment. For example, an oil company executive justified managers' behavior by external factors such as "capital shortage" and rising interest rates (Krasts 1982). In this "economic climate," his letter continued, "companies begin to feel uneasy as they view an uncertain future, and consequently they turn their attention toward increasing their cash inflow." Others expanded the accusations to shareholders, whose influence explained managers' strange behavior. The author of another letter to the editor lamented that nothing can be done to help the American manager, trapped in her relationship with "the American shareholder" under whose control she acts: "we remain deep in the woods because America's senior managers, who do understand the problem, must respond to a headless, mindless entity—the American shareholder—who demands immediate sacrifices of future productivity in favor of short-term earnings. Any manager who does not comply is terminated" (Friedman 1982). And others reacted to the role attributed to managerial tools such as discounting: "it is very clever to sharp-shoot the discounted cash flow techniques used to evaluate new programs, but the analysis is superficial. Japan's current prime rate is less than 7 percent. Use that number and discounted cash flow analysis works very well" (Lemkin 1982).

US managers, the tools that they use, and the shareholders in whose name they act: this threesome was at the center of the debate on the decline of US industry in the 1980s. To understand the links between these three entities, it is necessary to delve into the management articles on which the *New York Times* journalist based her piece: an article published by two Harvard Business School professors, Robert H. Hayes and William J. Abernathy, in a 1980 issue of the *Harvard Business Review* (Hayes and Abernathy 1980) and a sister paper that Hayes published with another colleague two years later in the same journal (Hayes and Garvin 1982). These two papers had a significant effect. The 1980 paper attracted "more attention than anything else published in the Review," according to an associate editor at the *Harvard Business Review* quoted in the *New York Times* article. It was reprinted in 2007 as one of the twenty most cited papers from the *Harvard Business Review* (Hayes and Abernathy 2007). The 1982 paper became a McKinsey Award winner. They both aroused vigorous reactions and harsh criticism.

DISCOUNTING CURIOSITIES

In 1980, Hayes was a forty-five-year-old professor at the Harvard Business School, specializing in the field of operations management. As he explained to me, his papers were a response to the contemporary debate about why US companies were doing worse than their European and Japanese counterparts while they faced the same "problems," such as oil prices and trade unions.[11] The statistics showed that key drivers such as productivity and investment slowed their growth. Through his consulting activities, Hayes had the opportunity to observe how companies actually made investment decisions; for example, decisions about expanding a plant, building a new plant, or implementing new production techniques such as flexible manufacturing systems. "I was astonished when I saw that to make these decisions, they used DCF," he shared with the discounting-sensitive listener that I was. He found "absurd" the very high discount rates that they used: rates such as 20 percent, for example, which "basically means that the future isn't worth considering." Moreover, they extended the analysis only to five or ten years and used terminal value, which "means that your window stops at year five."

The troubling consequence of the use of discounting was that companies were turning down investments, were not expanding, and were not buying new equipment. Hayes observed a similar effect in his teaching activities. He remembered a case study on the Schlitz brewing company where students were asked whether the company should invest in a new factory. They all returned saying: "No, because it's never going to be profitable. They should not expand. The best would actually be that they withdraw from this business!"

The case of Schlitz is interesting because it has become a narrative of what the search for short-term profits and investor satisfaction can do to a company. The story is nicely summarized in this post from a blog on the beer industry:

> At Harvard, the MBA program has a case study on how to kill a billion dollar company. It's called the demise of the Jos. Schlitz Brewing Co. By the early 1970's, Schlitz was trying to reduce costs and looked at building new, state-of-the art breweries. The Schlitz shareholders, however, refused to approve the change. The production department was then forced to create a new cost-cutting scheme: "accelerated-batch fermentation." The process added air to stimulate the yeast's growth, and reduced fermentation from twelve days, to less than four days, and allowed the brewmaster to cut the brewing cycle from 25 days, to two weeks. Corn syrup replaced corn grits; hop extract replaced hop pellets. Then the finance department raised prices in a high inflation market. By the mid 70's, with sales in a decline, an accountant took charge of running the brewery, and the marketing/sales executive, Fred Haviland, cleaned out his office and left." (Westapher 2013)

The moral of the Schlitz story is that although shareholder value rose in the short term (two to three years after the reforms started), it finally fell in the long term (ten years after), and the company eroded both its competitive position and its stock price. Of interest for us here is the link with discounting and the kind of transformations to which it gives rise: the implementation of "accelerated-batch fermentation," a shortened brewing cycle, a beer that consumers no longer seemed to appreciate, and the destruction of ten million bottles of beer that failed quality-control tests one year (Day and Fahey 1990).

It is effects such as these that most troubled Hayes and his coauthors. Driven by the use of discounting, US managers "found reinvestment in existing businesses less and less desirable" (Hayes and Garvin 1982, p. 63) and preferred buying pieces of other businesses in a general wave of mergers and acquisitions; they tended to "delay the replacement of a piece of equipment by another, more modern machine" (p. 64); they engaged more eagerly in expanding existing facilities than in building new ones. This, according to the authors, led to "ponderous, outmoded dinosaurs that are easy prey for the smaller, more modern, and better focused plants of competitors" (p. 63). They illustrated the claim by two examples that we may add to the short, young trees of Chapter 2 and the tasteless beer mentioned above in the cabinet of curiosities featuring entities shaped by discounting. The first was a manufacturing operation that, starting out as "a simple assembly operation in the 1920s," kept "expanding both the size and the numbers of its processes" until having "grown like Topsy," it "finds itself with a mammoth and uneconomical complex," even though "each addition made sense at the time." The second was a "collection of more than 40 multilevel buildings producing an extraordinary variety of low-demand items using equipment that dated back before World War II" that was forced to close down when faced with "the immense task of modernizing this outmoded plant, whose condition was the result of a series of apparently rational investment decisions over a long period" (pp. 63–64).

THE IRRATIONAL MANAGER

What was the link between discounting and curiosities such as a mammoth and uneconomical-manufacturing operation and a rationally constructed outmoded plant? Hayes and Garvin's demonstration hinged on the link between discounting and the willingness to invest. They showed that discounting calculations are likely to justify a policy of progressive disinvestment—a policy that they likened to the decision to operate "a goose that will lay each and every year golden eggs" (p. 56) so as to "remove its eggs prematurely, even though doing so impairs its future-laying ability (p. 58). The main problem, in their eyes, was that managers "appear to believe completely in the legitimacy of their investment decisions and in the techniques on which they are based" because of their "apparent rationality" (p. 55). These techniques, the authors argued, are based on a "combination of theoretical blind spots and economic misjudgments" (p. 55).

The central culprit at which the authors pointed was the discount rate. As we saw in Chapters 1 and 2, in the original theory of discounting, the discount rate is the interest rate that could be gained if the money was put in the bank instead of invested in, say, growing a forest. When extended to capital investments in the firm, the discount rate moves from the interest rate to "the rate of return that could be realized if the capital project were not approved and the funds were directed elsewhere" (p. 55). Managers called this the "hurdle rate." Calculated with the help of finance theory and the Capital Asset Pricing Model (CAPM), it was often situated in the range of 25 to 40 percent (p. 61). According to Hayes, the rule of the CAPM led to "an arbitrarily high cost of capital which made investments unnecessarily improbable."[12]

Discount rates were not only too high, but also "often used without question" (Hayes and Garvin 1982, p. 61). The rationality of discounting became its danger because "managers can all too easily hide behind the apparent rationality of such financial analyses while sidestepping the hard decisions necessary to keep their companies competitive" (p. 65). Hayes contrasted US managers, who were blindly following what discounting told them to do, to Japanese managers, who would simply say "we have to be in this market, even if the rate is lower," because they followed the prescriptions of a national industrial policy, and to European companies, who "would be thinking more holistically."[13]

Hayes and Garvin's criticism was addressed not only to the ways in which managers used discounting and the high discount rates that they practiced, but also to the basic rationale of discounting and the financial theories that inspired it. They emphasized two technical problems that have been discussed in the literature in economics: irreversibility and interdependency. Irreversibility refers to the implicit assumption made by discounting that investment processes are reversible, that is, that if one does not invest in a project now, she can always invest in it later. The classical example that shows the limitations of this assumption, Hayes explained to me, is that "if you delete

Notre Dame to build a parking lot, it's irreversible, you can't get Notre Dame back."[14] Interdependency referred to the links between different investment projects, which finance theory and discounting cannot take into account because they look at each project individually, as an autonomous asset that competes with other assets.

But the most salient criticism that Hayes and Garvin formulated, as we can judge from the reactions that it aroused among finance and management scholars, was addressed to the way managers "view the future through the reversed telescope of discounting cash flow analysis" (p. 51). It was the view of the future that discounting carried and imprinted on managers that was to blame. As they put it,

> capital investments represent an act of faith, a belief that the future will
> be as promising as the present, together with a commitment to make the
> future happen. Modern financial theory argues that under certain "rea-
> sonable" assumptions disinvestment is a logical and appropriate course of
> action. Today the future consequences of a disinvestment strategy, as seen
> through the reversed telescope of discounting, may appear inconsequen-
> tial; but once tomorrow arrives, those who must deal with it are certain to
> feel differently. (Hayes and Garvin 1982, p. 66)

The attack on finance theory was even more explicit in the other article that Hayes had published two years earlier (Hayes and Abernathy 1980), whose argument reached the columns of the *New York Times*. Entitled "Managing Our Way to Economic Decline," the article made a vigorous charge against "modern management principles" (p. 67), which the authors held responsible for the decline in the rate of productivity growth in the United States. These principles, described as a new "managerial gospel," favor "analytic detachment" over "hands on" experience, and "short-term cost reduction" over "long-term development of technological competitiveness" (p. 68). The demonstration built on two types of materials. Statistical data on the evolution of productivity growth, capital investment, and reserach and development (R&D) expenditures in the United States, Japan, and European countries showed that the United States was lagging behind. In addition, quotes from managers in non-US companies commenting on the practices of their US counterparts showed that American companies behaved strangely. They "act like banks," one "observer" shared with the authors because "all they are interested in is return on investment and getting their money back" (p. 68).

The authors were explicit about the academic origins of the new "managerial gospel." Two disciplines were identified as responsible for the "myopia" (p. 68) from which US managers suffered: finance and marketing. From finance, the authors argued, managers had inherited the fashion of decentralization, separating those who run the companies' operations from those who evaluate them, which creates the need for "remote control" and "management by the numbers" through "objectively quantifiable short-term criteria" (p. 70). From finance, too, they had inherited theories of portfolio management that transpose the workings of financial markets to the working of corporations: "When applied by a remote group of dispassionate experts primarily concerned with finance and control and lacking hands-on experience, the analytic formulas of portfolio theory push managers even further toward an extreme of caution in allocating resources" (Hayes and Abernathy 1980, p. 71).

According to the authors, the legacy of finance theory was increasingly penetrating US companies because top managers increasingly possessed expertise in finance and legal areas, rather than in production. Top managers had become "pseudo-professionals": individuals with no technical or industry-specific knowledge who can "step into an unfamiliar company and run it successfully through the strict application of financial controls, portfolio concepts, and a market-driven strategy" (p. 74). As Hayes shared with me, "I've been sitting on boards, and they don't know about the technologies, the markets; they see themselves as playing a fiduciary role: protecting the shareholders' investment."[15]

Hayes and Garvin (1982) blamed discounting for its "apparent rationality," behind which managers tended to hide in order to avoid making decisions. In Hayes and Abernathy's (1980) account, discounting was part of a set of management principles inherited from finance that had evolved into a "corporate religion" in which "the faithful" were encouraged to "make decisions about technological matters simply as if they were adjuncts to finance or marketing decisions" (p. 74). They shunned activities such as modernizing existing plants or building new ones and much more readily indulged in activities such as slicing up and merging companies and buying and selling corporate pieces. They were driven by excitement, the production of quick results, and "the appeal of the titles awarded by the financial community" (p. 75), dreaming to become the next "gunslinger," "white knight," or "raider." In place of the image of rational managers applying modern management principles, the authors substituted the description of a strange and frightening community halfway between a religious cult and a criminal gang. No wonder that the article "sent shock waves through American business" (Hayes and Abernathy 2007, editor's note) and triggered a vigorous counterattack led by finance scholars.

"WE LEFT IT TO ECONOMISTS AND FINANCE"

When I asked Hayes about what happened after the publication of his papers, he remembered that they received a "lot of criticism." Numerous letters to the editor criticized the argument and blamed the analysis for being too "simplistic." He also remembered how, shortly after the publication of his paper, a renowned professor of finance, famous for having contributed to the foundation of portfolio theory and the invention of the Capital Asset Pricing Model (CAPM)—a model that is used to determine the required rate of return of an asset in financial markets—came up to him at the Harvard Business School cafeteria and warned him: "I hope you don't mean DCF, but its application!"

Hayes and his colleagues decided to beat a retreat: "As a result, we got back to the things we were experts in. We retreated from this field and left it to economists and finance. Garvin made a study on comparing the defaults of air conditioners in the US and in Japan.... I wrote a paper…on why companies were not adopting flexible manufacturing systems and were lagging behind."[16]

That paper on flexible manufacturing systems (FMS), which Hayes coauthored six years later (Hayes and Jaikumar 1988), is significant for how the controversy evolved in the 1980s. Its first lines sound familiar: American companies are lagging behind because they have difficulty benefiting from new technologies such as FMS. And then the tone suddenly changes: the culprit no longer has to do with management principles inherited from finance theory and tools such as discounting, but with "obsolete organizations." The message is that companies need to organize better in order to reap the full advantages of the new technologies that they are implementing.

The article does contain a section on "the biases of capital budgeting," with the example of a metal products company that wished to implement a new heat-treating line. A capital authorization request was drafted, based on a DCF analysis of the project. However, because the benefits generated by this new manufacturing technology were difficult to predict, conservative estimates were used to calculate the project's annual cash flows. "Soft" benefits such as increased operating flexibility or the knowledge generated were not taken into account because they were difficult to quantify. Sales projections were made only for the first four years, which were deemed foreseeable, and then simply repeated for the additional sixteen years of the manufacturing line's expected life. The authors do not share with the reader the final decision made by the firm, but the reader expects that in such conditions, the project's NPV would be negative and that the investment would not be made. The consequences of the misfit between DCF and investments in new (radical, as we would say today) technologies are presented in a general way and with a much less worrisome tone than a reader of Hayes' previous work would expect: "Once they recognize what is going on, many companies simply force new investment by short-circuiting their standard capital-budgeting process; for example, top management steps in to take responsibility for making decisions about major capital-equipment acquisitions. But this top-down approach keeps the organization's lower levels from understanding how strategic issues may affect them" (Hayes and Jaikumar 1988).

The discrepancy with the conclusions drawn by the same author six years earlier is striking. Managers no longer appear as trapped in the "apparent rationality" of discounting and the "management gospel" it carried with it. Instead, they appear to make the right decisions and invest, and they do so against the guidance of discounting, through exceptional procedures. Discounting does not harm the prosperity of US industry; it harms the capacity of lower-level managers to understand strategic issues. So warning bells are no longer to be rung. Thus, it took only a few years for discounting to be rescued from its criticisms and its critics. How did this happen?

DISCOUNTING RESCUED

"I hope you don't mean DCF, but its application!" This sentence that a renowned finance professor told the younger and somewhat impertinent operations management professor Hayes while he was having lunch at the Harvard Business School cafeteria captures precisely the line of defense developed by finance scholars to counter the attacks on discounting: the problems described by Hayes and colleagues did exist, but they were not due to the tools with which finance theory provided managers. They were due to the erroneous ways in which managers used these tools.

This argument was developed by Stewart Myers, a professor of finance at the MIT Sloan School of Management, in an article that he published in 1984 in *Interfaces* (an academic journal in the field of operations research) and that was intended to reach a large audience beyond finance (Myers 1984). That Professor Myers took issue in the controversy over discounting was not incidental or without consequences. He is one of the leading scholars in the field of corporate finance and the coauthor of a textbook on corporate finance that has been edited twelve times since 1980 and, according to his biography, "is known as the "bible" of financial management."[17] When the controversy started in the 1980s, Myers's research was focusing precisely on questions related to capital budgeting, investment decisions within firms, portfolio theory, and the Capital Asset Pricing Model (e.g. [Myers and Turnbull 1977]). He also was engaged in a series of empirical studies on the measurement of rates of return to capital in the United States. The first edition of his textbook, *Principles of Corporate Finance*, was published in the same year as Hayes and Abernathy's "Managing Our Way to Economic Decline" (1980). Why did a figure such as Myers bother to enter the controversy over discounting, which, as he shared with me, was more akin to "journalistic commentary" than to "good economics"?[18]

> About that time, business people and commentators in the US had convinced themselves that the finance methods that were being used—like discounted cash flow—were systematically wrong and short-sighted and were leading US corporations to not invest in the long run. The thought of the 1980s was that Japan would take over the world because they supposedly were investing for the long run.... Everybody would assume that the US would fail and Japan and Germany and France would take over the world. Part of the argument was that they were not using these modern finance tools and that the US companies were stupid to use them because it just meant that they would lose out in this competitive race.

Myers was approached by colleagues in corporate strategy at MIT who asked him what he thought about that kind of argument, of which, as he explained to me, "those Harvard business review articles" were representative. "I said that my view was, and still is, that the problem wasn't finance.... It wasn't that finance was inherently short-sighted, it was the way these discounted cash flow tools were being applied that was inherently short-sighted."

In his article, Myers developed this argument in the following way. The critiques of discounting imagined US firms as being torn between two worlds: "the financial world" and "the real world" (Myers 1984, p. 129). They blamed US managers, especially those who held an MBA, for being too focused on the first world, relying "too much on purely financial analysis, and too little on building technology, products, markets, and production efficiency" (p. 129). This image, according to Myers, was incorrect because, first, the financial world is not inherently bad, and second, the financial world and the real world are not in opposition, but go hand in hand. "Financial values rest on real values" (p. 130), he argued, and financial economists are precisely trying to help the real world by attempting to "reform" managers' wrong "habits of financial analysis" (p. 129).

Helping managers meant correcting the misuse of discounting. For Myers, the misuse was twofold: first, managers often used discount rates that were "unrealistically high" (p. 132), and second, they sometimes used discounting in cases in which it was not applicable. Discount rates were too high not because they were defined as the cost of capital, but because they were artificially raised to reflect the riskiness of the evaluated project or to account for the overoptimism of the managers who sponsored it. This practice was faulty, but could be easily corrected if discount rates were based on "reasonable" estimates of the cost of capital:

> The opportunity cost of capital will always be difficult to measure, since it is an expected rate of return. We cannot commission the Gallup Poll to extract probability distributions from the minds of investors. However, we have extensive evidence on past average rates of return.... No long-run trends in "normal" rates of return are evident. Reasonable, ballpark cost of capital estimates can be obtained if obvious traps (for example, improper adjustments for risk or inflation) are avoided. (Myers 1984, p. 133)

Absent is discussion on the translation of the discount rate into the opportunity cost of capital and then into historical rates of return: the problem of the discount rate appears to be one of measurement and estimation, not of definition and justification. Absent also are indications of what "reasonable" discount rates might look like: the article instead invites the reader to abandon the search for a "normal" rate.

However, if one looks into the evidence on past average rates of return to which the article refers, she finds numbers that are quite distant from the double-digit discount rates that managers were reported using. In his empirical study of rates of return to capital, conducted with another professor of finance from MIT, Myers himself concluded that the real cost of capital for nonfinancial corporations seems to have been about 6 to 7 percent since the late 1950s (Holland and Myers 1979, 1980).[19] The other empirical study that the article refers to was conducted by Roger G. Ibbotson, who was then a senior lecturer in finance at the University of Chicago,[20] and Rex A. Sinquefield, a financial executive who earned an MBA from the University of Chicago, where, as he describes it, he studied under professors such as Merton Miller and Eugene Fama[21] (Ibbotson and Sinquefield 1976, 1982). They calculated year-by-year historical rates of return for different classes of assets in the United States, based on Standard and Poor's statistics. Their results indicated average rates of return for broadly defined classes; for the class defined as "common stocks," they found an annual return of 8.5 percent over the period from 1926 to 1974.

The other case of misapplication that Myers discussed was the improper use of discounting for the valuation of certain kinds of entities that displayed specific characteristics. We can observe again here a response to the critique of discounting that we have encountered in Chapter 1, which consists of delineating its domains of applicability. For Myers, discounting reached its "limits" when it came to valuing businesses with substantial growth opportunities, intangible assets, or pure research and development. In such cases, he argued, other approaches that are able to take into account the "links between today's investment and tomorrow's opportunities" (p. 134) should be implemented.[22]

The tone of discounting defenders stands in contrast with the viru-
lence of its assailants: it is peaceful and sympathetic, with financial
economists appearing as allies ready to help strategy scholars and
company managers who have misunderstood and misused financial
tools. There is one line of criticism, however, that Myers treated as an
offense: the idea that the problem with discounting resided not in the
improper use or the insufficient understanding of financial theory, but
in financial theory itself:

> "Finance theory, however, is under attack too. Some feel that any quantita-
> tive approach is inevitably short-sighted. Hayes and Garvin, for example,
> have blamed discounted cash flow for a significant part of this country's
> industrial difficulties. Much of their criticism seems directed to misap-
> plications of discounted cash flow, some of which I discuss later. But they
> also believe the underlying theory is wanting; they say that "beyond all
> else, capital investment represents an act of faith" [Hayes and Garvin
> 1982, p. 79]. This statement offends most card-carrying financial econo-
> mists. (Myers 1984, p. 130)

What was the finance theory that came under attack, according to
Myers? It consisted of a certain view of the firm and its investment projects. In this view, each investment project that the firm may wish to
carry out can be thought of as a "mini-firm, all equity financed" (Myers
1984, p. 127). The value of this project is then the "project's present
value to investors who have free access to capital markets" (p. 127). In
the eyes of the investors, the firm's investment projects compete with
the other securities that they could buy; therefore, the investor will be
willing to invest in them only if the firm "can do better" (p. 128).

Whether this view of the firm was true or not was not the issue at
stake. As Myers put it, "any time a firm sets a hurdle rate based on capital market evidence, and uses a DCF formula, it must implicitly rely
on the logic" of financial theory (Myers 1984, p. 128). His observation

shows how far the process of financialization in disguise had proceeded: if DCF users "implicitly" relied on finance theory, if managers
already had incorporated the investor's perspective, then the problem
was no longer whether this was right or wrong, but whether they had
done this correctly and broadly enough.

Myers thus reversed Hayes and Garvin's argument: the problem was
not that finance was having too much effect on firms' strategic planning and decision-making; the problem was that it was having too little
effect. He argued that finance should guide not only the selection of
individual investment projects, but also the strategy of the firm "as a
whole" (p. 128). He lamented that this was not the case yet and that even
for the selection of individual projects, the guidance of finance was not
always followed strictly: sometimes "low net present value projects are
nurtured" while "projects with apparently high net present values are
passed by" (p. 129), with the firm's "strategy" being the justification for
managers' temporary deviation from the precepts of finance theory.

Note that this rationale is different from Dean's moral argument
that managers should act in the name of the investor because they are
her trustees. Here, managers act as if they accepted finance theory, and
this appears as sufficient evidence for the relevance of finance theory.
The view of the world that it proposes (e.g. "think of each investment
project as a mini-firm") is observably adhered to, and this view can be
gradually extended to broader domains: "If the DCF formula works for
each project separately, it should work for any collection of projects, a
line of business, or the firm as a whole" (Myers 1984, p. 127).

The move is similar to what we saw in Chapters 1 and 2: if discounting works for forest land, *it should work* for the trees that stand
on it. If discounting works for goods such as forests or wine, it should
work for all kinds of economic goods (Fisher 1906). If it works for
projects, it should work for firms (Myers 1984). This move resonates with the potential of discounting to become a general form and
with the kind of evidence with which it is displayed, to which I will
now turn.

The evidence of discounting is deeply intertwined with a view of the dynamics of the economy and of the purpose of the firm. I asked Myers why one should discount at all, since as soon as one discounts, she automatically devalues the future, and this appears to create a problem of short-term orientation. He explained to me:

> Well, yes, that [i.e., discounting] should be, there is a rational reason to be: if you have an economy that is productive and is making investments that generate a positive rate of return, the economy is growing, and then of course a dollar immediately is worth less than a dollar in the future. If you have a dollar immediately, then you can put it to work, so any kind of a model of ideally efficient economy would have a discount rate.[23]

The obviousness of discounting did not seem to be in contradiction with the observation that it was actually a recent invention mediated by the intervention of finance theory and conditioned upon a process of learning. The way in which Myers narrated his encounter with discounting is telling in this respect:

> I started out as an MBA student in the 1960s; the concept was pretty clear by 1965, 1970; I didn't have any problem picking it up.... If you pick up the idea that the efficient financial objective of firms is to maximize value, they say OK, we are going to maximize value, maximize honest value at least, and the only question is what is the valuation? The valuation principle is obviously some kind of discounted cash flow—what else could it be? Then you add the capital asset pricing model...the theory of addressing the discount rate for the risk, and you are pretty much home free. Conceptually, I mean. It took a long time for people to get used to the idea for it to filter through to get practiced. Now, if you talk to CFOs everybody does it without even thinking, but it took a while. It actually took quite a while before it became second nature for people.[24]

If one posits that the economy is growing and that the purpose of the firm is to maximize shareholder value, then discounting comes "naturally," because it is "obviously" the valuation principle to follow, simply because, as Myers put it, "what else could it be?" Discounting can become "second nature for people" within a certain system of assumptions and a certain worldview dominated by the gaze of the investor who compares the returns generated by all kinds of projects anywhere. Once it becomes second nature for people, discounting continuously performs this worldview, for each time a manager sets a discount rate to value a project, she implicitly adheres to it, activates it, and further abolishes the gap between the "financial world" and "real world."

Eventually, the view proposed by financial economists was eagerly adopted by strategy scholars. I will give only one brief illustration: an article published by Robert S. Kaplan, professor of accounting at the Harvard Business School (Kaplan 1986). The article was published in 1986 in the *Harvard Business Review* and dealt the same problem as Hayes and Jaikumar's 1988 article discussed above, that is, the reluctance of US companies to invest in flexible manufacturing systems. Must such investments, its title asked, "be justified by faith alone?" The article starts with the example of a Japanese company installing a flexible manufacturing system that allows it to make savings in labor costs, floor space and inventory, and processing time. The project's return would be less than 10 percent per year. Such an investment would be impossible to justify for many US companies, which use discounting analysis and hurdle rates of 15 percent or higher. Referring to Hayes and Garvin, the author asks if the only way for US managers to make that type of investment would be to cast aside financial tools such as DCF "in a bold leap of strategic faith."

His answer is negative, and the argument that supports it is deeply inspired by the line of defense sketched by finance scholars. The argument goes as follows. Finance and strategy go hand in hand—there is no "fundamental conflict" between these two worlds. The only problem lies in the "poor application of DCF" to investment proposals such as flexible manufacturing systems. All managers have to do is to "apply the DCF approach more appropriately": in particular, stop setting "arbitrarily high hurdle rates." The paper gives the example of an actual capital authorization request where a discount rate of 20 percent serves to compare two alternatives: rebuild present machines or purchase new machines. Such a high discount rate, warns the author, leads to the rejection of longer-term investments because one dollar gets discounted to forty cents in five years and to sixteen cents in ten years. Instead, an appropriate discount rate should be based on "the project's opportunity cost of capital." The cost of capital is defined as "the return available in the capital markets for investments of the same risk." It can be estimated by "taking a weighted average of the current cost of equity and debt at the mix of capital financing typical in the industry." Building on one of the empirical studies I mentioned above (Ibbotson and Sinquefield 1982), the author concludes that a company's cost of capital "can be in the neighborhood of 8%" — a message about which, he suggests, "many corporate executives will, no doubt, be highly skeptical."

Like Myers, Kaplan argued that the problem with discounting is its application, not its theory. Finance theory was not even debatable because it presented itself with the kind of evidence that commands adherence and exempts it from the need of proof. "It is unlikely," the author wrote, "that the theory of discounting future cash flow is either faulty or unimportant: receiving $1 in the future is worth less than receiving $1 today." This sentence nicely captures how discounting survived the harsh attack that it endured in the 1980s, and became "second nature."

THE FUTURE OF THE FUTURE

The reinvention of discounting by the invention of DCF lies at the intersection of the history of the financialization of valuation (Chiapello 2015) and the analysis of discounting as a political technology. The intervention of discounting in the allocation of resources becomes blatant when DCF is used to compare alternative investment projects and select the ones that have the greatest present value. DCF has been an instrument for governments to "act at a distance" on companies' investment decisions by setting national discount rates (Miller 1991), and with the definition of the discount rate as the cost of capital such action at a distance was extended to investors.

This shift in the discount rate also affected the ways in which discounting described and produced the characteristics of the future. The future disappeared as a matter of concern because the justification of discounting no longer resided in the cost of time and the difficulty of waiting for the future to occur, but in the need to reward investors for the risks they take. And the future disappeared materially because free from the anchor of the interest rate, discount rates increased, and the future lost its worth.

However, the future still had a future. The reasons that spurred the critique of discounting in the 1980s lay in the observation of the "economic decline" of the US industry that was diagnosed to be lagging behind other economies, especially Japan. Such observations have vanished since then. Why?[25] One possible explanation, hinted at by some of the protagonists in this chapter, is that discounting spread worldwide, probably causing even what were then thriving economies to decline. Another possible explanation, however, is that the future was delegated to a different span of the US economy.

It may be no coincidence that the 1980s saw the emergence of an innovation-driven economy characterized by new modes of valuation that were radically future-oriented. To cite just one example, in 1976, scientist Herbert Boyer and venture capitalist Robert Swanson founded Genentech, the first biotechnology start-up. In 1978, Genentech and the pharmaceutical company Eli Lilly signed an agreement for the development of recombinant insulin, which resulted in the first approved biotechnology drug, Humulin. This agreement pioneered an entirely new business model and transformed research and development from a costly activity hidden inside the firm into an exciting opportunity for partnering and funding (Pisano 2006). In 2009, Genentech was sold to Roche for $43 billion. This example tells the story of the birth of a new economy whose essence can be captured through notions such as open innovation (Chesbrough 2006), in a more positive vein, and technoscientific capitalism (Birch 2020; Birch et al. 2020; Sunder Rajan 2006), in a more critical vein. The emblematic valuation device of this new economy has been the business model (Doganova and Eyquem-Renault 2009), and its characteristic dynamic has been that of promissory futures (Sunder Rajan 2006).

As we observed for forests in Chapter 1, the legacies of discounting can be identified not in the persistence of stable formulas and calculations such as Faustmann's, Fisher's, and now Dean's, but in certain ways of looking at things through the lens of their valuation as discounted future flows. Like discounting, business models are capitalization devices (Doganova and Muniesa 2015). Instead of rejecting discounting, technoscientific capitalism has made assetization its dominant form of valuation (Birch and Muniesa 2020). How discounting handles the innovation economy and what the future looks like there, if indeed it has not disappeared there, too, will be explored in the next chapter through what is certainly the most emblematic setting of technoscientific capitalism: the biopharmaceutical industry.

Discounting and the Valuation of Drug Development Projects: Versions of Uncertainty in the Biopharmaceutical Industry

Today, discounting is firmly anchored in the valuation and decision-making practices of corporations. Critiques of the effects of discounting on managers' investment decisions, on industries' innovation and productivity, and on national economies' prosperity have vanished. Today, the critique of discounting primarily focuses on the unreliability of the projections on which it relies and hence on its incapacity to calculate correctly the value of things and its corollary capacity to lend itself to manipulation. The idea that lies at the heart of contemporary critiques of discounting is that of *uncertainty*. The future is uncertain, the argument goes, and cannot be known. By attempting to look to the future, valuation devices such as discounting deprive themselves of the capacity to calculate. As observed ironically in a comment published in the *Financial Times* business and finance column "Lex," discounting creates the illusion that "it is possible to see the future. All you need is a spreadsheet" (Indap 2013).

The critique of discounting that puts forward the uncertainty of the future as an impediment to calculation resonates with a more general critique of rationality in situations characterized by uncertainty that can be found in the literature of sociology and economics. In economics, the critique of the rational economic actor remains out of the orthodox mainstream. It has nevertheless carved itself a significant academic and institutional space, and its relevance has been recognized by several Nobel Prizes, such as the one awarded to George Akerlof, who examined the consequences of uncertainty on the functioning of markets and put forward the concept of "asymmetric information" (Akerlof 1970), or the one awarded to Daniel Kahneman, who developed a "prospect theory" (Kahneman and Tversky 1979) claiming to account for the real behavior of agents "under risk" and the numerous biases from which their decisions suffer, in opposition to the incumbent "expected utility" theory and its "rational agents."

In sociology, the critique of the rational economic actor has been foundational for the discipline of economic sociology. It has served as a weapon against the hegemony of economics over the study of the economy. Sociologists wishing to turn their attention to economic objects such as markets or prices have justified their incursion into the territory of economics by debunking the myth of *homo oeconomicus* and his alleged rationality. Because there is uncertainty, the argument goes, rational behavior becomes impossible, and mechanisms other than calculation need to be mobilized in order to explain how the economy functions—mechanisms such as trust, networks, narratives, etc., that pertain to the domain of the "social" and hence belong to the territory of sociology.

This chapter argues that the critique of discounting (and of future-oriented valuation devices more broadly) needs to break from such a line of reasoning. The problem that we need to address is not why discounting does not work, the ready-made answer being "because uncertainty impedes calculation," but why it does work and what it does when it works. Addressing this problem requires a twofold shift. First, we need to abandon the aim of assessing whether the calculations of discounting are more or less truthful. Asking whether discounting produces the "true" value of something assumes that this "true" value exists and can be more or less closely approached by the instrument of discounting. If we accept that no value exists independently from the instrument through which it is measured, we should rather ask what value(s) discounting produces, how it operates in order to produce them, and what happens with these values once they are produced.

Second, we need to change the way we think of uncertainty. Uncertainty is often treated as a pregiven parameter that characterizes certain types of situations. This view assumes that situations in which the future is involved have a higher level of uncertainty than situations in which the present or the past are involved. Uncertainty is also often treated as an analytical category. This view assumes that uncertainty hinders calculability. Refusing to take these two assumptions for granted, this chapter proposes to approach uncertainty as an empirical object that can be seized through the methods of pragmatist sociology. This entails asking when and how uncertainty is mobilized and by whom, what forms it takes, and what effects it produces.

In order to do so, this chapter takes us to an industry where uncertainty is paramount: biopharma. Biopharma is a "science business" (Pisano 2006) firmly oriented toward the future, to which it relates through regimes that have been described in terms of "the promissory" (Geiger and Finch 2016; Sunder Rajan 2006) and "anticipation" (Montgomery 2017). Central in this industry is the research and development (R&D) of new drugs—a process that has the contingency of scientific work, may take as long as ten years, and is punctuated by market transactions in which promises of future drugs are being bought and sold between public research organizations, biotechnology start-ups, venture capitalists, and pharmaceutical companies. All these actors look to a more or less distant future in which the promises that they are exchanging might materialize in drugs entering the market and generating substantial revenues. They all talk about uncertainty: uncertainty about whether these future drugs will survive the preclinical and clinical phases of the drug development process, whether they will be able to claim a high enough price, and whether they will be successful once out there in the market. And they all calculate: determining the value of the promises of future drugs is a recurrent problem for actors in the biopharmaceutical industry as decisions about the

R&D projects to initiate or to abandon are made within companies and decisions about the R&D projects to buy, to sell, or to decline are made across companies. Unsurprisingly, these calculations of the value of promises of future drugs are made with discounting and the DCF formula and NPV criterion that we analyzed in the previous chapter: the costs and the revenues that the drug under development is likely to generate in the future are projected and then discounted in order to be brought into the present by means of the discount rate; their sum indicates the value of the future drug; if this sum is positive, the drug is worth developing.

In the biopharmaceutical industry, two different versions of uncertainty coexist and are intimately linked to discounting calculations in the valuation of drugs. The first is the one to which I have been referring in the preceding paragraphs: uncertainty as *lack of knowledge* (of the future). The second is certainly less present in common sense and in the academic literature, but recurrent in the narratives and calculations unfolding in the biopharmaceutical industry. Here, uncertainty becomes *the investor's concern*: a problem that the investor takes in charge, a sort of sacrifice that she undergoes by putting her money here, rather than elsewhere, and for which she deserves remuneration in the form of profit.

These two versions of uncertainty differ in their consequences: While the consequences of *uncertainty as lack of knowledge* are sought in its effect on calculability and reasoning, the consequences of *uncertainty as the investor's concern* reside in the distribution of rewards. They are both embedded in discounting calculations, but in different ways. Uncertainty as lack of knowledge is seen as a threat to discounting due to the fragility of projections of future flows of costs and revenues, and at the same time is integrated in the DCF formula through the addition of probabilities. It is mobilized in the critique of discounting either to argue that discounting calculations are unreliable, even dangerous, or to argue that the transformation of uncertainty into risk through probabilities violates the very definition of uncertainty that Frank Knight formulated a hundred years ago (Knight 1921) as what is not mere risk and cannot be measured. This form of critique, as we will see, abounds among both practitioners and academics. A critique of discounting that focuses on uncertainty as the investor's concern is much harder to find, and one of the objectives of this chapter is to make such a critique possible. To do so, this chapter explains how uncertainty is "capitalized"[1] in the biopharmaceutical industry through narratives that link the presence of uncertainty to the need for reward and through calculations that integrate the notion of uncertainty in the definition of the discount rate.

What follows is organized around a discussion of these two versions of uncertainty that delves simultaneously into the relevant academic literature, and into the narratives and discounting calculations that intervene in the valuation of drugs in the biopharmaceutical industry. It draws on two types of sources: public documents (reports, textbooks on valuation, scientific and press articles) and interviews (with managers from the partnership departments of two pharmaceutical companies and with consultants specialized in valuation in the biopharmaceutical industry) that I conducted as part of my doctoral research in 2008 and 2009.[2]

In the literature in sociology and economics, theoretical treatment of uncertainty as lack of knowledge is common and leads to a critique of discounting and of future-oriented valuation devices more generally that lies in their inability to calculate correctly. Critiques of this kind recurrently refer to Knight's definition of uncertainty as distinct from risk and unamenable to any form of measurement or calculation. An examination of his *Risk, Uncertainty and Profit* will show how his theory of knowledge (and the lack of knowledge) serves as a scaffolding for a theory of profit in which uncertainty is mobilized to justify the profit of the entrepreneur. In other words, in its early formulation, uncertainty as lack of knowledge was entangled with uncertainty as the investor's concern.

As an empirical matter, uncertainty as lack of knowledge in the biopharmaceutical industry can be observed in the case of the valuation of early stage drug development projects. The astonishment I felt when I started researching the biopharmaceutical industry as a doctoral student—asking myself how we could determine the economic value and set the price of entities that do not yet exist and whose characteristics are yet unknown or only vaguely defined—serves as a starting point for a journey in the search of uncertainty, with the, at first glance, disappointing result that the future turns out to be much less uncertain than it appeared to be initially. In the calculations of discounting, I gradually discovered, uncertainty does not have to do with predicting the future, but with determining rewards.

That is why, what follows then focuses on uncertainty as the investor's concern. I start by introducing narratives of uncertainty in the biopharmaceutical industry and show how the consequences of uncertainty are related to the calculations of discounting and in particular to the level of the discount rate defined as the internal rate of return (IRR) and the cost of capital. Then I delve deeper in the conundrums raised by attempts to integrate uncertainty in the calculation of the discount rate.

The chapter thus argues for the need to redirect the critique of discounting from uncertainty as lack of knowledge to uncertainty as the investor's concern, not just in the biopharmaceutical industry, but in financialized industries more generally. This shift is productive insofar as it allows engaging with contemporary debates such as those on the high price of drugs and extending the analysis of the future as a temporal and political domain.

UNCERTAINTY AS LACK OF KNOWLEDGE

A common criticism of discounting is the unreliability of the projections on which it is based. This criticism is widespread among practitioners. The comment in the *Financial Times* business and finance column "Lex" to which I briefly alluded above nicely summarizes the problem (Indap 2013). The comment reacts to the ruling of a Delaware court on the price of a biometrics company called Cogent acquired by 3M. The buyer and the seller did not agree on the price to be paid for the shares of Cogent, and the judge produced an opinion on the company's fair value using DCF. The comment argues that while DCF is "conceptually...correct," its use amounts to "seeing the future." Although seeing the future might be possible in a spreadsheet, it is not in the "real world," which is subject to unforeseeable changes: imagine, the author suggests, how the 2008 crisis made "a mockery of every DCF built in 2006." Management "might as well use a crystal ball," the comment concludes, at least then "everyone can see the process for what it is."

The journalist's analysis strongly resonates with more general theoretical work in the literature in sociology and economics that has discussed the consequences of uncertainty for decision-making tools and practices that attempt to take the future into account. Foundational here is the work of Knight (1921), who famously distinguished between situations characterized by "risk," in which statistics of past experience render uncertainty measurable, and situations characterized by "true uncertainty," such as those involving "the formation of those opinions as to the future course of events" (p. 233). In the latter, calculation becomes impossible, and decision-making can rely only on "estimates," at best.

What happens when economic agents turn to the future and deprive themselves of the possibility to calculate? John Maynard Keynes (1936) talked of "animal spirits" to describe the behavior of economic actors faced with situations such as those in which DCF users find themselves: situations such as "estimating the yield ten years hence of a railway, a copper mine, a textile factory, the goodwill of a patent medicine, an Atlantic liner, a building in the City of London" (chap. 12, sec. 3). Keynes argued more broadly that "enterprise" cannot rely on calculation because it is driven by the contemplation of future prospects, our knowledge of which amounts to nothing:

Most, probably, of our decisions to do something positive, the full consequences of which will be drawn out over many days to come, can only be taken as a result of animal spirits—of a spontaneous urge to action rather than inaction, and not as the outcome of a weighted average of quantitative benefits multiplied by quantitative probabilities. Enterprise only pretends to itself to be mainly actuated by the statements in its own prospectus, however candid and sincere. Only a little more than an expedition to the South Pole, is it based on an exact calculation of benefits to come. (Keynes 1936, chap. 12, sec. 7)

Keynes' argument was obviously addressed to the economic theories that he was criticizing: "the orthodox theory [that] assumes that we have a knowledge of the future of a kind quite different from that which we actually possess" and "makes the hypothesis of a calculable future" which, according to Keynes, led to "a wrong interpretation of the principles of behaviour" (Keynes 1937, p. 223). But interestingly, as we can see in the quote above, it is also addressed to what he calls "enterprise," epitomized by the entrepreneur who is considering whether a project is worth investing. Does the entrepreneur "pretend" to herself that her decision to undertake a project, in truth based on the action of "animal spirits," is based on "the exact calculation of benefits to come"? This is a question that the analysis of discounting practices or any other future-oriented valuation practices inevitably faces.

In a similar vein, Christopher Freeman, in his classic textbook on the economics of industrial innovation (1982) compared the use of evaluation techniques such as DCF to "tribal dances." His empirical study of the evaluation of innovation projects revealed "a process of political advocacy and clash of interest groups rather than sober assessment of measurable probabilities" (p. 151). The culprit was the uncertainty that weighs upon innovation projects: "The general uncertainty means that many different views may be held and the situation is typically one of advocacy and political debate in which project estimates are used by interest groups to buttress a particular point of view. Evaluation techniques and technological forecasting, like tribal dances, play a very important part in mobilizing, energizing and organizing" (Freeman 1982, p. 167). When oriented toward the future, calculation gives way to politics understood as power struggles.

Still in a similar vein, sociologists have argued that in situations of uncertainty, economic actors do not behave as economic theory would have them do. In such situations, rational decision-making based on the calculation of expected benefits and costs gives way to judgments whose formation can be understood only by resorting to extraeconomic explanations. For example, Karpik (1989) argued that when it comes to "incomplete" goods and services, which appear as "promises whose reality can only be tested by time" (p. 206), markets operate through social mechanisms such as trust and networks. The same holds for a whole range of goods that Karpik (2010) called "singularities," which are characterized by uncertainty and incommensurability (products such as wine or movies and services such as those provided by doctors or lawyers). The valuation of singularities relies on "judgment," instead of calculation, and markets operate thanks to "judgment devices" such as labels and certifications, critics and experts, prizes and hit lists, marketing and merchandising techniques, and interpersonal relations.[3]

A recent development of this line of sociological analysis can be found in Jens Beckert and Richard Bronk's introduction to an edited volume appropriately entitled *Uncertain Futures* (Beckert and Bronk 2018). Starting from G. S. L. Shackle's[4] observation (1972, p. 3) that "what does not yet exist cannot now be known," which is a plain definition of what I called uncertainty as lack of knowledge, the authors formulate the following question:

> The radical indeterminacy implied by innovation and novelty constitutes a major problem for economic actors: how are they to make decisions, and coordinate their actions with others, if they cannot know what future will follow? How can they form expectations of the future that may legitimately guide them? What is the role for rational analysis when

they cannot deduce from past regularities of behaviour and known constraints what the optimal course of action would be? (Beckert and Bronk 2018, p. 3)

So how do actors make decisions "if they cannot know what future will follow"? The answer that Beckert and Bronk provide inherits from their previous work and resorts to the notions of imagination (Bronk 2009), "imaginaries," and "fictional expectations," challenging the economists' notion of "rational expectations" (Beckert 2016). The terms are slightly different, but the underlying idea is the same: decisions involving the future face the problem of uncertainty; actors can no longer calculate; if they continue making decisions, it is because they mobilize fictions, imagination, narratives, and the like.

A question remains though. Empirical observation shows that economic actors do calculate. How can one account for the use of calculative tools in economic practices, including (and even more so) in practices dealing with innovation and its "radical indeterminacy"?[5] Do entrepreneurs "pretend" to calculate, as Keynes suggested in the quote above? In line with Freeman's "tribal dances," Beckert and Bronk understand the role of calculative tools as "social": they serve to "justify" and "legitimate" action *"despite* uncertainty about the future" (Beckert and Bronk 2018, p. 23, emphasis in the original). In their view, attempting to calculate the future with devices such as discounting and the net present values it produces is not only impossible, because the future cannot be known, but also dangerous, because it disguises foolhardy action as calculation and provides legitimacy to the wrong actors, which leads eventually to "devastating" results (p. 24) and events such as financial crises:

> This does not stop some economic actors *pretending* to themselves or others that such alchemy [transforming uncertainty into risk] is possible. In particular, the apparent mathematical precision of devices calculating probabilities or net present values is often harnessed to provide a degree of social or market legitimacy for bold action that is simply unwarranted

given the residual uncertainties involved: it enables the actors concerned to pretend (or act *as if*) they can know what the future holds sufficiently well to act in a way that would otherwise seem foolhardy. (Beckert and Bronk 2018, p. 23, emphasis in the original)

My observations of discounting practices in the valuation of drug development projects in the biopharmaceutical industry lead to a different account of the behavior of economic actors than these analyses in the literature of sociology and economics. I explore what economic actors actually call uncertainty, and to what extent and in which ways it constitutes a problem for them. As we will see in this chapter, this approach leads to a different form of critique, one concerned not with why actors calculate the future while they shouldn't, but with how they calculate the future when they try to do so and what effects this has on the future in question.

UNCERTAINTY AS THE INVESTOR'S CONCERN

As we've seen, analyses of uncertainty in the literature in sociology and economics such as the ones I briefly reviewed above commonly refer to the risk/uncertainty dichotomy put forward by Knight. Uncertainty, defined by Knight as the impossibility to calculate, has been of great help for nonorthodox economists and economic sociologists in their attack against orthodox economists' hypothesis that economic actors are characterized by rational decision-making and the ability to calculate in order to choose among different alternatives and maximize their utility. However, the objective that the definition of uncertainty served in Knight's theoretical elaboration was radically different: it was part and parcel of a theory of profit, scaffolded on a theory of knowledge, but directed at the justification of the rewards that entrepreneurs draw from their enterprising endeavors—rewards the levels of which have been both a theoretical problem for economists and a political problem for capitalist societies.

Revisiting Knight's demonstration in *Risk, Uncertainty and Profit* (1921) shows how he translates the problem of (lack of) knowledge into the problem of (need for) reward. Knight's argument was an intervention in the distribution controversy that took place among economists at the end of the nineteenth century, and more broadly, in the academic and political debate on distribution and social justice, as Pierre-Charles Pradier and Davi Teira Serrano (2000) have shown.[6] A key issue in this debate was the explanation of the rewards that different economic actors draw from their participation in economic activities—and the justification of the high rewards accruing to some of these actors. The problem with which Knight's book is concerned is that of the existence of profit, and uncertainty is an analytical tool for addressing this problem. The book opens with the following puzzle: theoretically, competition is supposed to eliminate profit and bring the value of economic goods to equality with their cost; however, this is not verified empirically. "The key to the whole tangle," Knight argues, is the concept of "uncertainty." By introducing uncertainty, Knight proposes a new interpretation of profit that views the revenue of the entrepreneur as a reward for the uncertainty she bears.[7]

Knight's distinction between risk and uncertainty is functional rather than ontological: "it refers to two things which, functionally at least, in their causal relations to the phenomena of economic organization, are categorically different" (p. 19). Risk (or "measurable uncertainty") and uncertainty ("unmeasurable" or "true" uncertainty) (p. 20) differ in their economic effects. The economic effect of risk lies in the development of "organizational devices" that reduce measurable uncertainties to complete certainty by grouping cases into categories (p. 232). The economic effect of the "higher form of uncertainty not susceptible to measurement and hence to elimination" is far more radical: "It is this *true uncertainty* which by preventing the theoretically perfect outworking of the tendencies of competition gives the characteristic form of 'enterprise' to economic organization as a whole and accounts for the peculiar income of the entrepreneur" (Knight 1921, p. 232, emphasis in the original).

In Knight's writings, uncertainty is the cornerstone of an economic theory of entrepreneurial profit in which it serves to explain "the peculiar income of the entrepreneur." His concept of uncertainty is inseparable from a theory of knowledge and a theory of profit that are absent from and, as we will see, sometimes even at odds with sociological theories built on the Knightian concept of uncertainty. Indeed, the distinction uncertainty versus risk has been entangled in subsequent sociological theories with distinctions such as the future versus the present or judgment versus calculation. However, such distinctions make little sense in Knight's theory of knowledge. For Knight, conduct is always forward-looking: "we do not react to the past stimulus, but to the 'image' of a future state of affairs" (p. 201). The future in question is not radically different from other temporal domains because "we know the absent from the present, the future from the now, by assuming that connections or associations among phenomena which have been valid will be so; we judge the future by the past" (p. 204).

It follows that the relevant distinction to be made is not between different temporal orientations and the knowledge they allow for.[8] Instead, Knight distinguishes between different sites and ways in which knowledge is produced: on the one hand, "knowledge as the scientist and the logician of science uses the term" and, on the other hand, "the convictions or opinions upon which conduct is based outside of laboratory experiments" (p. 230); on the one hand, "the formal processes of logic which the scientist uses in an investigation" and, on the other hand, "the ordinary decisions of life [that] are made on the basis of 'estimates' of a crude and superficial character" (p. 210). He also distinguishes between situations that are unique and situations that can be grouped into categories. Statistical probability rests on the empirical classification of instances and the calculation of frequencies. By contrast, when "there is no valid basis of any kind for classifying instances," all we have are estimates (p. 225). Estimates are not a rare exception but rather the general rule. For Knight, they characterize most business decisions because these decisions "deal with situations which are far too unique, generally speaking, for any sort of statistical tabulation to have any value for guidance" (p. 231), "the same obviously applies to the most of conduct, and not to business decisions alone" (p. 226).

The translation of Knight's theory of knowledge, which depicts the pervasiveness of uncertainty in business decisions and human conduct, into a theory of profit, hinges on the link between uncertainty and sacrifice and reward. He proposes to "treat all instances of economic uncertainty as cases of choice between a smaller reward more confidently and a larger one less confidently anticipated" (p. 237). The reward in question should be commensurate with the sacrifice made and hence with the uncertainty felt by the man who is acting forward: "We shall assume, then, that if a man is undergoing a sacrifice for the sake of a future benefit, the expected reward must be larger in order to evoke the sacrifice if it is viewed as contingent than if it is considered certain, and that it will have to be larger in at least some general proportion to the degree of felt uncertainty in the anticipation" (Knight 1921, p. 236).

The man in question takes shape in the figure of the "entrepreneur." This figure appears as Knight discusses the main methods for "dealing with uncertainty." Methods such as "consolidation"[9] (p. 239) or "control of the future" and "increased power of prediction"[10] (p. 260) consist in reducing uncertainty. Conversely, the method of "specialization" consists of delegating the problem of uncertainty to a category of individuals through the "selection of men to 'bear' [uncertainty]" (p. 239). In a system of "free enterprise," Knight explains, the problem of anticipating the future is "taken out of the hands" of consumers and of "the great mass of producers" and "placed in charge of a limited class of 'entrepreneurs' or 'business men.'" (p. 244) Uncertainty produces the following effect: "doing things, the actual execution of activity, becomes in a real sense a secondary part of life; the primary problem or function is deciding what to do and how to do it" (p. 268). This is the problem embraced by a "special social class, the business men," whose emergence is described as "a direct result of the fact of uncertainty" (p. 271). "With the specialization of function goes also a differentiation of reward," which justifies that the "special social class" formed by entrepreneurs deserves a special kind of income, which is profit:

> Profit arises out of the inherent, absolute unpredictability of things, out of the sheer brute fact that the results of human activity cannot be anticipated and then only in so far as even a probability calculation in regard to them is impossible and meaningless. The receipt of profit in a particular case may be argued to be the result of superior judgment. But it is judgment of judgment, especially one's own judgment, and in an individual case there is no way of telling good judgment from good luck. (Knight 1921, p. 311)[11]

The causal link between uncertainty, a special form of reward, and a special figure who deserves this reward because she bears the uncertainty is the major conceptual innovation in Knight's *Risk, Uncertainty and Profit*. Uncertainty is not an exceptional situation, but the general rule; sometimes it can be transformed into measurable uncertainty (what Knight calls "risk") through consolidation or the production of information, but what matters most is "the economic effect" produced by uncertainty, which lies in the justification of the existence of a particular type of actor who requires a particular type of reward—the "entrepreneur" or the "business man." As we will see, today, the figure to which the rewards entailed by uncertainty are associated is the "investor."[12] I will therefore call this second version of uncertainty, which serves as a justification for the distribution of rewards, uncertainty as the "investor's concern."

(NOT) KNOWING THE FUTURE:
HOW ARE DRUG DEVELOPMENT PROJECTS VALUED?

The problem of not knowing the future is exacerbated in the case of the biopharmaceutical industry and in the valuation of drug development projects in particular. Valuing a drug development project with DCF requires the estimation of the sales of the future drug. When the project is at an early stage, the prospect of sales is distant in time because the first sales (if the project runs successfully through all the clinical trials to the moment when it can be put on the market), may occur as far as ten or fifteen years ahead. Moreover, the very characteristics of this future drug that are supposed to generate these sales (which indication it targets, how it compares with similar drugs, what kinds of medical benefits it has been able to demonstrate...) are often unknown at the moment when the valuation of the project is performed.

In assessing this situation, scholars and practitioners alike adopt a critical tone, pointing to the fragility of DCF projections and the impossibility to forecast accurately. As we've seen, it's said that discounting and its users act *as if* they could foresee the future, and calculation becomes a kind of façade while economic actors indulge in the production of narratives, acts of imagination, the search for legitimacy, and political battles.

Studying this industry was how I first encountered discounting, and something bothered me about the situation, but not what had concerned these critics. Why were the pharmaceutical firms using discounting in the first place? I was studying the partnerships that biotechnology start-ups established with pharmaceutical companies, and I was trying to understand how the prices at which pharmaceutical companies bought the R&D projects sold by biotechnology start-ups were set. How could the two parties agree on the price of what was often no more that the promise of a future drug? The question was all the more puzzling to me that the prices of these promises of future drugs were far from negligible, often ranging in millions of euros. For example:

> For its contribution, [Biotech] will receive approximately 25 million euros in a combination of an upfront payment, R&D funding and preclinical milestone payments during the three-year period. [Biotech] will also be eligible for remuneration of developmental and regulatory milestones (up to

approximately 25 million euros per drug candidate, from first [Investigational New Drug Application] to first commercial sales), as well as to royalties on future product sales. [Pharma], already a minority shareholder in [Biotech], will also invest 10 million euros in new [Biotech] equity, whereby [Pharma]'s ownership share of [Biotech] will be around 20%.[13]

One can find the same type of figures in most press releases announcing the establishment or extension of partnerships between biotech start-ups and pharmaceutical companies. The price at which the promise of a future drug is exchanged has a specific structure: it is composed of an "upfront payment" (a sort of admission fee, which is paid for the collaboration to begin), R&D funding (corresponding to the number of researchers who will devote their time to the joint project), "milestone payments" (which will occur when and if the project reaches a given stage in its development, e.g. phase 1 of clinical trials), and royalties (the percentage on sales that the pharmaceutical company will transfer to the biotech start-up if the project succeeds and results in the commercialization of a new drug). This price reflects both knowledge about the future drug and the right to continue its development and commercialize the drug when and if it is ready to be introduced to the market.

The calculation of the different components of the price of a future drug becomes all the more complicated as some projects are bought and sold while they are still in a very early stage of development. In this case, there is actually no drug to buy or to sell. The object of the transaction is a compound, a molecule, or even no more than a new target mechanism that may prove to be efficient in one (or more) therapeutic indication(s) and give rise to a new drug one day—a number of years after the transaction has taken place. If we take again the press release quoted above, the object worth tens of millions of euros is described rather broadly as molecules able to act on natural killer (NK) cells, which are one of "the body's first lines of defense against cancer and infections": "the companies will collaborate for at least the next three years to develop new molecules—chiefly antibodies—that stimulate or inhibit NK cell activity. Although the partnership covers all therapeutic indications, drug candidates will be developed primarily in cancer, autoimmune disorders and infections."

How do the transacting parties then manage to calculate and agree on the price of molecules whose identity and characteristics are unknown, whose odds of successfully moving through all the phases of clinical trials are often derisory, and whose market potential will be known only in what may be as long as ten years' time? Intrigued by what seemed to be an impossible calculation, I addressed this question to one of my interviewees, in charge of the partnerships of a French pharmaceutical company.[14] "You should know that we are not completely disarmed. There are books," he answered, taking a few books off the shelves in his office.

PRICING, VALUATION, AND DCF

Let us open one of these books, entitled *Early-Stage Technologies: Valuation and Pricing* (Razgatis 1999). The book gives itself the objective to help companies answer questions such as "to develop or not to develop; to license or not to license; what price will be a true reflection of the product's value from both the buyer's and seller's point of view?" The help it provides consists of introducing managers to a number of valuation methods, presented in order of increasing sophistication: industry standards, scoring, DCF, advanced techniques (Monte Carlo simulations, decision trees, real options), and auctions. DCF, I was told by the managers whom I interviewed, was the most widespread of these valuation methods.

However, moving from the question "How are the prices of future objects calculated?" to the answer "With valuation methods such as DCF" only partly satisfied my curiosity. If DCF determines the value of drug development projects (and hence their price) by estimating the future flows of costs and revenues that they are likely to generate, how were these projections of the future—only loosely coupled to the entities being valued because their characteristics were only broadly defined, as in the example of molecules targeting natural killer cells above—made and agreed upon?

The literature of sociology and economics would have directed me toward several possible conclusions. I could have concluded that the sophisticated valuation methods from the books, bound to fail in the face of uncertainty (because nobody knows what will happen in the future), served only to give some form of legitimacy to managers who, behind the façade of the calculation, always ended up proposing the same ranges of round numbers, referring to comparable "deals" that had recently occurred in their field,[15] in the same way that you know that the price of one euro that you are asked to pay for a baguette in a Parisian bakery is reasonable because this is more or less what you will be asked to pay for a baguette in all the bakeries nearby. There is no need to delve into mathematical reflections on what the "value" of this particular baguette is.

Alternatively, I could have concluded that the sophisticated valuation methods from the books served as a weapon that the actors who found themselves in a less powerful position in the negotiation could mobilize to try to move the price in their favor. It was probably a weak weapon, though, if one considers the discrepancy between the clout of the pharmaceutical companies sitting on one side of the negotiation and the financial fragility of the biotechnology start-ups sitting on the other.[16] Imagine how helpful it would be to devise an alternative calculation based on expectations of the future in a situation where you engage a negotiation with the tax administration over the amount of your taxes or a negotiation with a vendor on a crowded market over the price of this little bag you really like, while there are only a few such bags left and a lot of other interested buyers impatiently waiting behind you.

In my view, these different conclusions on the use of future-oriented valuation tools, which echoed the interpretations I could find in the academic and practitioner-oriented literature, led to a dead end.

The same question kept popping up: If it seems rather obvious that these valuation calculations are not only untrue, but also useless, why do managers use discounting and engage with the calculations it produces? Are they, to rephrase Harold Garfinkel, "valuation dopes" (Garfinkel 1967; Lynch 2012)? Or are they shrewd manipulators, able to act *as if* they could foresee the future while at the same time grounding their decisions in legitimacy or power considerations? Because none of these answers seemed satisfactory, I was urged to delve further into the use of discounting in the valuation of drug development projects with the aim to understand how the uncertain future was dealt with in the process of calculation, or, conversely, how a different form of a certain future was produced.

THE PRODUCTION OF CERTAIN FUTURES

Delving further into the use of discounting in the valuation of drug development projects was not a straightforward task. Valuation exercises are extremely sensitive, protected by walls of confidentiality and hardly ever opened to an outside observer. The observational standpoint I could find allowed me to look at the use of discounting through the eyes of pharmaceutical managers and consultants involved in the valuation of drug development projects. My view was necessarily limited and was deflected by my interviewees' concerns, yet it yielded important insights on how the incursions of discounting into the future unfold in practice. "There are books," I was told, and I chose to follow as a guide the textbooks to which my interviewees referred. Our guide here will a textbook titled *Valuation in Life Sciences: A Practical Guide* (Bogdan and Villiger 2007), authored by two consultants who specialized in this field.

The textbook presents the two major quantitative valuation methods used in the biopharmaceutical industry: DCF, which it says has been "the gold standard" for years, and real options, which can be regarded as a "possible alternative" (p. 6). DCF allows the calculation of the net present value (NPV) of a drug development project,[17] and most often the risk-adjusted net present value (rNPV), which includes probabilities in the calculation in order to account for the risk that cash flows may not occur. I will revert to the inclusion of probabilities below; for the moment, let us continue with the DCF formula for calculating the rNPV (p. 32):

$$rNPV = -I_0 + \sum_{t=1}^{T} \frac{p * CF_t}{(1+r)^t}$$

Figure 4.1. The DCF formula for the valuation of drug development projects (Bogdan and Villiger 2007, p. 32).

The formula computes the rNPV of a project by summing up the future "cash flows" (CF) that it will consume (negative CF, that is, costs) or generate (positive CF, that is, revenues) in the future, with each cash flow being adjusted by its probability to occur (p) and then discounted, that is, reduced by a discount rate (r), which is itself raised to the power of the distance in time of the CF (t). From this sum is subtracted the amount of the initial investment (I_0). A simple rule is then applied: if the resulting rNPV is positive (that is, if the sum of the adjusted and discounted future flows is greater than the amount of the initial investment), the project is worth investing in.

The difficulty, as explained to me by one consultant, lies in "estimating the input parameters," that is, "development duration (how long will the development phases last?), the costs of the development for each phase, the probability of success for each phase…the sales expectations…and the discount rate."[18] This difficulty quickly dissipates, though, because available statistics transform what looks like an impossible exercise of projecting the future into what seems to be a copy-and-paste task of replicating what is known from the past. Indeed, numerous publications (textbooks, articles published in scientific journals and in the specialized press, newsletters, consultants' reports, etc.) gather data on the mean values of each of these parameters. Putting averages and probabilities in the valuer's hands, textbooks transforms the exercise of reading a crystal ball into a classic calculation process.

The first input parameter that DCF requires relates to time. How many years will cash flows be spread over? The textbook provides information about the mean duration of drug development phases: discovery (or research) and clinical trials (preclinical, phase 1, phase 2, phase 3, approval phase, phase 4), resulting in a total duration ranging between 116 to 154 months. Crucial here is the very possibility to think in terms of phases. Time in the biopharmaceutical industry is modeled after the image of the "pipeline": a long, tubular conduit through which the drug development process flows, transforming the entering promise of a future drug, into a drug on the market (fig. 4.2).

The image of the pipeline embodies a peculiar vision of the future: a linear process consisting in a series of phases that can be chronologically located and whose attributes can be known. Indeed textbooks provide data on average costs and "success rates" for each of the phases that constitute the pipeline. The certain future thus produced is a variation on the past: the pipeline is both a synthesis of what has happened so far and a projection of what will happen. It uses past data and patterns to project the path of a particular drug development project that is about to begin.

AVERAGES AND PROBABILITIES

With the time image of the pipeline in mind, let us ask again: How could the cash flows, composed first of a series of R&D costs and then of a series of revenues equal to the sales generated by the drug once launched on the market, minus the corresponding operational costs, be calculated while the very identity of the drug to be developed and commercialized is only vaguely defined? For R&D costs, the issue can be easily solved: one can read the costs incurred by each development phase on average in textbooks and other publications. Average

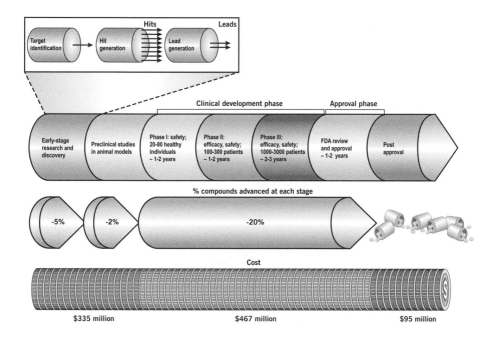

Figure 4.2. The drug development pipeline. Redrawn by Virge Kask from Cath O'Driscoll, "A Virtual Space Odyssey," *Nature Horizon: Charting Chemical Space*, 2004.

numbers, drawn from the records of past drug development projects, are associated to each phase; for example, our guide textbook informs us that phase I trials last between eighteen and twenty-two months and cost between $1 million and $5 million.

Estimating sales is trickier. The more distant, "post-approval" time is less standardized, and drug prices are more variable. As one consultant explained to me:

> There's no standard way of defining peak sales, so everybody can come up with a different figure. Everybody will come up with a different figure. I have never seen one standard way. I've been at forecasting conferences to see what they are doing and everybody is doing it differently. It's not only how high the sales are, it's when they're going to be reached, how quick they will be reached, how quick they will be lost. The whole curve that you are expecting, every year, you can fight for.[19]

Averages, again, appear as a solution. For early stage projects, when little is yet known about the characteristics of the future drug and its potential market, textbooks suggest using the average sales of a basket of comparable drugs that are currently on the market or even the average sales of all drugs that are currently on the market. The consultant who depicted how every year of sales is something "you can fight for" also mentioned two standard approaches to estimating sales. A "top-down approach," appropriate for early stage projects, relies on averages derived from the past: "If we do not even know what the indication is, we can take the average sales in this pharmaceutical domain. In cancer, for example, a molecule makes 500 million dollars of peaks sales on average."[20] Conversely, a "Bottom-up approach" can be applied in advanced projects in which the characteristics of the drug to be valued are better defined:

> In advanced projects, we know relatively well the drug profile, the formulation, the indication, etc. We then apply a bottom-up approach: how many patients are there, how many have access to doctors, how many will

be diagnosed, how many receive a medical treatment, how many will be treated with our drug, for how long, and how do we penetrate the market? This is the standard procedure. It is described in [this] book on pharmaceutical forecasting.[21]

Averages are also applied to uncertainty itself, transforming it into measurable probabilities. This process—akin to what Knight describes as the transformation of uncertainty into risk—more precisely is applied to one form of uncertainty, which our guide textbook calls "technical uncertainty" and defines as follows:

> It is not known in advance, whether a cash flow will happen at all. The reason for uncertain cash flows is usually caused by failure and quantified by attrition rates. Attrition rates are purely value destructive. If a cash flow has only a probability p to happen, then you cannot count with the full cash flow, but only with its expectation, i.e. p times the cash flow. For valuation purposes, a cash flow must always be multiplied with its probability to happen. (Bogdan and Villiger 2007, pp. 29-30)

"Technical uncertainty" is transformed into risk through the instrument of probabilities: that is, "success rates" or, conversely, "attrition rates." Conventional wisdom holds that only around 10 percent of drug development projects make it all the way from the first phase of clinical trials to approval by regulatory bodies. A growing body of academic and gray literature (research produced by organizations other than those of commercial or academic publishing) that builds on the statistical analysis of past data tends to confirm this number and furthermore provides success rates by phase of development and by therapeutic area (Hay et al. 2014; Kola and Landis 2004). Let us take a report published by the biotechnology industry association (BIO), Biomedtracker, and Amplion that presents itself as "the largest study of clinical drug development success rates to date." In it, one can learn about the probability of a drug to move from one phase to the next ("phase transition success") in sixteen disease areas (Thomas et al. 2016). For example, for a drug candidate in oncology, the probability to move from phase 1 to phase 2 clinical trials is 62.8 percent. Overall (for all diseases), success rates are estimated at 63.2 percent for phase 1, 30.7 percent for phase 2, 58.1 percent for phase 3, and 85.3 percent for moving to final approval. This results in a total success rate from phase 1 to approval equal to 9.6 percent, in line with conventional wisdom's 10 percent.

Using success rates drawn from the past to assess the probabilities that future events (here, cash flows) will occur is akin to using averages drawn from the past to estimate what these events (here, the amount of cash flows) will be. Both contribute to producing a form of certain future: a linear, pipeline-like future that makes itself knowable as a variation on the past.

HOW SHOULD WE THINK ABOUT UNCERTAINTY AS LACK OF KNOWLEDGE?

Some see this production of a future as an erroneous operation because it consists in confusing uncertainty and risk and acting as if the future is knowable. The use of averages as a shortcut to knowing the future has been criticized in the literature of management and sociology. For example, in *The Flaw of Averages: Why We Underestimate Risk in the Face of Uncertainty*, Sam Savage, a consulting professor of management science and engineering at Stanford University, argues against managers' penchant to look for forecasts based on single numbers and to use average values (measures of central tendency, instead of variations or distributions) to come up with this single number (Savage 2012). "The Flaw of Averages typically results when someone plugs a single number into a spreadsheet to represent an uncertain future quantity" is how one ad summarizes the description of the book. The someone in question, who strikingly resembles the manager using DCF to value a drug development project, then faces the peril of making the wrong decision, like the statistician who, the joke goes, drowned while crossing a river that was three feet deep "on average." One of Savage's key arguments is the need to distinguish uncertainty from risk: "two concepts [that] are often used interchange-ably but they shouldn't be" (p. 52).[22]

This argument resonates with the sociological analyses that I reviewed earlier. They similarly criticize the lack of distinction between uncertainty and risk, building on Knight's theory of knowledge. In their perspective, when actors use averages and probabilities to predict the future (such as the DCF user calculating the rNPV of a drug development project), they are actually confusing uncertainty with measurable risk and therefore missing Knight's point because "no amount of calculation and careful analysis of known constraints and causal mechanisms can (in Knight's terms) turn genuine 'uncertainty' into objective probability functions or knowable 'risk'" (Beckert and Bronk 2018, p. 23). Consequently, when actors deal with the uncertainty of the future through probabilities drawn from the past, they do something wrong.

As we saw above, this critique is not only epistemic (calculating the uncertain future produces incorrect results), but also moral (actors "pretend" to themselves and to others, act in a "foolhardy" manner, and make decisions that endanger not only their personal wealth, but the economy as a whole). Indeed, there is no reason to believe that uncertainty about the technological breakthroughs and scientific advances that are likely to occur in the future could be amenable to systematic regularities that can be measured through averages and transformed into probabilities.

Envisaging the future as a variation on the past is certainly not the only way to envisage the future. However, it is what users of discounting in the pharmaceutical industry do, and what is of interest for our argument here is that translating uncertainty by means of averages and probabilities is one way (be it correct or not) in which DCF users engage with the future. When they do so, as far as they are concerned, the future produced by discounting is linear, known on average, and likely to happen.

However, as we will see next, actors in the biopharmaceutical industry still actually talk about "uncertainty" incessantly. Regarding projections of future sales in particular, stories about overestimated or underestimated sales are abundant. A well-known example is Pfizer's Viagra, whose indication and sales potential were unforeseen. Retrospective studies comparing sales forecasts to actual sales show that most forecasts are indeed wrong; for example, a study of analysts' forecasts conducted by the consultancy company McKinsey under the evocative title "Pharmaceutical Forecasting: Throwing Darts?" found that "more than 60% of the forecasts" examined "were either over or under by more than 40% of the actual peak revenues" (Cha et al. 2013).

While the metrological structure provided by discounting addresses uncertainty as lack of knowledge by producing a form of a certain future, however inaccurate it may prove to be in retrospect, uncertainty nevertheless remains a central concern in the pharmaceutical industry. What's at issue here is why and for whom. If we take seriously the ability of actors involved in attempts to foresee the future to acknowledge the fragility of their projections and refuse to analyze them, more or less explicitly, as beguiled with illusions or prone to an "as if" behavior, and if we look instead at where and how uncertainty appears in calculative practices, we find that uncertainty appears in a wholly different way. It appears not as a concern in making decisions about future drug development programs whose costs and revenues are yet unknown, but as a concern for investors. For investors, discounting doesn't operate as a way of producing a form of a certain future when faced with a lack of knowledge, but as a way of justifying the rewards they seek for investing.

RISK AND REWARD: UNCERTAINTY
NARRATED, CALCULATED, CAPITALIZED

"Drug development is fraught with uncertainty"—this is a phrase that those who study the biopharmaceutical industry have often heard and repeated. To take one example, the opening plenary of the March 2017 edition of the BIO-Europe meeting discussed the "mounting uncertainty [that] threatens research and innovation in medicines" (Righetti 2017).[23] Speakers talked, "on top of the usual financial and biological risks of drug development," about uncertainties such as the possibility of regulatory reform, Brexit, a proposed cut in the funding for the US National Institutes of Health, Donald Trump, travel bans and restrictions on immigration, "alternative facts" and the "crisis of ignorance," firms "agonizing over scenario plans around uncertainty" and "putting all (their) time and energy in trying to navigate these ambiguities," and even political action and resistance. A representative from Genentech, the iconic biotechnology company,[24] summarized the consequences of this "mounting uncertainty" in the terms of a "huge cost" borne by the industry: "We are in the business of risk, but when you layer on additional regulatory risk and jurisdictional differences, this can easily become a distraction that steers us off the course of what we are really trying to do which is discover and develop next-generation medicines. There is a huge cost to us for that" (Righetti 2017).

Uncertainty in the biopharmaceutical industry is not only narrated, sometimes with a certain sense of drama, but also calculated, in more or less precise ways. How is this possible, if the whole point of uncertainty is about the impossibility to calculate? A report published in 2014 by the consulting firm Deloitte in collaboration with the pharmaceutical company Janssen illustrates a possible answer to this question (Deloitte 2014). Aptly named "High Value, High Uncertainty," the report compares "the level of uncertainty" encountered by the biopharmaceutical industry with other industries and concludes, in short, that this level is "higher" and "increasing." It is worth saying a few words about how this conclusion was reached. The report starts by identifying three trends that are likely to "increase uncertainty" in the industry: "market access challenges, fragmented and complex regulation, costs and challenges of scientific advancement." These trends are translated into seven metrics[25] on which the report builds an "uncertainty index" that serves to compare the biopharmaceutical industry to five other industries (automotive manufacturing, commercial aircraft manufacturing, consumer electronics, food manufacturing, and generic pharmaceuticals). Unsurprisingly, the biopharmaceutical industry scores highest on most of the metrics.

The uncertainty thus quantified serves as a "background" to shine a light on the "contribution" that the biopharmaceutical industry provides and, reciprocally, the "reward" that it deserves: "It is against this background of uncertainty that innovative biopharmaceutical products make an essential contribution to improvements in population health. Bringing new treatments to patients thus involves managing high levels of risk. However, the value to medical advancement provided by biopharmaceutical innovation can only emerge if it is possible for the industry successfully to negotiate the demands of the business process while also maintaining an appropriate level of reward" (Deloitte 2014, p. 19).

What does "maintaining an appropriate level of reward" mean? The report models the effect of "current and future uncertainties" on the revenues of biopharmaceutical companies. The uncertainties are translated in six scenarios affecting the three trends previously identified: increases in the costs of scientific advancement (with the scenarios of phase 3 attrition rates increasing from 31.5 to 45 percent and phase 3 length increasing by one year), more stringent regulation (with the scenarios of approval delayed by one year and the requirement for two more phase 4 studies), and harder market access (with the scenarios of a two-year delay in the time to reach peak revenue and a five-year decrease in the exclusivity period). The report then calculates "the revenue increases that would be required to maintain the internal rate of return constant (baseline case) under the six scenarios" (p. 27).

Enter discounting. As we discussed in Chapter 3, the internal rate of return (IRR) is the discount rate that brings the net present value of a project to zero. According to the report, the IRR of the biopharmaceutical industry needs to remain constant so that the industry can "mitigate the increased risks posed by these scenarios and keep innovation sustainable at the current level of investment" (p. 27). This would require increases in revenues ranging from 15 percent (for the scenario in which approval is delayed by one year) to 55 percent (for the scenario in which the exclusivity period is decreased by five years). The report concludes with what sounds as a warning to public authorities:

> There is need for greater understanding on the role that revenue increases play in safeguarding innovation.... Payers would have to pay a higher price per unit of medication sold, or alternatively commit to allowing access to medication for a larger volume of patients, either through a longer exclusivity period or by no longer restricting authorisations of new drugs to narrowly defined sub-populations.... [A vicious circle] will be created if nothing is done to mitigate the increasing risk exposure of the biopharmaceutical industry. (Deloitte 2014, p. 28)

COSTS, RISKS, AND REWARDS

Such warnings, pleading for higher drug prices, are not new, and "payers" have not remained insensitive to them. Twenty years before the report by Deloitte attempted to make the link between "high value" and "high uncertainty" in the biopharmaceutical industry, a report published by the Office of Technology Assessment (OTA) of the United States Congress set out to explore the costs, risks, and rewards of pharmaceutical R&D:

> OTA's study of pharmaceutical R&D grew out of a long-standing congressional debate over the prices of ethical drugs. Increases in real (inflation-adjusted) drug prices and perceived high prices for new drugs have been a concern of congressional committees for more than 30 years. The industry's collective response to charges that drug prices are too high or are increasing too fast has been to point to the high and increasing cost of pharmaceutical R&D and their need to repay investors for their substantial and risky investments. (US Congress, Office of Technology Assessment 1993, p. 3)

The objective of the report was to provide evidence on drugs' development costs in order to intervene, from an expert position, in the debate on their high prices. Its conclusion is that the rewards that pharmaceutical companies have drawn from the drugs they have developed exceed the costs they have incurred for R&D. More precisely,

> each new drug introduced to the U.S. market between 1981 and 1983 returned, net of taxes, at least $36 million more to its investors than was needed to pay off the R&D investment....
>
> Over a longer span of time, economic returns to the pharmaceutical industry as whole exceeded returns to corporations in other industries by about 2 to 3 percentage points per year from 1976 to 1987, after adjusting for differences in risk among industries. (US Congress, Office of Technology Assessment 1993, pp. 1–2)

These conclusions of course can be and have been challenged. Of interest for our argument here is the kind of reasoning that holds together the high prices of drugs, the rewards required by investors, and the risks and uncertainties of pharmaceutical R&D. Albeit emanating from a public authority, the report espouses the point of view of the investor, considering pharmaceutical R&D as an investment:

> In this perspective, pharmaceutical R&D is an investment. The principal characteristic of an investment is that money is spent today in the hope that even more money will be returned to the investors sometime in the future. If investors (or the corporate R&D managers who act on their behalf) believe that the potential profits from R&D are worth the investment's cost and risks, then they will invest in it. Otherwise, they will not. (US Congress, Office of Technology Assessment 1993, p. 3)

To know whether a R&D investment is worth it, investors calculate its net present value (NPV) by means of the DCF formula. The three most important components of R&D investment, the report explains, are "money, time, and risk" (p. 7). Investors "look ahead" (p. 9) and care about how much money they will get back in exchange for the money they put into a R&D project, about when these money outflows and inflows will occur, and about how risky they are, because "the present value of $100 that is expected next year but with a great deal of uncertainty is even lower than the present value of a risk-free investment" (p.8). This last component appears as particularly important for pharmaceutical R&D: "Pharmaceutical industry executives often emphasize the particular riskiness of R&D. Analogies to drilling for oil are common: R&D involves many dry holes and a few gushers. According to one industry executive, pharmaceutical R&D is like 'wildcatting in Texas....' Data on the dropout rate for drugs under development support these notions that R&D is, indeed, an uncertain and risky undertaking" (US Congress, Office of Technology Assessment 1993, p. 8).

The report nuances the industry's claims about uncertainty by resorting to finance theory and recalling the difference between diversifiable and undiversifiable risks, to which we will revert in the next section. It calculates the discount rate relevant for pharmaceutical R&D, which is defined as the cost of capital because it is supposed to account for the riskiness of the investment.[26] This discount rate is then used to "capitalize" to their present value on the day of market approval "all outlays required to achieve the successes" in order to calculate the "full cost of past R&D projects" (p. 10).

In her analysis of how Merck dealt with suspicions and then lawsuits over the adverse effects of its drug Vioxx, Linsey McGoey (2009) develops the notion of "capitalized uncertainty" to refer to "the strategy of purposefully exploiting scientific doubts over the risks of a commercial product or a course of action" (p. 152). Uncertainty, she argues, is generative and performative insofar as it "creates a demand for resolution" and "it demands attention, debate, funding, and most crucially experts" (p. 155). We can now recast McGoey's analysis in a new light by moving from a definition of uncertainty as lack of knowledge, or "scientific doubt," which may be exploited strategically, to a definition of uncertainty as a justification for reward. This latter uncertainty is "capitalized," that is, integrated in the discounting calculations that transform promises of future drugs into their "present values." The translation of uncertainty into reward hinges on the discount rate.

THE CONUNDRUMS OF HIGH DISCOUNT RATES

The textbook *Valuation in Life Sciences* that we used as a guide above mentions, next to the "technical uncertainty" that can be taken into account through the inclusion of probabilities in discounting calculations, another form of uncertainty that concerns not the likelihood that a cash flow occurs, but the accuracy of the estimate itself: "We do not know in advance, how large a cash flow will be. Many factors like competition or regulation influence the actual size of the cash flow. This uncertainty can be negative, if for instance a competitor launches a better product. But the uncertainty has also an upside; imagine that the product sells better than anticipated, or costs are lower than expected" (Bogdan and Villiger 2007, pp. 29–30).

This type of uncertainty is taken into account in the determination of the discount rate. The raison d'être of the discount rate is twofold. First, the discount rate is supposed to reflect the "time value of money": the idea that a dollar today is worth more than a dollar in the future due to the alternative scenario of putting this dollar in the bank and earning interest on it. The time value of money is measured by the risk-free interest rate (our guide textbook uses the yields of treasury bonds of the United States or the eurozone, which range, for example, between 1 percent and 5 percent in Europe). Second, the discount rate is supposed to reflect uncertainty: "uncertain investments should reward the investor at a higher rate than safe investments" (p. 24). Why? Because of "risk-aversion," which the textbook describes as an attitude common to most people, "who tend to dislike under-performance or loss more than they do like over-performance or gain" (p. 24).[27] The reward for investors takes the form of a "spread" that is added on top of the risk-free interest rate. The notions of the time value of money and of risk aversion are packed together in the determination of the discount rate.

According to the textbook, the spread can range from 0 percent to

20 percent and is typically situated between 5 percent and 8 percent (p. 24). A table with published discount rates used by companies (p. 66) shows rates ranging between 7 percent and 28 percent. The highest discount rates in the table are the rates used by the biotechnology company Genentech in 1990 (20 to 28 percent). Discount rates appear to decrease as companies grow older (and therefore probably less uncertain about the future): ten years later, Genentech used considerably lower rates (16 to 19 percent in 1999). Similarly, pharmaceutical companies use lower discount rates than biotechnology companies. For example, in the acquisition of the biotech Cambridge Antibody Technology by the pharma Astra Zeneca in 2006 (at the price of 832 million euros), the biotech used a discount rate of 12.5 percent while the pharma used a discount rate of 8 percent.

Where do these numbers come from? It is widely acknowledged that the discount rate has a significant effect on the result of the valuation and therefore requires great attention. In a newsletter devoted to the calculation of discount rates for biotech companies, a consultancy company (that was founded by the authors of our guide textbook), explains how important the discount rate is and how difficult it is to determine:

> Via the discount rate a cash flow is translated into value. The discount rate must be determined with the utmost care, because usually the value of a project or a company is very sensitive to this parameter. It is generally accepted that more risk comes along with a higher discount rate. But when it comes to determining what risk corresponds to what premium in the discount rate practitioners and academics struggle and there is still no broadly accepted method to elaborate the premiums. They therefore invoke models to determine the discount rate (or the cost of capital).[28]

What are these models that practitioners and academics "invoke" when they are faced with the problem with determining the discount rate? We have seen in Chapter 3 how in the 1970s, the discount rate was redefined from the rate of interest into the "cost of capital."

I insisted then on the justification advanced for the definition of the discount rate as the cost of capital: the project being valued is seen, through the all-encompassing view of an investor, as an asset similar to all other assets in which the investor may or may not invest. To trigger the investor's attention, the project, aka asset, must perform better than all these other assets to which it is made comparable. At issue, then, is how this cost of capital is calculated and the extent to which financial theory is able to explain the high discount rates observed in the biopharmaceutical industry.

THE COST OF CAPITAL

The cost of capital is calculated by means of a formula called weighted average cost of capital (WACC).[29] According to the WACC, the cost of capital is equal to the weighted average of the cost of debt and the cost of equity. The cost of debt and the cost of equity refer, respectively, to the returns required by two types of investors: those who hold the firm's debt and those who hold the firm's equity, or, in other words, the firm's creditors and its stockholders. The model most widely used to calculate the rate of return of the firm's equity is the so-called Capital Asset Pricing Model (CAPM).[30] The CAPM calculates the required rate of return of an asset from the point of view of the investor who has to decide whether or not to add this asset in her portfolio. The rate of return of an asset is envisaged in relation to its risk, where it is equal to the risk-free rate of return plus a "risk premium" that is positively related to the risk of the asset. Importantly, the CAPM distinguishes two types of risk: risks that are specific to the asset, which can be diversified within a large and well-built portfolio, and risks that are specific to the market, which are nondiversifiable—micro risks and macro risks, respectively. It is only for the latter type of risk, macro risks, which pertain to the market as a whole, that the investor should be rewarded and that are therefore included in the calculation of the "risk premium." In other words, the macro risks affecting a firm (e.g., inflation, energy costs, etc.) are taken into account in its cost of capital, while the micro risks that are specific to the firm are not taken into account in its cost of capital because they are supposed to "wash out" in the investor's diversified portfolio.

As we have also seen in Chapter 3, the shift from the rate of interest to the cost of capital as the definition of the discount rate entailed a significant rise in the level of discount rates. Still, the discount rates of biotech companies remain strikingly high. In particular, they are significantly higher than the discount rates of pharmaceutical companies, although they operate in the same market and therefore their investors bear a similar macro risk and should be rewarded with a similar risk premium. For example, the consultancy company's newsletter to which I referred above notes that observed discount rates tend to decrease with the degree of maturity of a company: from 20 percent for a start-up or a company in the discovery stage to 8-10 percent for a company that has a project on market or pharmaceutical company.

Empirical studies that apply the CAPM on publicly available data to infer firms' cost of capital arrive at similar conclusions, although the discrepancies between pharma and biotech companies appear to be less important. A chapter coauthored by Stewart Myers (whom the reader met in Chapter 3) for an edited volume on competitive strategies in the pharmaceutical industry published by the press of American Enterprise Institute found that in 1990, the cost of capital was on average 15 percent for major pharmaceutical companies and 19 percent for smaller biotechnology companies, or respectively 10 percent and 14 percent in real, that is, inflation-adjusted, terms (Myers and Shyam-Sunder 1996).[31] Scott Harrington (2012) found slightly lower numbers for the periods 2001 to 2005 and 2006 to 2008: respectively 10 percent and 9 percent for pharmaceutical companies and 14 percent and 12 percent for biotechnology companies (in nominal terms).

Myers and Lakshmi Shyam-Sunder (1996) explicitly address the problem of the higher levels of the discount rates of smaller companies specialized in pharmaceutical R&D (aka biotech start-ups). They observe that "the most obvious risks facing pharmaceutical R&D are 'micro,'" and precisely because they are micro, following the theory of the CAPM, they "do not require a higher cost of capital" (p. 214).

So are biotech firms wrong when they use higher costs of capital? Or is the CAPM wrong? To what extent can the notion of uncertainty, redefined as the investor's concern and backed with modern financial theory, serve as an explanatory resource for the high discount rates observed in the biopharmaceutical industry and in particular the high discount rates of biotechnology companies?

THE LIMITS OF UNCERTAINTY AS THE INVESTOR'S CONCERN

Part of the answer lies in the epistemic role devoted to the CAPM. Myers and Shyam-Sunder (1996) defend their use of this model in terms of practicality rather than "truth":

> We use the CAPM in the empirical section of our study not because it is truth—it has both theoretical and empirical weakness—but because it reflects the main ideas of modern valuation theory, it is widely used, it seems, to generate sensible discount rates, and other models are extremely difficult to implement in practice. The following CAPM-based empirical analysis expresses good current practice, and we believe that it generates cost-of-capital estimates in the same ballpark as those corporate financial managers actually use. (Myers and Shyam-Sunder 1996, pp. 214–15)

In other words, the CAPM works because the results that it generates are "in the same ballpark as those corporate financial managers actually use." At the same time, the results of the model are intended to serve as "benchmarks" that "current practice...would adjust up or down to set the cost of capital and discount rate or 'hurdle rate' for particular classes of capital investments" (p. 208). These "adjustments" are not condemned by financial theory here,[32] but instead interpreted in terms of the exceptionality of certain types of projects:

> Higher returns are demanded for riskier projects, but the adjustments are judgmental and implicit. For example, managers may discount at a

company's cost of capital for an especially risky project, yet penalize the project for its risk by working with especially conservative cash flow forecasts.

None of that excuses us from considering the discount rates that should in principle apply to investment in pharmaceutical R&D. Those rates may be implicit in practice and not quantified here, but they are clearly higher than the benchmark rates given above [i.e., the discount rates calculated with the CAPM]. (Myers and Shyam-Sunder 1996, p. 230)

Here is another part of the answer to the discrepancy between the discount rates derived from the theoretical model and those observed in practice: the model does not apply to certain types of projects because they are too risky. Interestingly, the notion of uncertainty as the investor's concern that lies at the heart of the theory linking risk and reward does not suffice to explain the rewards required by investors precisely for uncertain projects. My objective here is not to criticize financial theory, but to emphasize the fragilities of the notion of uncertainty as the investor's concern, which is often presented in the self-evident terms of "risk deserves reward."

Discount rates, finance theory argues, need to account not only for the time value of money, but also for the uncertainty from which the investor suffers because she does not know whether the cash flow she has projected to receive will be the cash flows that she actually will receive. The CAPM is supposed to account for the risk borne by the investor: it calculates the expected return on an asset in relation to its risk. The only risk that deserves a premium, though, is the risk that the investor cannot diversify: that is, the "macro risk" or "market risk," which is not specific to the asset being valued. In what ways does this risk relate to the kind of "mounting uncertainty" that characterizes the biopharmaceutical industry according to participants in the BIO-Europe panel I evoked above? It turns out, not many: "Most of the risks that trouble a pharmaceutical manager or scientist are technical or regulatory and have nothing to do with the macroeconomic risks that move the stock market and therefore concern diversified investors" (Myers and Shyam-Sunder 1996, p. 230).

Put differently, as we've seen all along, the uncertainty that concerns the investor has little to do with the uncertainty that concerns the manager who has to value a drug development project. In my reading, this observation could have led to two opposite conclusions: either that investor-specific uncertainty should not be considered in the discount rate, which would bring the discount rate back to the level of the rate of interest, because there would no longer be a risk premium for the investor or that manager-specific uncertainty should be integrated into the discount rate in addition to its integration into cash flows in the form of probabilities, which would further increase the discount rate. From the observation of the discount rates practiced by companies, it appears that the latter conclusion has prevailed.

Trying to catch up with this practice, new models are being developed to account for the higher cost of capital in the biopharmaceutical industry. One example is the market-derived capital pricing model (MCPM), which instead of using historical data, like the CAPM, adopts a forward-looking approach.[33] The MCPM results in significantly higher discount rates for biotechnology companies; for example, the relevant cost of equity capital for a biotech such as Genset moves from 10.5 percent with the CAPM to 34.8 percent with the MCPM (McNulty et al. 2002).

Here is an observation made by the authors of the MCPM on why the higher discount rates produced by their model matter: "If a company routinely applies too high a cost of capital in its project valuations, then it will reject valuable opportunities that its competitors will happily snap up. Setting the rate too low, on the other hand, almost guarantees that the company will commit resources to projects that will erode profitability and destroy shareholder value" (McNulty et al. 2002, p. 5). The observation underlies the way in which, in the biopharmaceutical industry, we must continually be assured, little shareholder value is destroyed. And the safeguard of shareholder value is precisely uncertainty: uncertainty defined as the investor's concern and integrated into the calculation of the discount rate through models such as the CAPM. That version of uncertainty permeates the valuation of drug development projects.

CONSEQUENCES

The preceding analysis has shown the need to direct the critique of discounting from uncertainty as lack of knowledge to uncertainty as the investor's concern. Uncertainty as lack of knowledge has been largely discussed in the literature of sociology and economics as an obstacle faced by all future-oriented valuation devices, resulting in the impossibility to calculate and, worse, in manipulation by those able to act as if the future was known. Examining how discounting valuations are performed in the case of drug development projects, where such uncertainty is supposed to be at its highest, shows how the existing metrological infrastructure, made of rules, textbooks, standardized time, averages, and probabilities, transforms what appears first as consulting a crystal ball into a routine calculation exercise. Rather than being disarmed by the uncertainty of the future, discounting produces a form of a certain future, envisaged as a variation on the past.

However, uncertainty as the investor's concern has received a much poorer theoretical elaboration. Its foundations were laid, quite surprisingly, by the author whose name is generally associated with the first version of uncertainty—sociologists and economists even talk of "Knightian uncertainty." Knight's functional, rather than ontological, definition of genuine uncertainty as distinct from mere risk produces a focus on its economic effect, which resides in the existence of a special class of actors, the entrepreneurs, who assume the burden of uncertainty and, in exchange, are entitled to a reward in the form of profit. His theory of knowledge thus serves to scaffold a theory of profit in which uncertainty as lack of knowledge is translated into uncertainty as the investor's concern. This translation is visible in the biopharmaceutical industry, where uncertainty is narrated, calculated, and capitalized, acting both as a justification for and a measure of the reward that investors deserve, and the key operator in this process is the discount rate, defined as the cost of capital.

How does this matter? As noted in a *Harvard Business Review* article that I quoted above, high discount rates are said to be necessary to ensure that resources are not committed to "projects that will erode profitability and destroy shareholder value" (McNulty et al. 2002, p. 5). At the same time, high discount rates annihilate the value of early stage projects, which may lead managers either to abandon these projects, falling prey to the kind of short-termism that we examined in Chapter 3, or simply to "not trust their valuations and disregard the recommendation retrieved from the valuations," generating "a general refusal of quantitative methods" (Bogdan and Villiger 2007, p. 6). All this may of course be detrimental to the quality of decision-making and the amount of innovation in the biopharmaceutical industry. But there are also other consequences that reach well beyond the world of biotechnology start-ups, pharmaceutical companies, and financial markets.

The first one has to do with drug prices. As we saw in our discussion of the OTA's report on costs, risks, and rewards in pharmaceutical R&D, the high prices of drugs have been an issue for many decades. The pharmaceutical industry has typically responded to criticism by citing the costs of R&D, exacerbated by the long time scales and the uncertainty of drug development. Studies that have attempted to measure these costs have reached varied results and attracted various critiques, but one thing that they have clearly shown is the importance of the cost of capital. Among the most influential studies of this type are those conducted by the Tufts Center for the Study of Drug Development: in 2014, they assessed the cost of development of a new drug at $2.6 billion, of which $1.2 billion—that is, almost half—corresponded to the cost of capital. The numbers were quite similar in their previous study, conducted in 2001: $400 million out of a total of $800 million corresponded to the cost of capital (DiMasi et al. 2003, 2016).

More recently, pharmaceutical companies have turned to a different kind of argument in the justification of the high prices of drugs: rather than the costs incurred in the past, they point to the value that new drugs will bring in the future and argue for "value-based pricing" (Doganova and Rabeharisoa 2022). Reacting to the backlash triggered by the price of $2.1 million that Novartis claimed for Zolgensma, "the most expensive drug ever" (Stein 2019), the president of the biotech start-up that led its development before selling itself to Novartis for $8.7 billion in 2018 explained that "we should be pricing these medicines on the value they bring to society and sharing that value between the innovator and society" (Green 2019). The reader of this chapter by now should have understood that the argument of uncertainty and the technology of discounting are likely to play a crucial in how this "value" is determined and what portion of it will accrue to "the innovator" and hence the investors for the sake of whom he is mandated to innovate and financially enabled to do so.

The second consequence has to do with the relevance of critique. Preoccupied with uncertainty as lack of knowledge, critique tends to focus on the denunciation of practices that are deemed wrong because they deviate from some kind of truth, such as the real value of a project or the genuine unknowability of the future. Turning to uncertainty as the investor's concern, critique tilts over to a different objective: unbind the discursive and calculative chains that hold together the uncertainty of the future and the figure of the investor. Rethinking the critique of discounting in terms of uncertainty is an integral part of rethinking the future as a temporal and a political domain, as this book urges us to do. This chapter has attempted to demonstrate that uncertainty is part and parcel of the analytical arsenal through which discounting gives the figure of the investor control over the future. The next and final chapter will pursue this argument in a different empirical and analytical direction: examining the introduction of discounting in the Chilean mining law, it will discuss its capacity to grant investors control over the future by providing certainty.

Discounting and the State-Investor Relationship: From Owning to Valuing Chilean Copper

Chapter 4 discussed the entanglement between future-orientation and financialization in the biopharmaceutical industry. Another markedly future-oriented industry is oil. This is where, in the 1950s, Joel Dean's consultancy firm found the first users of discounting and transformed discounted cash flow (DCF) into a product, as we have seen in Chapter 3. Indeed, drilling for oil and developing new drugs are often compared when it comes to demonstrating the uncertainty bearing upon them; for example, when discussing the "particular riskiness of R&D," the report of the Office of Technology Assessment (OTA) of the US Congress on pharmaceutical R&D compared it to "wildcatting in Texas" and noted that it "involves many dry holes and a few gushers" (US Congress, Office of Technology Assessment 1993, p. 8). The oil company Shell is well known as the inventor of business scenarios, a technology that "seeks to address an uncertain, and in some respects unknowable, future" (Jefferson 2012, p. 186). The theme of the uncertain future is equally present in recent analyses of the extractive industries more broadly. Echoing the descriptions of the biopharmaceutical industry, social scientists have portrayed the uncertainty faced by mineral exploration, "with its distant temporal horizons, high stakes, and low probability of success" (Olofsson 2020a) and, consequently, the use that such industries make of technologies of the future such as predictions (Olofsson 2020b), promises (Merlin et al. 2021), or anticipation (Weszkalnys 2014).

This chapter takes us to the field of extractive industries in order to explore one final facet of discounting. Discounting is certainly part of the technologies of the future that play a role in mineral exploration, and this role can certainly be analyzed along the same lines as the ones I drew in the previous chapter, paying attention to how a version of uncertainty defined as lack of knowledge is translated into a different version of uncertainty defined as the investor's concern and exploring how this transforms discounting problems such as the reliability of future projections and the justification of high discount rates.[1] However, this is not what I am going to do here. I would rather move to the other end of the process of mineral extraction and consider the moment when exploration has already occurred, investors and states have been convinced by promises of future rewards and have allowed for mining activities to begin, and entrepreneurial projects have evolved into industrial installations and entered the phase of exploitation, similar to when a new drug has finally entered the market and is being delivered to millions of patients on a regular basis. Does the future have any role to play at this end of the process, when routine seems to have superseded uncertainty and the distant future seems to have been absorbed into an expanding present?

In situations that cannot be easily disentangled from their history, the extent to which the future matters and, as a corollary, the extent to which discounting appears as an appropriate measure of value, becomes more complicated. The gesture made by Irving Fisher when he proclaimed that "the value of any article of wealth or property is dependent alone on the future, not the past" (Fisher 1906, p. 188) loses some of its force. To use his own example: imagine how fragile the statement that the value of the Panama Canal is dependent only upon its future expected services, and not upon the past cost of building the canal, can become when future services and past costs are embodied and connected to the actors who experience these flows of money—those who have incurred the costs of building the canal and those who will benefit from its future services. In other words, how easy is it to purge the problem of valuation from the temporality of the past in moments that cannot be entirely defined by the forward-looking gaze of innovation, in moments when history resists the future?

Such a moment, in which the past and the future collide in the quest for the value of something, broke out twice in Chile in response to the following practical question: What is the price of a copper mine? Or more precisely, what is the compensation that should be paid to the company operating the copper mine in case it is expropriated by the state? The question was, essentially, quite similar to the one that triggered the "invention" of discounting in forest management in the nineteenth century: What is the price that a state should pay to an economic actor—whether a private forest owner or a multinational corporation—in order to take its place in the exploitation of natural resources? Providing an answer in this case, however, proved to be much more controversial.

Two radically opposite answers were given to the question of the price of a copper mine in Chile: first, by Salvador Allende, who nationalized Chilean copper mines in 1971, and, ten years later, by José Piñera, minister of mines in Augusto Pinochet's government and author of the Constitutional Mining Law of 1981. Allende's valuation is well known mostly for the result at which it arrived: a price equal to zero, which outraged the US multinationals that owned the mines and the US government itself and, directly or indirectly, caused dramatic consequences for Chile. Here, I am interested not so much in the seemingly shocking result of a zero price, but in the reasoning and the calculation that led to it.

Allende's valuation was firmly oriented toward the past: the accounting past of the mining operations of the multinational companies that were being expropriated, but also the political past of Chile and the exploitation of its natural resources. José Piñera's valuation, by contrast, was firmly oriented toward the future and made standard and explicit use of discounting and present value. In many ways, it will sound familiar to the reader, who has encountered the same formulas and the same kind of justifications of the value of things in the previous chapters. What will be novel, rather, is the ways in which discounting was celebrated. In his writings, Piñera refers to "Present Value," with a capital P and a capital V,[2] as the "sword" that enabled him to cut the "Gordian knot" of attracting foreign investors while maintaining the public ownership of mines. What will be novel, also, is the institutional embedding of discounting. In Chapter 4, I argued that discounting produces certain futures because it has been embedded in a calculative infrastructure made of textbooks, standardized time, averages, and probabilities. Here, discounting produces certain futures because it has been institutionally embedded: Piñera not only imported discounting from economic science to the mining industry, but also crafted the object whose value discounting could determine (the "concession"), and inscribed both—what is valued and how it is valued—in law. The certain futures that discounting produces in this case are for an investor whose expectations about the future are guaranteed to be met, no matter what the future actually turns out to be.

What now appears to me as a crucial and yet little-known episode in the development of discounting came to me by chance. It is probably not a surprise that a book interested in an economic technique enacting the temporalities of neoliberalism ends up in Chile, a country whose recent history has been analyzed as a laboratory of neoliberalism and a powerful illustration of the performativity of economics, both during and after the period of Pinochet's government and its "Chicago Boys" economists (Ossandón and Ureta 2019; Valdes 1995). It was the study of performativity that brought me to Chile in 2015.[3] As part of my research visit, I gave a talk on the performativity of valuation devices in which I presented my preliminary research on the use of discounting in the pharmaceutical industry. Going through the details of the economic formula, I was hoping not to lose an audience composed of sociologists and anthropologists who, I thought, had never heard about discounting before. The discussion that followed proved me wrong. An anthropologist in the audience shared that many people in Chile actually knew about this formula.[4] We can see it in the Chilean mining law established by Piñera, he said, which stated that to be expropriated, companies that owned mines had to be paid a compensation equal to the amount of the future benefits that the mine would have generated. I had never heard of Piñera, and I was surprised to find that the economic formula I was tracking had been inscribed in law and was widely known in a place so distant from those to which my investigation had brought me so far. Intrigued by this unexpected discovery, I decided to delve into the history of Chilean mining legislation.

This chapter therefore provides a brief and cursory account of the long and illuminating history of the relationship between the Chilean state and the foreign investors willing to exploit its copper resources, as revealed through the narrow but powerful lens of the use of discounting and competing valuation methodologies in the country's mining legislation. I insist on the narrowness of my lens, which will exclude issues related to mining regulation more broadly, such as the calculation of royalties and taxes, the industry's environmental impact, or its relationship with national governments and local populations. But I also insist on its potential. Indeed, the question of the valuation of the "damages" inflicted by national governments to international investors in situations ranging from expropriation to the implementation of stricter regulation is not specific to the Chilean mining law. It has been debated in international law more broadly since the early twentieth century and is becoming more and more pregnant with implications now (Marzal 2021).

Like the other chapters of the book, this chapter attempts to understand the kind of problem to which discounting came as a solution, or, to use Piñera's terms, the kind of knot that it allowed cutting. However, the light in which discounting features in this case is novel. Here, discounting appears as a tool shaping the relationship between states in search of development and corporations in search of returns on their investments. By analyzing the role played by discounting and the alternative valuation approaches it has been competing within in the state-investor relationship, this chapter will show that the politics of discounting is also to be found in its ability to reformulate a problem of ownership into a problem of valuation and, relatedly, to reformulate a problem of the past or the present into a problem of the future.

VALUATION FUTURES

José Piñera Echenique was one of the "Chicago Boys" who joined the Chilean government after the military coup d'état in 1973 and designed many of the policies that were implemented by Pinochet. Trained in economics, Piñera served as minister of labor and social security and then as minister of mining. In a book entitled *The Principles of the Basic Constitutional Law on Mining Concessions,* he explains the reasoning behind the Constitutional Mining Law of 1981 when he conceived it, putting particular emphasis on the role played by discounting.

The problem that Piñera was faced with when he became minister of mining was privatizing the mines that Allende had nationalized ten years earlier seemed politically impossible, but then how to attract the investors that nationalization had chased away? The solution he found lay in the present value of discounted future cash flows, which he described as the sword that cut the Gordian knot formed by the public ownership versus foreign investment dilemma. What was that knot that present value allowed cutting?

Piñera recalls the mission he was entrusted with when he became minister of mining on December 29, 1980.[5] The constitutional reform that President Allende had introduced in 1971 gave the state the "absolute, exclusive, inalienable and imprescriptible" ownership of mines (Law 17450, Reforma la Constitucion Politica del Estado, 16-07-1971). Many expected that the new constitution prepared under Pinochet would cancel this measure and "reestablish traditional property rights." However, the new constitution approved in 1980 failed to do so. Numeral 24 of article 19 stated that "the State has absolute, exclusive, inalienable and imprescriptible domain [over] all mines," keeping the Allende's formulation (Chile's Constitution of 1980 with Amendments through 2012). However, Numeral 24 continued, certain substances may be "objects of concessions of exploration or of exploitation." These concessions "will always be constituted by judicial resolution," and only "ordinary tribunals of justice" will have the competence to declare their extinction. A law of a "constitutional organic character" will specify the duration of these concessions, the rights that they confer, and the obligations that they impose.

It is to this constitutional law that Piñera devoted his efforts. The challenge, as he saw it, "was to draft a constitutional law that would provide firm mining property rights, to secure presidential and legislative approval for it, to obtain the assent of the constitutional tribunal as it was required, and to convince local and international entrepreneurs of its rationality, as well as to persuade the public that the national interest had been safeguarded."

The challenge, to put it differently, was to reconcile public ownership and private investment, attracting the latter without questioning the former. The question, in Piñera's view, was not whether the state company Codelco, which owned the large Chilean mines since their nationalization, should be privatized. Privatization would have set off a "holy war." What was needed was "considerably more practical and concrete." At that time, Codelco produced 85 percent of Chile's copper. Between 1980 and 1996, the share produced by publicly owned companies shrank from 84 percent to 39 percent of output while that produced by privately owned companies rose from 6 percent to 54 percent (Spilimbergo 1999). Judging by these numbers, the effects of Piñera's legislation resembled those of privatization, but the "considerably more practical and concrete" strategy through which they were achieved was different: it sought to "open the way for private production of copper (and other minerals) to grow to the point where it predominated, through a legislation which would encourage the discovery of new deposits and the expansion of existing ones, thereby creating new wealth."

"Growth" and "value creation" (to give Piñera's "creating wealth" motto a contemporary twist) aptly describe what happened in Chile in the 1980s. According to a working paper of the International Monetary Fund, foreign direct investment in the mining sector increased by a factor of nine: from the equivalent of $90 million (the yearly average for the period 1974 to 1989) to $803 million in 1990 (Spilimbergo 1999). The author attributes this increase to "the constitutional protection to the right of private ownership of mines…[and to] a fiscal regime for mining with no royalty payments and low tax rates on profits." Such "strong incentives" certainly helped. But they were not the solution to the key problem that Piñera was struggling with. Let us return to his account of the events.

THE SWORD: "PRESENT VALUE" AND THE "FULL CONCESSION"

Piñera explains that "the knot" that the "sword" of discounting enabled him to cut was not the problem of property, but that of expropriation:

> I have always believed that the correct identification of a problem is the first decisive step towards solving it. The "knot" impeding the development of private mining was the question of a fair indemnity in the event of expropriation of the mining concession. . . .
>
> Soon I came to the conclusion that the Gordian knot which was strangling mining in Chile could not be "untied." It had to be cut. The "sword" I found embedded in a concept of economic science. It was the Present Value of the net cash flows of an asset or company.

One might wonder, at a first glance, what the link is between expropriation, the "question of a fair indemnity," and the concept of "Present Value." I wondered, too. What does it mean to owe something? Part of the answer to this complex question relates to the temporality of the relationship established with the thing being owned. In the investor's eyes, the thing is capital, that is, a stream of future cash flows. What matters to her is that these flows accrue to her. What matters, therefore, is not the ownership of capital in the present, but the control over the revenue it will produce in the future. We tend to think of these two dimensions—the orchard and the harvested apples turned into cash flows, the mine and the extracted copper turned into cash flows—as inseparable. But they are not. Armed with his Present Value sword, Piñera granted investors not ownership of the present, but control over the future. He granted them a stream of cash flows that even the dramatic event of expropriation could not interrupt because the indemnity they would receive would be equal to the sum of the future revenues that they would have received from the mine.

To Piñera, the reasoning of discounting appeared "simple." He gave the following example. Imagine a multistory parking structure at the South Pole: its value is much less than what it cost to build. Imagine a shop on the best corner in central Santiago: its value is much more than what it cost to build. The conclusion is straightforward: "An asset... has value to the extent that it can generate future profits." These future profits arise at different points of time; to be summed up, they need to be made commensurate; for this, they need to be "discounted to the present at the appropriate rate of interest."

Albeit simple, this reasoning was demanding. It required a certain definition of the object to which it could be applied and a certain temporal disposition in which the object valued had a future. Piñera introduced simultaneously the type of valuation technique, discounting, and the type of object that this technique could value, the concession. The concession was modeled so that the Present Value formula could be applied to it. As he explains:

> In order to apply this formula in the case of the mining concession, the concession right had to incorporate the right to exploit and to continue to exploit the mine, and that is how we drew it up. As an expropriation deprives the owner of the concession of the possibility of future exploitation and of the ensuing cash flows, the loss occasioned to him by the expropriation of the concession is the same as the Present Value of the net cash flows which it is capable of generating.

The object that Piñera's team designed so that it lends itself to Present Value calculations was called the "full concession," an invention that had "all the legal attributes required to provide guarantees to the private Investor as well as to safeguard the national interest." In his account, Piñera highlights five of these attributes. First, the concession is defined as a property of its owner; as a result, the only way to detach the concession from its owner is by means of "expropriation."[6] Second, such expropriation should be "fairly indemnified," and for an exploitation concession, the indemnity should be equal to the "Present Value of its future net cash flows." Third, to permit "the rational operation of a mine," management is free from controls by government. Forth, the concession is given without any expiration date; the concession right has an "indefinite life," conditioned only on the payment of an annual fee per hectare (*la patenta minera*). Fifth, the concession is not "a political creation"; it is up to the judge, rather than to legislative or executive powers, to decide whether a concession should be given or withdrawn.

Piñera submitted the draft of the constitutional law to Pinochet in August 1981, together with a report that was reproduced in his book. The report included an appendix that explained the calculation of the present value of a copper mining concession and the industrial facility exploiting it. Imagine a concession that produces a given amount of copper (500 pounds) per year, at a certain cost of production ($320), which it sells at a certain price ($1) and for which it pays a certain level of taxes (50 percent income tax). After taking into account a few other factors such as the depreciation of the equipment, a simple subtraction shows that the concession will generate net cash flows of $100 per year. (The parameters are supposed to remain constant over 50 years.)

Imagine then that "due to public utility or national interest, a law authorizes...the expropriation of the exploitation concession right and of the activities of the mining industrial facility destined to exercise this right" (Piñera 1981b, p. 56). The following formula allows calculating "the Present Value" of the future cash flows (fig. 5.1):

$$Present\ Value\ =\ \sum_{i\,=\,1}^{i\,=\,50}\ \frac{F_i}{(1+r_i)^i}$$

Figure 5.1. The Present Value formula for the calculation of the amount of compensation in case of expropriation (Piñera 1981b, p. 56).

A discount rate of 10 percent is indicated, whose level or meaning are not discussed. According to Piñera (personal communication), such rates were used in evaluating investments projects in Chile at that time because "capital was scarce in Chile." Unlike the Present Value formula, the discount rate is not inscribed in legislation because it is a "parameter" that varies with market conditions, and it is determined ad hoc for each case, either by agreement between the parties or by the judge following the advice of experts. At a discount rate of 10 percent, "the Present Value" of this imaginary concession is equal to $99,150. This number indicates the indemnity that should be paid to the owner of the concession in the year when expropriation occurs.

DISCOUNTING IN THE LAW

The constitutional law received unanimous approval both from the legislative body and the Constitutional Court. According to Piñera (personal communication), there were no major objections raised during the review process, "but many questions to fully understand the Present Value concept and why it would both protect property rights and ensure the national interests." The law was published on January 21, 1982, as Law No. 18.097. Present Value features in article 11, which specifies that the owner of an exploitation concession has the right

> to be indemnified, in case of expropriation of the concession, for the property damage effectively caused to him, which consists in the commercial value of the ability to start and continue the extraction and the appropriation of the substances that are object of the concession. In the absence

of agreement, the value of this damage will be determined by the judge, using the prior opinion of experts. The experts, in order to determine the amount of the indemnity, will establish the value of the concession, by calculating, on the basis of the reserves of the substances of the concession that the expropriated party proves, the present value of the net cash flows of the concession. (Law 18097, Ley Organica Constitucional sobre Concesiones Mineras, 21-01-1982)

Thus, discounting entered law as the valuation methodology to calculate the price to be paid to the owner of a mining concession in the event of expropriation. In a speech he made on December 2, 1981, announcing that his law had just been approved, Piñera gave particular mention to this twin invention: the full concession, ending "a decade of uncertainty in mining rights," and the present value of net cash flows, "a modern concept that comes from economics and is very useful in determining the value of an asset" (Piñera 1981a). He had learned the Present Value concept at Harvard while getting a PhD in economics (personal communication). While preparing the law, his team of lawyers reviewed mining legislation in other countries and reported they could not find any mention of this concept. While notions of future profits and discounting were well established in economic theory and in firms' practices by that time, the Chilean mining law of 1981 appears as the first instance in which such calculations were inscribed in legislation, and even more significantly, in legislation of a constitutional order.

Taking account of future profits to determine compensations in case of expropriation was not completely novel, though. This approach to valuation has been supported by corporations and developed states since it was first formulated by the US Secretary of State Cordell Hull in a letter he wrote to the Mexican government in 1938 following the expropriation of agrarian properties owned by American citizens "without adequate, effective and prompt compensation being made therefor" (Hull 1938). According to this view, "adequate" compensation should reflect the "full value" of the assets, taking into account the future profits that would have been generated by the expropriated party if its activities had not been ended (Weller 1986). Two valuation methods could allow reaching, or at least come close to, the determination of such a "full value": the fair market value method, equal to the price that the corporation would have received for its assets in an open-market transaction (if a market in which its assets could have been sold existed), and the "going concern" method, which is calculated "by multiplying either the past annual earnings or estimated future earnings by a capitalization factor" (p. 327). Among the arguments put forward by the proponents of this view was the need to assure investors that the agreements they have signed will be enforced and that the expectations they have formed will be met. Other arguments focused on the efforts that corporations had put into developing the assets they had invested in, thereby acquiring "an interest in the land to which the concession applies, as well as the natural resources present in the land" (p. 330).

In his recent and pioneering research on the use of discounting in investor-state dispute settlement, Toni Marzal (2021) has meticulously traced the spread of DCF and the associated principles of "full compensation" and "fair market value" in arbitral practice. He situates the shift to DCF in the late 1980s. Until then, he explains, DCF was seen as a "speculative" method and alternative methods were preferred, such as book value—a "backward-facing" valuation method, since "contrary to DCF, it is based on past expenditure rather than future income" (p. 274).

The debate that led to the change was triggered by the Amoco decision of the Iran-United States Claims Tribunal in 1987. The decision rejected DCF because of its orientation toward the future: "no reparation for speculative or uncertain damage can be awarded" (Amoco International Finance Corp v Islamic Rep of Iran, Partial Award No 310-56-3 [July 14, 1987] 15 IUSCTR 189, para. 238, quoted in Marzal 2021, p. 274). This decision was criticized in a separate opinion arguing that although the legal principle against compensation for speculative losses applies, once the investor's loss has been proven, the assessment of the compensation should be performed with the help of "the best available evidence, even though this process be inherently speculative"—and here, rejecting DCF is based on a "misunderstanding of economics" (Concurring opinion of Judge Brower, Amoco v Iran [n 142] para. 26, quoted in Marzal 2021, p. 275). As Marzal tells the rest of the story, this separate opinion

> is regularly cited to support the proposition that there is no contradiction between legal principles (such as the non-compensability of speculative losses) and the use of the DCF method.... The tables first turned in the Phillips Petroleum award, rendered only two years after Amoco, with the Tribunal embracing the DCF method. Crucially, the majority opinion justified this, not on the basis of legal principle, but on the perception that DCF is the method that a hypothetical investor would have relied on to determine the purchase price. Two further decisions followed, where the Tribunals also turned to DCF to determine compensation. The World Bank Guidelines then [in 1992] gave their blessing: on the basis of the then current "consensus" and "best practices"...they advocated for the DCF method in determining the FMV [fair market value] of "a going concern with a proven record of profitability. (Marzal 2021, pp. 275–76)

The inscription of discounting in Chilean mining law in 1981 was precocious with regard to the broader history of the calculation of compensation in investor-state arbitration. Its precocity is certainly related to the particular context of the government of Pinochet, which gave economists—the Chicago Boys—the mandate to rewrite the law. As Marzal shows in his work, the spread of discounting as a measure of the "fair market value" that allows expropriated investors to be "fully compensated" for their loss is deeply related to a shift in the understanding of "value" from a legal to an economic concept. In current arbitral practice, "value" has come to be seen as "an objective concept with an economic content" (Lauterpacht 1990, p. 249, quoted in Marzal 2021, p. 269), and discounting has become the appropriate instrument to measure this value in a manner "consistent with the principles of modern finance" (Simmons 2013, p. 233, quoted in Marzal 2021, p. 279). According to a study published by PwC, the accounting firm PricewaterhouseCoopers, today, DCF is the valuation methodology most frequently adopted by tribunals, showing that "the trend over time was for Tribunals to prefer forward-looking, income based approaches over reliance on historical figures" (PwC 2017, p. 6).

VALUATION PASTS

Piñera's knot stemmed from the public ownership of mines that had been inscribed in the Chilean Constitution since 1971, when Allende nationalized the mines owned by the US multinationals Kennecott (known as Rio Tinto today) and Anaconda (which later became part of British Petroleum). Nationalization was a political promise that Allende made during the presidential elections and that, once he was elected, faced a practical problem: how to calculate the price that the buyer (Chile) should pay to the seller (multinational companies) in exchange for the shares that it got? The answer that Allende announced caused a tremor: the price to be paid, he said, was zero.

This price was the result of the following calculation. The value of mining assets is equal to their book value. While present value is oriented toward the future, book value is anchored in the past, for it refers to the price at which the assets of the company were initially purchased. Allende further anchored the calculation of value in the past by taking into account the past behavior of the mining companies and in particular what he called the "excess profits" that they had been able to generate thanks to Chile's friendly regulation and the booming price of copper. The difference between the companies' excess profits over the previous fifteen years and a reasonable level of profits, according to international profit levels, was deducted from the book value of the companies' assets. The result of this mathematical operation

Figure 5.2. Larrea Vicente, "Chile se pone pantalones largos, ahora el cobre es chileno," 1971 (Library of Congress).

was negative: it turned out that it was the companies that owed money to Chile, instead of Chile owing money to them. Consequently, Chile decided to nationalize Kennecott's and Anaconda's holdings without compensation.

SOVEREIGNTY AND INTERNATIONAL ORDER

Allende, too, had a Gordian knot to cut, but his looked quite different than Piñera's. The problem he was facing was not that of attracting private investment versus safeguarding the national interest. It was that of regaining Chilean sovereignty while respecting international order. Sovereignty in this case involved control over the country's natural resources. International order involved the relationship between Chile, a "host country," in the parlance of international law, and its no-longer-welcome guests, the multinational companies that had invested in the exploitation of its natural resources. The solution of the problem thus framed lay in the calculation of the "just" compensation that the corporations should receive in exchange for "their" mines.

The threads of Allende's knot permeated the everyday atmosphere in Chile as it prepared for nationalization. In July 1971, when the reform was unanimously approved and the law was promulgated, the country was covered in posters claiming "Chile se pone pantalones largos, ahora el cobre es chileno"—"Chile puts on long pants, copper is Chilean now" (Dupoy 1983) (the image is reproduced in fig. 5.2).

In the midst of the fervor generated by the prospect of regaining sovereignty, Allende repeatedly insisted on the importance of a "just" compensation to ensure that nationalization would conform to international law. An article in *The New York Times* reports Allende saying, "We will pay if it is just, and we will not pay what is not just" in front of a crowd of miners in Rancagua as well as on radio and TV (De Onis 1971). A French journalist in Chile similarly reports:

> On December 21, 1970, at the Constitution Square in Santiago, Allende signed publicly the project of the reform that would allow the nationalization of copper, in front of thousands of people who applauded him

frantically when he declared: "… This is not an aggression against the people or the government of North America. Neither is it an aggression against the companies themselves, because the compensations will be just and the nationalization will be done in conformity with the law." (Dupoy 1983)

What was a "just" compensation was still an open question in 1970, in sharp contrast with the current consensus on the concepts of full compensation, fair market value, and DCF. As Marzal (2021, p. 265) writes, "not so long ago, an international tribunal's determination of the right amount owed to the investor was generally understood to necessarily involve some reliance on equitable judgment" through the adjudicator's "subjective perception of what was just or equitable" (p. 265) or "an external correction to the valuation process" (p. 266). In the speech he made when the initial nationalization proposal was delivered to congress, Allende referred to the United Nations' notion of permanent sovereignty over natural resources: "We emphasize that with the nationalization of copper begins our second independence. We will realize this nationalization by exercising our rights as recognized in the United Nations Charter and as recognized by the Supreme Court of the United States. This is not an act of vengeance against anyone, but rather the exercise on the part of Chile of her supreme right to be free, united, prosperous, and sovereign" (Allende 1970, translation from Fleming 1973, p. 605).

UN General Assembly Resolution 1803 on permanent sovereignty over natural resources, which was adopted in 1962, stated that the profits derived from the exploitation of natural resources must be "shared in the proportions freely agreed upon, in each case, between the investor and the recipient State" (article 3). It addressed specifically the issue of nationalization and the compensation due by the state to the investor in such cases (article 4): "Nationalization, expropriation or requisitioning shall be based on grounds or reasons of public utility, security, or the national interest which are recognized as overriding purely individual or private interests, both domestic and foreign. In such cases the owner shall be paid appropriate compensation, in accordance with the rules in force in the State taking such measures in the exercise of its sovereignty and in accordance with international law" (United Nations General Assembly Resolution 1803, Adopted on December 14, 1962, on Permanent Sovereignty Over Natural Resource).

While the UN resolution states that compensation should be "appropriate," in spite of the United States' attempts to amend the text, it does not mention the "prompt, adequate, and effective" formulation, linked to valuation approaches that account for future profits, that has been supported by developed states and corporations (Fleming 1973). Article 4 also notes that cases of controversy will be settled by the jurisdiction of the nationalizing state and, under the condition of the state's agreement, through arbitration or international adjudication. This again is significant in terms of valuation approaches because arbitration tribunals have been much more inclined to use methods, such as fair market value, going concern value, or present value, than national jurisdictions, which have favored the book value method (Weller 1986). These two specifications in the resolution, related to how and by whom the price to be paid to foreign investors should be determined, were key in the defense of Allende's calculation and in the demonstration of its conformity with international law.

A DIFFERENT SWORD: BOOK VALUE AND EXCESS PROFITS

Law 17450, published on July 16, 1971, reformed the Chilean Constitution so as to allow for the nationalization of copper. In addition to stating that mines are under the "absolute, exclusive, inalienable and imprescriptible" possession of the state, the amended text of the constitution dealt with the problem of compensation: "The amount of the compensation, or compensations, as the case may be, may be determined on the basis of the original cost of such assets, less amortization, depreciation write-offs (*castigos*), and devaluation through obsolescence. All or part of the excess profits the nationalized companies have obtained may also be deducted from the compensation"

(Law 17450, Reforma la Constitucion Politica del Estado, 16-07-1971, article 1, c, translation from Fleming 1973).

Compensation was further addressed in the transitory provisions specifically related to the nationalization of the enterprises that constitute large-scale copper mining or "Gran Minería del Cobre" (Kennecott's El Teniente, Anaconda's Chuquicamata, El Salvador, and Exotica), as well as the Compañía Minera Andina (owned by Cerro). In order to determine an "adequate compensation," the text described the following procedure. First, the comptroller general will determine the amount of the compensation that has to be paid to the nationalized companies. The amount of the compensation will be equal to the book value of the assets as of December 31, 1970, minus a number of deductions that are listed in the text (for example, the revaluations made by the companies after 1964 or the value of the assets that the state may receive in poor condition of utilization). Second, the president of the republic can instruct the comptroller also to deduct from the compensation "all or part of the excess profits that the nationalized companies and their predecessors have accrued annually since the enactment of Law 11.828, considering especially the normal profits they may have obtained in their overall international operations or agreements which the Chilean State may have entered into on the subject of maximum profits of foreign companies established in the country" (Comptroller General 1971, p. 1241).

In order to determine the book value of the nationalized companies and the deductions that were within its scope (that is, all deductions among those for excess profits), the controller general's office mobilized its Department of Auditing and Department of Studies, constituted technical commissions, visited the mines, and requested from Codelco and the National Mining Enterprise data on the tangible and intangible assets necessary to calculate the deductions it was in charge of, as well as the balance sheets and annexes necessary to calculate the book value. The book value was determined "pursuant the following formula" (fig. 5.3):

$$Capital + Reserves + Net\ results\ as\ of\ December\ 31,\ 1970$$
$$- Transitory\ dividends\ paid = BASE\ BOOK\ VALUE$$

Figure 5.3. The book formula for the calculation of the amount of compensation in case of expropriation (Comptroller General 1971, p. 1247).

From the book value thus obtained were made a number of deductions, the most significant part of which was constituted by the excess profits calculated by the president of the republic (see fig. 5.4 below). On September 28, 1971, Allende decreed that the comptroller general should deduct $410 million from the value of El Teniente Mining Company, $300 million from the value of the Chuquicamata Copper Company, and $64 million from the value of Salvador Copper Company (Decree Concerning Excess Profits of Copper Companies, Sept. 28, 1971). For the first two, the amount of excess profits was higher than the book values of the companies: in other words, it is the companies that owed money to Chile for the profits they had unduly accrued, instead of Chile owing the companies a compensation for expropriating them.

The decree does not provide many details about the level of "normal" profits in comparison to which "excess" profits were defined. It mentions four points of comparison that were considered in the calculation: the profits obtained by Anaconda and Kennecott in their international operations, the profits of other mining companies, other examples of profits made on investments, and cases of limits placed on foreign investors' profits.[7] It appears that the first point served as a key reference for defining what level of profits is normal and what is excessive. The Allende administration gathered data from the companies' accounts and observed the following discrepancies: between 1955 and 1970, Anaconda earned an average profit of 16.68 percent (21.51 percent at Chuquicamata and 11.84 percent at El Salvador), as compared with 3.67 percent on average in its international operations apart from

	CHUQUICAMATA (ANACONDA)	EL SALVADOR (ANACONDA)	EXOTICA (ANACONDA)	EL TENIENTE (KENNECOTT)	MINERA ANDINA (CERRO)
BOOK VALUE	242	68	15	319	20
TOTAL DEDUCTIONS	318	70	5	629	1.9
AMONG WHICH EXCESS PROFITS	300	64	0	410	0
RESULT	−76.5	−1.6	10	−310.4	18.3
COMPENSATION TO BE PAID	0	0	10	0	18.3

Figure 5.4. Calculation of the compensation to be paid to nationalized companies. Table based on Comptroller General's Resolution on Compensation 1971.

Chile. Kennecott earned 52.87 percent at El Teniente, in comparison with 9.95 percent internationally (Fleming 1973). Another estimation, building on a different source, reports slightly different figures but still pointing in the same direction: 20.2 percent versus 7.2 percent for Anaconda and 34.8 percent versus 11.6 percent for Kennecott, in annual average profits as percentage of book value between 1955 and 1970 (Fortin 1975).

The threshold that Allende retained to distinguish normal from excess profits varies, depending on the accounts, from 10 percent on book value (Novitski 1971), to 12 percent (Fortin 1975) or 15 percent (Falcoff 1989). In his address to the General Assembly of the United Nations, Allende explained profits above 12 percent had been deducted from the compensation and gave the examples of Anaconda's profits of 21.5 percent per year on average and Kennecott's profits of 52.8 percent per year on average, reaching above 100 percent in certain years or even 200 percent in 1969 (Allende 1972) (fig. 5.4).

Unsurprisingly, the results of the comptroller's calculation triggered controversy. The companies questioned the method by which book value was estimated, as well as the deductions made from book value. Conversely, the State Defense Council pointed to other deductions that the comptroller should have taken into account in his calculations (Fleming 1973). They both filed legal briefs with the special tribunal that had been established to deal with appeals relating to the issue of compensation, in accordance with the constitution's transitory dispositions. At stake was not only the amount of deductions, but the very nature of the calculation of excess profits and the authority of the law over that matter. In March 1972, the special tribunal declared that the presidential decree was of political and not jurisdictional nature and refused to review appeals related to the calculation of excess profits (Fleming 1973).

Kennecott also challenged book value as an appropriate measure of a company's value. In a memorandum of August 16, 1971, prepared by the law firm of Covington and Burling, the company argued that its assets have "substantial additional value as part of a going concern," complaining that "the past, current and future income potential of the mining companies" was not recognized in legislation (Kennecott Copper Corp., *Expropriation of El Teniente, the World's Largest Underground Copper Mine* [1971], reprinted in Lillich, ed. 1975, quoted in Weller 1986, p. 341).

THE LIMITS OF THE PAST

Allende's sword, honed with book value and excess profits, pointed in the opposite direction than Piñera's sword, honed with present value: toward the past, instead of the future. Several pasts were entangled in his calculations, defining a space of relationships that went beyond the state/investor couple and complexifying the meaning of "just" compensation. A first temporal line was drawn to encompass the past fifteen years, mainly for reasons related to the availability of data on profits. Excess profits were to be computed since the enactment of Law 11.828, that is, after May 5, 1955. This limit was chosen because before Law 11.828—which created Chile's Department of Copper that later became Codelco, the Copper Corporation of Chile—data on profits were considered unreliable (Fleming 1973). In fact, there was no audit, and it is the companies themselves that provided the figures published by the Ministry of Mines (Moran 1974).[8] The Department of Copper began collecting statistics on production, prices, taxation, profits, etc., with data being provided, again, by the companies, but also being analyzed and checked by the experts in the department. The other important effect of Law 11.828 of 1955, which might well be relevant, too, with regard to the measurement of profits, was the introduction of a series of fiscal and other advantages aimed at attracting investors, which significantly increased copper companies' profits.[9]

A second temporal line was drawn further back in the past, meant to reflect a much larger span of Chile's history, viewed through the lens of foreign exploitation. The decree explained that deductions for excess profits aimed at "rectifying a historic past that permitted the exploitation of basic natural resources of major copper mines by private investors" and "restoring to the country the legitimate participation it should have obtained from said natural resources" (Decree Concerning Excess Profits of Copper Companies, Sept. 28, 1971, p. 1238). In his address to the General Assembly of the United Nations, Allende looked back at the last forty-two years, in which companies made more than $4 billion in profits while their initial investments were less than $30 million (Allende 1972). In the message with which he initiated the constitutional reform project on December 23, 1970, Allende estimated that "the three largest North American mines alone have siphoned abroad some $10.8 billion in the last sixty years of operations. In contrast, the entire Chilean national patrimony has been evaluated at only $10.5 billion" (Allende 1970, quoted in Fleming 1973). And a few days earlier, in a declaration he made at Constitution Square in Santiago while signing the project of the reform that would allow the nationalization of copper, just before addressing the question of the "just" compensation, Allende stated: "Since 1930, the large copper companies have generated profits reaching $3.7 billion, which represents 40% of the total wealth of Chile. We cannot forget this" (Dupoy 1983).

The decree positioned the calculation of excess profits not only in the past, but also in a space of relationships that reached beyond the couple formed by the host country and the foreign investor. The act of investment was not depicted as a contractual agreement between an investee and an investor who, albeit of profoundly distinct nature (a state, a corporation) benefited from rights that could be considered as equivalent. Quite the contrary, it was depicted as a part and parcel of a system of "international economic relations existing between poor and wealthy countries":

> Foreign investment—so it is said—is one of the mechanisms that can contribute to raising the standard of living and increasing the rate of development in the under-developed countries. As a matter of fact, however, this mechanism has been converted into just one more element which, in conjunction with financial dependency and unequal interchange, has served to mold the subordination of backward nations to the economically powerful countries. (Decree Concerning Excess Profits of Copper Companies, Sept. 28, 1971, p. 1239)

While the concept of Present Value was embedded in a narrative of clarity, rationality, universal acceptance, and modernity, the justification of excess profits appealed to social justice. According to Fleming (1973, pp. 619-20), nationalization was viewed as an effort "to restore to public ownership assets of superior import to the Chilean people which had been 'unjustly' held and exploited by foreign entrepreneurs." He quotes a government brief mentioning that "respect for acquired rights" ignores "the most elemental principle of justice which demands taking care of the necessities of others who have not consolidated their situation in any way."

Key here was the distinction between nationalization and expropriation on which the Allende government insisted when preparing the constitutional reform. Eduardo Novoa, who was in charge of the legal aspects of the reform, conceptualized nationalization as different from expropriation both in the objectives that it pursues and in the amount of compensation that it requires (Novoa 1972; see also, Etchegaray

2017). This reasoning could also be found in the debates that took place among international law scholars: nationalization rests upon the idea that the state is sovereign, and its needs are overarching; if full compensation threatens the satisfaction of these needs and hence the very objective of the act of nationalization, it can no longer be justified. (For a further analysis of these debates, see Fleming 1973.)

Critique of excess profits went well beyond the dispute between the Chilean state and the two multinationals. It was situated at two levels that resonated with the temporalities and spaces of relationships drawn by Allende: the accounting past of companies' business operations and the history of international relations. Two responses in radically different registers illustrate the larger stakes that were involved.

In his "critical history" of Chile in the 1970s and 1980s, Mark Falcoff, then a resident scholar on Latin America at the American Enterprise Institute, summarizes some of the arguments against excess profits: there is no accepted definition of "normal profits," periods of high profits may be balanced by periods of lower profits over the long run, companies have never been asked by the Chilean government to restrict their profits, and alternative estimates of the companies' profits made by "American economists" are much lower than the estimates decreed by Allende (Falcoff 1989).

The critique made by the US president and recorded in the Nixon tapes collection was more straightforward. Having been informed by Secretary of the Treasury John Connally that Allende "said that the copper companies owe $700 million…and…doesn't intend to compensate for the expropriated properties," President Richard Nixon summarized the situation to Secretary of State Henry Kissinger in the following terms: "Allende, according to Connally, is really screwing us now.... I'm goin' to kick 'em. And I want to make something out of it" (*Nixon Tapes*, conversation No. 584-003, October 5, 1971). A few days later, Kissinger informed Nixon that he had warned the Chilean foreign minister that "if they go through with that, certain consequences will follow" (*Nixon Tapes*, conversation No. 287-007, October 11, 1971).

Consequences did follow, through the action of both the United States and of the companies that had been nationalized, and they dramatically changed the history of Chile.

APPROPRIATION THROUGH VALUATION

Did Piñera's sword cut the Gordian knot his government was facing? In his view, it did, and it helped cut other similar nodes in Chile and abroad. He describes the consequences of his law with great enthusiasm. Foreign investment and production activity increased as soon as the approval of the law was announced. Subsequent administrations did not question or try to alter the law. It showed other countries, Piñera notes, that "there is a way to make the nominal State ownership that is written into their Constitutions compatible with a robust property right over a 'full concession,' and thereby to open new fields for the creation of wealth through the activity of private entrepreneurs." The "intellectual framework" of the law helped the privatization of state-owned companies in the telecommunications and power sectors in Chile. The "concession system" was extended to Chile's infrastructure sector, "which had traditionally been part of the so-called 'public works' carried out by the State."[10]

Abroad, the Chilean mining law reform was heralded as a success. For example, in a report published fifteen years later, the World Bank (1996) used the case of Chile as an illustration of "the most successful mining reforms" in Latin America (p. 11). Three of its characteristics were put forward. First, the report emphasized that the "cornerstone" of the Chilean reform was constitutional reform with the explicit protection of private property rights in the constitution. Among the key constitutional provisions ensuring the "Protections for Private Investment" was the "guarantee against expropriation of private property except for public necessity as determined by legislation, and upon prompt payment of the fair value of the property in convertible currency" (p. 11). Moreover, the report highlighted "the unique Chilean adjudicative mining law regime," which it contrasts with the administrative and contractual regimes prevalent in other Latin American countries. In an adjudicative regime, mineral rights are handled by judges, instead of by the ministry in charge of mining or by contractual agreements. According to the report, "adjudicative regimes have, in theory, the attractive quality of a judicial officer authorized to grant and extinguish mineral rights completely independently of any state mining interests" (p. 12–13). Finally, in the World Bank's eyes, what contributed to Chile's "attractiveness" was the creation of a "stable" environment in which investors' economic evaluations were not altered by unforeseen changes.

STABILITY AND THE PRODUCTION OF CERTAIN FUTURES

It is precisely to this idea of stability that Piñera attributes the effectiveness of Present Value. When I asked him how his sword succeeded in cutting the Gordian knot he was facing, he explained:

> By introducing into legislation, at the highest level, a rigorous concept already well established in economics, the "Present Value concept," that guarantees, both the private owner and the State, that the compensation in case of expropriation would be grounded in justice and reason. This concept is clear, rational and can be translated into an accepted formula. Whenever you have clear and fair rules in case of possible expropriations, you remove a huge uncertainty to private investors, domestic and foreign, and thus obviously attract investments while at the same time safeguarding the national interest. (José Piñera, personal communication)

The concept was "powerful" and "just," he added, and once its logic was fully understood, it became "universally accepted." As a proof, he pointed to the fact that thirty-seven years after it was passed, the law remained intact: "there has not been even a change of a comma in the Mining Law, and zero proposals to change or touch the Present Value concept."[11]

In what ways does discounting "remove a huge uncertainty to private investors"? In the quote above, Piñera referred to the uncertainty regarding which valuation method will be applied to calculate the compensation paid to investors. We have seen, however, that even when it is "translated into an accepted formula," discounting gives its users plenty of leeway when it comes to estimating the future cash flows and determining the discount rate. And one could argue that the same effect could be achieved if another valuation method, such as historical cost, had been used to achieve stability in lieu of discounting. However, there is another kind of uncertainty that discounting removes for investors: the uncertainty over the flows of revenues that the investment will generate in the future. The compensation calculated with discounting is the monetary translation of a future scenario that may or may not have occurred, but for which the investor is rewarded now, with certainty. Unlike past-oriented valuation methods such as historical cost, discounting gives the investor the guarantee that her expectations will be met.

Toni Marzal (2021) convincingly develops this argument in his critique of the use of DCF in international investment arbitration. DCF is supposed to measure the fair market value (FMV) of the investment for which the investor is to be compensated, that is, an estimate of the price that the investment would be sold for in an open market when such a market does not exist. Marzal shows that fair market value is a "legally constructed 'fiction'" (p. 291) corresponding to an idealized market—with less risk and more liquidity—that does not exist either in the present or in the future. Thus, "the legal interpretation of FMV serves to construct a fictional but-for scenario—and thus leads to, somewhat paradoxically, allowing investors to obtain via remedies what they could not have obtained had the State not breached its obligations" (p. 291). In other words, it provides investors with a future—more precisely, the present value of that future—that may well have not occurred, but whose relevance is justified by the mere fact that it was expected.

To what extent is one entitled to a future, translated into its present value, for the reason that she formed expectations about that future? Whether these expectations are "rational," as economists put it, or "fictional," as sociologists do, is not the key question. The question, if we follow Marzal, is whether these expectations are "legitimate," that is, "built on some basis of a particular quality," or more precisely, "grounded on a promise or guarantee or duty that the legal system chooses to render enforceable" (p. 299). Instead of weighing investors' expectations by the probability of future profits to occur (as in the drug development projects we examined in Chapter 4), tribunals should consider "whether the investor could be said to have any legitimate claim to those future profits" (p. 304) and to a particular level of these profits.

Marzal reminds us of "the often forgotten truism that the level of profits of any particular business (and hence its economic value) is largely determined through law," in particular, through tax law, price capping, or limits on profits (p. 306). Consequently, the level of the future profits expected by the investor is subject to decisions made by the state. So the investor may well have a "subjective expectation" of the "full stream of profits that at any particular time an investment is predicted to generate in the future," but not a "legitimate" expectation, "since their realisation is in the discretionary hands of the State" (p. 307). By treating the action of the state as "regulatory risk" to be taken into account in the discount rate (again, as in the valuation of drug development projects that we discussed in Chapter 4), tribunals are actually granting investors the extraordinary privilege to be entitled to the future that they expected, simply because they expected it.

Marzal limpidly draws out the implications of this implicit view on the significance of state prerogatives and the principle of sovereignty over natural resources to which Allende was referring in his valuation:

> They [tribunals] are thus ignoring that the existence of legitimate of State prerogatives does not only affect the probability of that chance becoming true, but more fundamentally the legitimacy of the investor's claim to it. Indeed, how can it be said that the revenue of, say, a mining concession may be subject in the future to redistribution via increased taxation, and

at the same time that the termination of that concession will entitle the investor to the entirety of current projections of profits? Similarly, does it not make a mockery of the principle of sovereignty over natural resources, to allow the State to retake control over the concession whilst simultaneously awarding the investor the full value of the mineral reserves? (Marzal 2021, p. 307)

TURBULENT TIMES AND UNCERTAIN PASTS

Because indeed "the level of profits of any particular business (and hence its economic value) is largely determined through law," it is worth looking into investors' expectations against the backdrop of the broader past in which their expectations were continuously revamped by the Chilean state's "discretionary hands." I will use Theodore Moran's (1974) account of the confrontation between multinational corporations and the Chilean government over the exploitation of copper to show how the state/investor relationship evolved from a focus on the problem of profits, to that of prices, and then to property. Discounting was instrumental to a new shift: from owning to valuing Chilean copper.

Kennecott and Anaconda arrived in Chile in the early twentieth century, following the explorations of William Braden, a North American mining engineer and entrepreneur, and the investments of the Guggenheims. In 1916, Kennecott acquired El Teniente in the Andes Mountains, which became the largest underground copper mine in the world. In 1923, Anaconda acquired Chuquicamata in the Atacama desert, which became the largest open-pit copper mine in the world. Their investments were initially viewed as "blessings" because of the employment that they provided. They were no less blessings for the companies, which enjoyed a period of high profits and low taxes. The state levied an income tax of 6 percent, starting in 1922; it was raised several times (to 12 percent and then 18 percent), but remained low until World War II. In the late 1920s, Kennecott and Anaconda obtained annual returns on their investments equal to between 20 and 40 percent for Kennecott and 14 percent for Anaconda. In the companies' eyes, high profits were justified as compensation for the risks they had taken and for the contribution to Chilean wealth that they were uniquely able to make. As Moran puts it: "The companies measured their contribution to the country against what the country would have had if they had never come to invest. Until the day they were nationalized, Anaconda and Kennecott were recounting feats of risk and endurance in the lonely deserts and treacherous mountains that had occurred fifty years earlier" (Moran 1974, p. 25).

After World War II, the picture started to darken. Arguments derived from economic theories of monopoly denied that the companies' profits were a legitimate award for the risks that investors had taken in the past. Neither were they a "blessing" that the companies would automatically share with the country through the taxes they paid. Instead, profits came to be seen as "too high." They were made possible by the companies' "monopolistic" positions—so in a way, they were unfair—and furthermore, they had a deleterious effect on the development of the Chilean economy.

Another economic theory further darkened the picture, introducing the issue of prices. The Prebisch model of declining terms of trade (also known as the Prebisch–Singer hypothesis) argued that the prices of primary products (such as the copper that Chile exported) decline relative to the prices of manufacturing products (such as those that the country imported).[12] It gave Chile the impetus to achieve *precios justos* (Moran 1974, p. 72) for its copper—prices that would be able to reverse the trend toward the decline of its terms of trade. Chilean politicians, economists, and businessmen alike made claims against the copper companies, which they saw as keeping prices artificially low, and envisaged various reasons and instruments for government intervention on copper prices.

Evidence for the problem of "low prices" was provided by the US government's and the multinational companies' doctrine of "moderation in pricing policy." Moderation was ensured by the setting of price ceilings during wartime, to prevent the excessive price peaks that might appear due to shortage. During World War II, the price of copper was fixed by the Allied governments at a figure about equal to or slightly lower than late-Depression levels. During the Korean War, US officials in conjunction with representatives of the US copper companies unilaterally set a ceiling of 24.5 cents per pound on the price of Chilean copper, without consulting the Chilean government. During peacetime, moderation was ensured by the so-called system of "producers' prices," through which the companies guaranteed a stable level of prices to their regular customers at a level often below that of the major open markets, the London Metal Exchange and the New York Commodity Exchange.

The Chilean government's response to the problem consisted of a series of attempts to gain control over prices. At a conference in Washington gathering the ministers of foreign affairs of North American and Latin American states in 1951, Chile achieved an increase in the Korean War ceiling of 3 cents per pound and the right to sell up to 20 percent of its output independently. Most of the copper sold independently went to the European "free" market at a price of about 54 cents per pound. One year later, Chile annulled the Washington agreement and established a state monopoly over all copper sales. As Moran (1974, p. 88) notes ironically, "with two local functionaries, two secretaries, and a man who worked half-days, a single small office in the Banco Central began trying to price and sell 13% of the world's copper output to customers on four continents." Faced with the difficulty of finding new customers and disentangling the companies' regular customers from the system of "producers' prices," the Chilean policy of state control over prices was considered a failure and was replaced by the diametrically opposed policy of the Nuevo Trato (New Deal), which took up again the narrative of alignment between the interests of host countries and foreign investors.

The period of the Nuevo Trato was inaugurated by Law 11.828 of

May 5, 1955, which established provisions related to the Grand Minería companies, created the Department of Copper, and codified a series of advantages granted to the copper-producing companies in terms of lower taxes. Its purpose was to create a "good investment climate" that would attract investors by allowing them to make high profits. Its logic was that of incentives and stimuli, which would automatically transform lower taxes into higher profits, hence more investment, hence more output and more returns to Chile. However, the effects of the Nuevo Trato policy did not reach its objectives, having only a weak effect on the level of production and investment, but a very strong effect on companies' profits, which approximately doubled, leading the Socialist senator Raúl Ampuero to conclude that "our interests and the interests of the foreign copper corporations are in permanent contradiction" (quoted in Moran 1974, p. 114).

Disappointment with investors and doubts as to the automatic alignment of their interests with that of the country paved the way for a novel treatment of the state/investor relationship in which the focus shifted from profits and prices to the issue of property. In 1964, Eduardo Frei was elected president with a program of "Chileanization" according to which the state would purchase 51 percent of the Grand Mineria companies. On April 25, 1966, Law 16425 created the regulatory framework allowing for state participation through the creation of joint companies. In 1967, Codelco bought a 51 percent equity interest in El Teniente for a price of $80 million (which was based on, but higher than, the company's book value), complemented by a number of other arrangements, including reductions in tax rates and government contributions to financing the expansion plans of the mine.[13] The state also signed agreements with foreign companies for two new mines, following which it owned 25 percent of Anaconda's Exotica mine and 30 percent of Cerro's Andina.

In 1969, the state reached an agreement with Anaconda for its two other mines, Chuquicamata and El Salvador. Having "refused to submit to Chileanization," the company had increasingly come under attack and ended up proposing to be "nationalized with compensation" because it thought the process would end there anyway (Moran 1974, p. 146). Referred to as "negotiated nationalization," the agreements with Anaconda gave the Chilean State 51 percent ownership in the joint companies created, as well as the option the purchase the remaining 49 percent after 1973. The price for the first 51 percent was determined on the basis of the new joint companies' book value (respectively, $140.5 and $34.1 million). The price mechanism envisaged for the next 49 percent, if the state exercised the option to buy them, was different: "by multiplying Anaconda's share of the average annual earnings of the companies after taxes by a factor dependent on the date of the transaction" (Fleming 1973, p. 599) or, according to a different source, "a factor of eight" (Fortin 1975). Frei called the agreement signed with Anaconda "Chile's Second Independence" (Moran 1974, p. 146).

TEMPORAL APPROPRIATION

What did Piñera's sword cut? It cut the Gordian knot that he faced by translating mines in the present, owned by the state, into flows in the future, owned by investors. Discounting performs a "fundist" definition of the mine as capital: it "dematerializes" capital by transforming it into future flows (Levy 2017). In so doing, it erases any past agency involved in the constitution of capital as such: both states, understood as owners of national resources and drafters of regulations, and corporations, understood as production and profit-making units. We have observed the same gesture in Chapters 1 and 4: capitalization brushes off the technical and political battles involved in the construction of the Panama Canal and the long process of developing drugs through public and private research.

The past is full of agency and claims. In contrast, the future appears as void, waiting to be populated—for some, with future generations, and for others, with flows of money. Turning away from the past to look to the future as the source of value places the investor in a position reminiscent of that of the colonizer. Colonial land appropriations were justified by an apprehension of land as empty space: *terra nullius*. This argument has been recently mobilized to account for new forms of appropriation in the Anthropocene (Folkers 2020; Pottage 2019). It can be extended to embrace not only the spatial, but also the temporal dimensions of appropriation. Such spatiotemporal reasoning can be found in discussions about future generations. Thomas Jefferson famously compared a generation to a nation and the wish of present generations to rule those of the future to the wish of people of one nation to rule those of another (Nordblad, 2021, p. 367). Innerarity (2012, p. 12) likens the preference for the present to "a temporal version of the privilege that some people want to establish in space, a type of time-based colonialism." He also compares the "influence that previous generations wielded over the current generation, the privilege of the dead versus the freedom of the living" (p. 13), which the revolutionary ideal sought to annihilate, to the influence on the future that we, "the coalition of the living," are exercising today, enjoying "a type of impunity in the temporal zone of the future, where we can recklessly deplete other people's time or expropriate other people's future" (pp. 12–13).

A similar form of temporal appropriation occurs with discounting. By looking to the future instead of the past and at the same time blurring the image of that future and lightening the weight of the entities that inhabit it, such as future generations, discounting creates what we could call a *tempus nullius* prone to appropriation. This form of temporal appropriation is not about ownership, but about valuation. What did the introduction of discounting in Chilean mining law give investors the right to? Not to continue exploiting a concession in the future, because they could still be expropriated, but to receive the flows that this concession would have yielded in the future, translated into their present value at the moment of expropriation. Discounting thus operated a shift from spatial to temporal appropriation: it translated a problem of ownership (Who owns the mines in the present?) into a problem of valuation (Who is entitled to value the future?).

When I asked Piñera what, with hindsight, were the most important elements of the Constitutional Mining Law of 1981, he cited, in addition to the role given to the courts (and not the government), "the strong protection of property rights, thanks to the Present Value formula in case of expropriation." The link that he makes between discounting calculations and the problem of property sheds light on the defining characteristic of discounting with respect to other valuation techniques. How can we formulate this specificity?

To Piñera, the defining characteristic of discounting is its greater clarity, rationality, and acceptability. The historical sociology of discounting that this book has developed should have made this explanation insufficient. To other authors, the defining characteristic of discounting lies in its ability to produce higher valuations and hence help investors obtain higher compensations (see, for example, Weller's [1986] note on the recovery of future profits in a case of expropriation). Indeed, valuations including future profits often produce higher results than alternative valuation methods such as book value.[14]

However, the history of copper mining in Chile shows something more radical: that the defining characteristic of discounting lies in its ability to translate a problem of ownership into a problem of valuation. As we have seen throughout, within the temporalities of discounting, what matters is not who has control over the present (by holding the proverbial 51 or 100 percent of an asset), but who has control over the future, and it is precisely such a control over the future that discounting gives to the figure of the investor. It provides investors with a future—more precisely, the present value of that future—that may well not occur. The only raison d'être of this future is that it was "expected" by the investor when she made the decision to invest.

The appearance of discounting in the calculation of compensations in international law, juxtaposed with its appearance in the calculation of drug prices in pharmaceutical markets via the notion of "value-based pricing" on which I touched at the end of Chapter 4, is illuminating in several respects. It shows that while discounting has become dominant in public policy and corporate management, through now stabilized tools such as cost-benefit analysis (CBA) and net present value (NPV), it continues to expand into new places and in doing so to trigger controversies. This expansion proceeds either by direct applications of the DCF formula (which is discussed as such in the literature in investor-state dispute settlement) or by variations on the reasoning that it carries (as in the notion of value-based pricing). The new places in which discounting enters are neither public policy, with its CBA and its social discount rate, nor corporate management, with its NPV and its cost of capital. They are found at the junction of these two worlds and more precisely in the relationship between states and investors.

At this juncture, new questions arise. If discounting is a way of looking to the future, can states' and investors' perspectives on the future—materialized in a longer or shorter time frame and in a lower or higher discount rate—be reconciled, and if not, whose perspective should prevail? But also, is an orientation toward the future the relevant perspective in places where the investment process ends rather than starts? In places where drugs have already been researched and developed and minerals have already been explored and extracted? In places where the issue at stake is no longer whether development or extraction should be done or not done, but how investors should be rewarded or compensated for what they have done or not done. Here, discounting asks how investors should be rewarded or compensated for what they will do or will not do. How should they be rewarded for the benefits that a drug will bring to patients and society? How should they be compensated for the minerals that they could have extracted but will not extract? Discounting moves not only to new places but also to new times. The alteration of the temporality of problems through the reformulation of questions about the past into questions about of the future is part of discounting's expansion.

The Ministry for the Future:
Sketch of a Program

Mary: Dick, what are you and your team doing to make current economics more helpful for the people of the future?

Dick: We've looking at discount rates....

Mary: How does this relate to future people?

Dick: It's very central. We discount the future generations. It works by analogy to how we treat money....

Mary: So how much is the discount? How does it work?

Dick: The rate varies.... If you go out fifty years, that hundred euros you would get then is worth half a euro today.

Mary: That seems like a steep rate!

Dick: It is.... But steep rates are pretty common. Someone once won the pseudo-Nobel in economics for suggesting a four percent discount rate on the future.... The time value of money, it's called.

Mary: But this gets applied to other things?

Dick: Oh yes. That's economics. Since everything can be converted to its money value, when you need to rate the future value of an action, to decide whether to pay to do it now or not, you speak of that value using a discount rate.

Mary: But those future people will be just as real as you and I. Why discount them in the same way you do money?

Dick: It's partly to decide what to do....

Mary: So given that, how do you pick a discount rate?

Dick: Out of a hat....

Mary: So the higher the discount rate, the less we spend on future people?

Dick: That's right.

Mary: And right now everyone chooses a high discount rate.

Dick: Yes....

Mary: But if the numbers lie?

Dick: They do lie. Which allows us to ignore any costs and benefits that will occur more than a few decades down the line....

Dick: No one denies future people are going to be just as real as us. So there isn't any moral justification for the discounting, it's just for our own convenience. Plenty of economists acknowledged this....

Mary: But we do it anyway.

Dick: We kick their ass.

Mary: Easy to do when they're not here to defend themselves!

Dick: True. I like to think of it as a rugby match, with present-day people as the New Zealand All Blacks, playing against a team of three-year-olds, who represent the people of the future. We kick their ass....

Mary: But what do you do?

Dick: We're the Ministry for the Future. So we step in and play for the three-year-olds. We substitute for them.

Mary: So... is there a way to make the calculations better?

Dick: This is where India comes into it. Since the heat wave, they've been leading the way in terms of re-examining everything. So regarding this issue, you could just set a low discount rate, of course. But Badim tells me in India it is traditional to talk about the seven generations before and after you as being your equals.... Now they are using that idea to alter their economics. Their idea is to shape the discount rate as a bell curve, with the present always at the top of the bell.

(Stanley Robinson 2020, pp. 129–32)[1]

This dialogue occurs in the near future. The excerpt is taken from Kim Stanley Robinson's climate fiction novel *The Ministry for the Future*. It nicely synthesizes most of the issues that this book's exploration of discounting has raised. And it poses a question.[2] In light of the consequences that discounting has had on our ability to act on the future, what is to be done about it?

The answer depends on how we answer two different, but related questions. First, what does the future look like through the lens of discounting? Second, are discounting and the future it produces amenable to change, and if so, what is the best way to do it? The answers to these questions will help us envisage a program for the Ministry for the Future—that is, a way to reinvent the political technologies needed to govern the future as a political domain.

A DISCOUNTED FUTURE, A CONTESTED PRESENT

What does one see when she looks to the future through the lens of discounting? What does a discounted future look like? Unlike most technologies of the future, such as plans, scenarios, models, foresight exercises etc., discounting does not actually attempt to know the future, to imagine what it will, it might, or it should look like.[3] Instead, discounting relates to the future by means of valuation. It is not interested in the forms that the future will take, but in how distant this future is and hence what worth it deserves to be granted. The future that matters to discounting is made up only of flows of costs and benefits or revenues whose contents and scope are largely derived from the observation of the present and the past. What a discounted future looks like is blurred, not so much because it is uncertain and therefore hard or even impossible to know, but because its precise contours and its literal contents are immaterial when viewed through the lens of discounting. What is at stake with discounting is not the accuracy of projections, but the possibility of translating future flows into their value in the present. The future that matters is not warmer or cooler, greener or grayer. It is a future that triggers action in the present insofar as its worth justifies and guides the making of a decision.

I started the Introduction by asking why we can or cannot act on the future. One of the things we have seen in ample measure is that discounting is one of the reasons why we do not do so. That is because discounting appears first and foremost as the reason why we do or do not act in the present. And as we also have seen, while discounting gives priority to the present, there actually is not much present in discounting. The present is exhausted in the moment when the valuation of the future is made. While the future is blurred, the present is elusive: it is immediately thrown into the future, projected into flows of costs, revenues, and benefits, and then these future flows are brought into a present that has no tangible presence other than the urge to act, that is, precisely, to alter the state of the present.

While there is not much present in discounting, there surely is a contestation of the relevance of the present as a temporality for valuation. Discounting explicitly criticizes the present of the market: the true value of things, it argues, is not to be found in the prices that can be readily observed in the market, but in the intrinsic capability of things to produce future flows and to be capitalized, that is, to become capital (Muniesa and Doganova 2020).

Discounting is also recurrently associated with the contestation of another kind of present: not that of a place or an institution, such as the market and the prices that it produces, but of a type of actor, an actor who, like the investor, is defined by her temporal orientation, but, unlike the investor, is oriented toward the present. In much of the economic literature, actors with this kind of temporal orientation are associated with figurations of them as "the poor." Stuck in the present and unable to embrace the future, poor individuals and poor countries alike are said to behave in economically irrational (or at least nonoptimal) ways, which ultimately makes them fall deeper into poverty and contributes to environmental degradation.[4]

Economists have attempted to provide theoretical and empirical evidence of the relationship between poverty, high discount rates, and investment—both in economic activities and environmental conservation. In particular, experimental economists have measured the discount rates of people in poor countries (often through questions asking respondents to choose between consumption of this now and consumption of this same thing at a later moment in time), usually concluding that the poor discount too much. For example, a study that estimated rates of time preference of rural households in Indonesia, Zambia, and Ethiopia found that these rates are very high and get higher the poorer people are—a conclusion deemed worrisome because such high rates "can be a potential disincentive to investment...thus also to investment in conservation" (Holden et al. 1998, p. 106). Another study—provocatively titled "An Optimal Path to Extinction?"—modeled the link between resource degradation and poverty. It examined how the balance between agrarian and pastoral activities would evolve if, in an open agrarian economy as a result of variations in the prices of inputs and outputs, agrarian income decreases below the poverty line. It noted that people's discount rates will rise so much in such a case that they will ignore future consequences and narrow their focus down to the present exclusively: "When the need to stave off starvation governs all current production decisions it may be expected that people will ignore the future consequences of these decisions. Poverty may be expected to drive up their rate of time preference to the point where all that matters is consumption today" (Perrings 1989, p. 20).

Such descriptions resonate with descriptions of the inability of precapitalist societies to look to the future. It is precisely this awakening to the future that has been analyzed as one of the drivers or consequences of the advent of capitalism. Learning to look to the future was an integral part of the adaptation of the labor force during the Industrial Revolution. In his study of the genesis of modern management, economic historian Sidney Pollard (1965) has described how managers had to transform workers—described by contemporaries as "improvident," having "no care for the morrow" (p. 196)—so that they enlarge their time horizons beyond the present day and at the same time turn "obedient to the cash stimulus" (p. 161), ambitious and respectable (p. 195), rational and forward-looking. Learning to look to the future was also a "temporal disposition" (Bourdieu 2000) that precapitalist societies had to acquire as they entered into capitalism. In his analysis of the social structures of the economy, Pierre Bourdieu beautifully describes this "transformation of worldview" required by the Kabyle traditional society as it was "thrown into an economic universe imported and imposed by colonization" (p. 5). I will quote him at length:

> The economic agents I was able to observe in Algeria in the 1960s had to learn or, more exactly reinvent, with greater or lesser success depending on their economic and cultural resources, everything economic theory considers (at least tacitly) as a given, that is to say, everything it regards as innate, universal gift, forming part of human nature: the idea of work as an activity procuring monetary income, as opposed to mere occupation on the lines of the traditional division of activities or the traditional exchange of services; the very possibility of impersonal transactions between strangers, linked to a market situation, as opposed to all the exchanges of the economy of "good faith," as the Kabyles call it;...the notion of long-term investment, as opposed to the practice of putting in reserve, or the simple anticipation that forms part of the directly felt unity of productive cycles; the modern conception...of lending at interest and the very idea of a contract, with its previously known deadlines and formal clauses, which gradually supplanted the honorable exchange between men of honour that excluded calculation and the pursuit of profit, and involved an acute concern with fairness etc. (Bourdieu 2005, p. 4)

All these new elements, Bourdieu argues, concurred in a novel "representation of the future as a site of 'possibles' that are open and susceptible to calculation" (p. 4). Learning to look to the future went hand in hand with the emergence of a new vision of the future: an "open" and "calculable" future (Bourdieu 1963, p. 27). The precapitalist future was "virtually enclosed in the perceived present, a future within easy reach, such as the consumption goods that the peasant surrounds himself with and that constitute the guarantee of his security." It was engaged with through the practice of constituting reserves and demonstrating foresight, prudence, and provident care.

The capitalist future, by contrast, is "distant and abstract" while at the same time amenable to "calculative and rational forecast," a future for which goods can be "reserved," but not so as to be preserved and consumed later if needed. Keeping things for this new future meant envisaging their "productive use," putting them to work, unleashing the flows they could yield—that is, transforming them into capital.

Recent works in sociology have demonstrated the tensions between the openness of the capitalist future, on the one hand, and its calculability, on the other. Pointing to the argument of uncertainty, economic sociologists have criticized the hypothesis of rational decision-making posited by economists and argued for the inclusion of other explanatory variables, such as networks, trust, or imitation, that fell under their disciplinary jurisdiction. Judgment replaces calculation in sociological accounts of the operations of markets (Karpik 2010), and more recently, the role of fictional expectations about the future has replaced expectations of rational behavior in sociological accounts of the dynamics of capitalism (Beckert 2016). Sociologist Jens Beckert defines fictional expectations as "the imaginaries of future states of the world and of causal relations that inform actors' decisions" (p. 62). Because they are contingent—not determined by a situation, but inspired by an open future—they can be influenced and "used instrumentally." This is where Beckert sees room for influencing a "politics of expectations" (p. 79) about the future.

This book has taken a different route. The politics it explores are not those of "the imaginaries of future states of the world," but the politics of the very act of looking to the future and the politics of the kind of future that then is seen when that is done. We have seen that there is as much politics in what looks like rational calculation as in what looks like the fictions and imaginaries of the future. The route I have followed was laid out by sociologist Michel Callon in *The Laws of the Markets* (Callon 1998a), reacting to the critique that economic sociology made of *homo oeconomicus*. Callon has invited economic sociologists to consider a different perspective, one that redefines the concept of *homo oeconomicus* by attempting to explain how economic behavior is made possible: *"homo economicus* does exist, but is not an ahistorical reality; he does not describe the hidden nature of the human being. He is the result of a process of configuration...[that] mobilizes material and metrological investments, property rights and money [and] the essential contribution of economics in performing the economy" (Callon 1998b, pp. 22–23).

In a similar vein, this book has probed the existence of *"homo prospectus,"* as psychologists have termed the way in which projecting and evaluating future possibilities drives thought and action (Seligman et al. 2016). *Homo prospectus,* too, is the result of a process of configuration. The historical sociology of discounting proposed in this book has shown that this process is contingent and contested. As in my earlier work on valuation devices (Doganova and Eyquem-Renault 2009; Doganova and Muniesa 2015), I have not been interested in whether discounting represents truthfully or usefully the future and the value of things, but in what it does when it is mobilized—to what kind of debates it gives rise, what kinds of actors it features and brings forward, and to whom it gives more or lesser money, strength, legitimacy, and power.

A PATH TO A DIFFERENT FUTURE

The question whether the future is worth less than the present and whether it is the relevant temporal order to characterize what happens in our epoch and/or in our economic system is an empirical question whose answers, as we have seen, emerge in particular situations. Discounting has certainly become dominant in public policy and corporate management. Nevertheless, it also continues to be questioned, and the question of the right discount rate—or more broadly, whether the future is worth less than the present—is still open, as we saw in the debates on climate change policy and firm innovation. The same holds for the other assumption of discounting—the orientation toward the future, although debates here are less visible, as in deliberations over drug pricing and investment arbitration. Such conclusions are almost as far as an empirical approach to these issues can take us.

"Almost," because looking at discounting in the way we have done has exposed alternative conceptions of the past, present, and future that the claim of discounting to be a general form of addressing the future has in some cases provoked as critiques and in other cases has simply occluded. The cases we've examined here have brought us to a point where we can say what these alternatives are, compare them, and assess them as ways to engage with the challenges of the present that encourage, rather than discourage, action to meet those challenges. If there ever is to be a Ministry for the Future, what should it do in order to speak for the future? The answer depends on how we, now, today, in our present epoch of crisis—the ecological crisis, the energy crisis, the crisis of capitalism—approach determining the future.

One such way of conceiving of and valuing the future—an approach that discounting discounts—appears in the figure of the poor. As we have just seen, the figure of the poor, viewed through the lens of discounting, has two incarnations that differ in their relationship with the discounted future. On the one hand, there are the poor who stand at the economic margins of capitalism, but within it, such as the rural populations that in the nineteenth century stood at the margins of the scientifically managed forest and at the margins of its long-term future. They are said to be entrenched in the present because they lack the material capacity to project themselves into the future, to wait for that future to occur, and in doing so, to allow it to happen. It is here that we find the reform proposals that I evoked in the beginning of Chapter 1. Designed by researchers in experimental economics, these proposals aim at measuring the discount rates of people living in poverty and reducing them by means of commitment devices that are supposed to extract these individuals from their present needs and open them to the future, transform them into entrepreneurs and, hence, the argument goes, foster both economic development and environmental conservation. The path to the future that these reforms sketch begins with transforming individuals—often individuals characterized by their otherness. The *Stern Review*'s proposal to decrease discount rates in order to enable climate change policies can be analyzed as a similar experiment. The expertise that it mobilizes, however, is that of environmental economics, and the entities that it aims at transforming are the national economies of developed countries. The opposition that it triggered also was much more vivid than reactions to experiments on the discount rates of poor individuals—experiments whose ethical grounds and intrusive mode of operation were no less questionable.

The parallel between these two experiments on purposefully decreasing discount rates—the discount rates of poor individuals, on the one hand, and of rich states, on the other hand—reveals the limits of this path to the future. It is a path that seems to be reserved for "the other": those who live at the economic margins of capitalism and are encouraged to join a capitalistic future, only a slightly less discounted one. It is a path that "we" do not seem to be ready to take because we remain entrenched in a view of the discount rate as an expression of a truth that markets reveal to us. This view goes with a certain comfort. We are reassured that we act rationally. It is deeply entangled with the view of acting on the future as a form of investment. Even in proposals that argue for a prescriptive use of discount rates, the idea that we should act on the future because this action now will generate returns later is latent. The *Stern Review* explicitly proclaimed that climate policy must be viewed as an investment. In fact, the justifications that governments have put forward in their decisions to decrease discount rates in the last two decades, often in relation with the figure of future generations and the issue of intergenerational justice, have espoused this same rationale—the rationale of the investment.[5]

But why and how do public decisions about our economy or society—the emissions we produce, our way of living and consumption style, the distribution of wealth among different social groups and parts of the world—become comparable to an investment decision? This book suggests the following answer: because questions in the form "What should be done?" are reformulated as questions in the form "Is it worth it?" Questions about, say, justice or responsibility are transformed into valuation questions. Considerations about whether these actions are just, or responsible, or simply needed or impending give way to the critical examination of actions in terms of their "returns." The key issue here is not so much the higher or lower level of the discount rate, but the very reasoning that discounting entails.

The fundamental characteristic of discounting resides precisely in this entanglement between a focus on valuation as the relevant criterion for action and a focus on the future—the impact, the effects, the costs and benefits or revenues that action will generate—as the relevant temporality for action. Discounting involves turning our back on the past—a past saturated with agency and claims—to embrace the future, a void future, drip-fed with the "impacts" of our actions, but only so as to translate that future back into the present in terms of its value. The idiosyncratic relationship between temporality and valuation that discounting constructs helps explain the general form that it has taken.

On the other hand, there are the poor who stand at the historical margins of capitalism, and outside it, such as the precapitalist societies that the advent of capitalism aimed to convert to a temporality set free from cycles and repetitions, unchained from the past and directed to an open future to be filled from scratch. They have been described as not discounting at all, as not seeing the future as an unchartered territory, but as a recycling of the present and the past. Doing so makes them strangers to the kind of future that capitalism requires and thus makes our past one place to look for alternative ways of conceiving our future. These poor treat the future as the next present: a future that can be preserved, a future for which reserves can be accumulated, things that are visible and tangible in the present—a future for which resources are kept intact—which also means, unproductive because they are maintained as stocks instead of being transformed into flows.

From the historical margins of capitalism, but beyond it, it thus is possible to reconstruct a relationship to the future, free from discounting, that the arrival of capitalism stripped from precapitalist societies. It is to this conception and valuation of the future that today's notions of scarcity, abandonment, "degrowth," frugality, and sustainability inevitably lead us. For there to be an alternative to the general form of discounting as represented in the figure of the investor, in this future, we would have to break free from the notion of present sacrifice for future rewards, a notion that, as this book had reminded repeatedly, has been successfully mobilized in the figure of the one who takes the future in charge and, in exchange for her loss, for the present she sacrifices, requires to be rewarded, regardless of what that future might actually hold.

The concern for future generations can be read as one attempt to reinvent a future to which we relate not as a separate temporal domain, but as just another instantiation of the present. However, the ways in which we relate to future generations today, that is, through the attempt to make them count in the present while still imagining them as radically "other" (having more wealth or more knowledge, or conversely, being more vulnerable to the threat of climate change) is still caught in the mechanics of discounting. This is why the concept of future generations can also be mobilized with the exact opposite purpose: it has been argued that discount rates should be high because future generations will possess more knowledge and more wealth and hence will be better equipped than us to deal with problems like climate change—a vision intimately linked to the ideas of economic growth and technological progress that has been present for decades in debates about the disposal of nuclear waste (Barthe, 2006).

As Nordblad (2021, p. 366) shows, concepts of future generations differ on "the question of how much qualitative newness the future can be expected to bring and thus to what extent future generations can be known." Will they be richer and smarter? What will they want? Can we, present generations, decide for them, future generations? The question works both ways: Can we leave them a damaged planet, but as well, can we assume that they will not like living on a damaged planet, which they may not consider as damaged at all? A "politics of the future," argues Innerarity (2012, p. 17), should extend our temporal horizon through "the introduction of longer time frames and the consideration of the rights of future generations" (p. 17). A major difficulty in creating this politics of the future relates again to the knowability of the future: "since the future cannot be known, responsibility does not generally factor in" (p. 18).

This book has argued that an exploration of discounting urges us to renew the analytical repertoire on which we draw to think about the future. The problem of knowability and the figure of future generations are one modality of giving consistency to the future, which often ends in complex discussions about how we could be responsible for what we do not know because it does not yet exist. The conceptualization of time in terms of generations and degrees of knowledge rests on the assumption that the past, the present, and the future are distinct temporal domains, akin to distinct spatial domains. This assumption is central to the reasoning of discounting that contests the present, erases the past, and is concerned with the future only as a source of value. However, discounting can also serve to undermine this assumption.

The separation of the present and the future is one possible, but not unique configuration: setting the discount rate to zero means eradicating the frontier between the present and the future. The differences between temporal domains are blatant when they are analyzed in terms of the degree and type of knowledge that they allow for. However, they become a contingent effect of the discount rate when these temporal domains are analyzed in terms of their valuation. Then there is no longer a reason to distinguish between present and future generations. There is, instead, the need to investigate the conflicts of temporalities within present generations and the delineations they draw between the actors who are denied the ability to act on the future and those who proclaim their own ability to do so.

To put it another way, conceptions of the future can be articulated only from within the present. If we seek a path to the future free from the problems that trouble discounting, that path begins with discounting itself. And ironically, discounting can help us here. It can do so when the political qualities of discounting that I have emphasized throughout are taken seriously.

The present and the future are not only temporal, but also political domains, and as such, they can hardly be treated as separate. By making things valuable, by determining the choice of the series of uses to which anything may be put, in its use as a "technology of government" and more generally in its ability to define the characteristics of the future and the ability to act on it, discounting is a site where the present produces the future and thus a site where the particular characteristics of the future can be contested. When the future is seen as a political domain and discounting is understood as a way of contesting the future, the future becomes open to the present in a variety of ways. Traveling that path encounters obstacles, but it is precisely in encountering such obstacles that contesting the future occurs. And the principal obstacle is one that this book has set out to contest by uncovering its particular and contingent history and development—the naturalization of discounting as a general form.

One of the ways in which the future becomes open to the present when contested from within discounting approaches discounting as something that should be restricted to certain places and replaced by alternatives temporalities of valuation in other places. In this perspective, the expansion of discounting is akin to the expansion of marketization from the realm of the market to the realm of, say, nature or life. Critique is then focused on the preservation of niches from which the logics of marketization is banned. Appeals to the general form that discounting has taken on constitute the principal obstacle that this approach has encountered. As we saw, in the original formulation of Irving Fisher, everything is capital or, rather, everything can be capitalized as soon as it is engaged in a particular relationship with time and envisioned through the valuation of the future flows that it is likely to produce. A factory is capital because it is likely to produce a flow of goods, but also nature is capital, "natural capital," because it is likely to produce ecosystem services, and life is capital, "human capital," because it is likely to produce flows of costs and revenues.[6]

Likewise, the hostile reaction to *The Stern Review*'s proposal to decrease discount rates in order to enable climate change policies is another example of the ways in which the appeal to discounting as a general form is deployed against efforts at reform. The truth of the discount rate, claimed William Nordhaus, is to be found in the description of reality (as expressed in the operations of capital markets) rather than in the prescription of political will. In this same vein, in pharmaceutical markets today, endeavors to reform drug pricing by taking into account past costs, rather than future value, are often faced with the implacable argument that incumbent valuation techniques express some kind of economic truth—the truth of discounting according to which prices are based on value, and value comes from the future (Doganova and Rabeharisoa 2022).

That discounting is a particular and contingent development within the history of capitalism and that it is a way in which particular kinds of future can be produced can be demonstrated empirically. No empirical study can determine what the future *ought* to look like, and the objective of this book certainly has not been to reach the conclusion that the future, or the past, or the present, is the appropriate temporality of valuation. What my analysis can establish, however, is the way in which the present contains resources for contesting what the future *will* look like and that those resources are to be found within discounting itself. That is the value of a critique that approaches discounting from the inside, as I have done. At stake here is using discounting against itself, rather than replacing it—expanding its use to contest its effects, rather than restricting it.

Consider, in that light, a thought experiment that was suggested to me by a student who did research on the calculation of the compensation paid by TotalEnergies to the populations in Uganda whose land it needed to purchase in order to proceed with the construction of an oil pipeline. To calculate the price of land, the company appeared to abandon the future-oriented temporalities of valuation that it espoused in its presentations to investors. It valued the land of affected households on the basis of the cost of replacement and the prices observed in the market, that is, by adopting the present as the temporality of valuation. What if, the student asked, Ugandan families contested the compensations that were offered to them by espousing the dominant future-oriented temporality of valuation that TotalEnergies had momentarily forsaken? What if they claimed that their land was worth as much as the present value of the future flows of costs and benefits that it was likely to yield if mobilized in oil exploration? What if they adopted the figure of the investor (Feher 2009, 2018)? Couldn't that ultimately lead to reconsidering if oil exploitation was worth it by putting greater weight on the proximate costs that this investment would incur, thereby decreasing its present value and deterring the decision to act, in this case, to exploit resources? Wouldn't then discounting be subverted into constructing a future at odds with its assumptions?

If there is to be a Ministry for the Future that governs the future as a political domain, discounting will be a tool that it can use. The bell curve discount rate encompassing seven past and future generations imagined in Stanley Robinson's novel is just one way that can happen. The investor figure that we can imagine adopted in Ugandan families' valuation of land is another way of using discounting against itself. I dare believe that this book will provide resources for more such tactics to be conceived of and experimented with and thus not only help to free actors from the truth claims of discounting as a general form, but also extend what Horacio Ortiz has called "the limits of financial imagination" (Ortiz 2014a). To me, such endeavors can provide a crucial contribution to the much-needed rearrangement of the ties of time and value in the political technology of discounting.

Acknowledgments

This book would not have come into existence without the intellectual and moral support of Michel Feher and Fabian Muniesa. I have been impressed by their benevolence and their insight. The inception of this book occurred on March 10, 2017, when Fabian Muniesa invited me to present my preliminary research on discounting at the seminar on capitalization that he organized at the École des Mines de Paris. Michel Feher luckily happened to attend this seminar and thought that the fragments I shared could well be the ingredients for a book. The process took seven years. I thank Michel Feher and Zone Books for their patience and their confidence.

Seven years is the age of my son, Thomas. It is striking to imagine that for his entire life, I have been writing this book. I thank Thomas and my husband, Alexandre, for their endurance and their cheerfulness, which have sustained mine. It is a joy to look to the future with them.

The ideas developed in this book have grown on the fertile ground of the Centre de Sociologie de l'Innovation (CSI) at the École des Mines in Paris, where I have been conducting research, first as a doctoral student and later as an assistant and associate professor. I thank all the members of the CSI for all these years of shared academic life. I am grateful in particular to Madeleine Akrich, who trusted in my project to become a sociologist; to Michel Callon, who taught me how to do so; to Fabian Muniesa, who has guided me in my thinking ever since; and to Brice Laurent, who has urged me to explore new empirical and theoretical terrains.

I acknowledge financial support from two projects in which I participated in the initial and the final stages of my research on discounting. From 2011 to 2015, I worked together with Horacio Ortiz and Alvaro Pina Stranger in the project PERFORMABUSINESS (Performativity in Business Education, Management Consulting and Entrepreneurial Finance) led, with brio, by Fabian Muniesa and funded by the European Research Council (ERC). This project allowed me to conduct fieldwork in the United States. The data I collected there through interviews at MIT and at the Harvard Business School and archival research at the MIT library and the Harvard Law School library have nourished Chapter 3 of this book. The conversations with my colleagues in this project formed my analysis of discounting as a political technology, developed in Chapter 1.

Since 2020, I have worked together with Nassima Abdelghafour, Stine Engen, and Marie Stilling in the project VALUETHREADS (Tracing the economy as technology and culture in an emergent value economy) led, with brio again, by Kristin Asdal and funded by the Research Council of Norway. This project allowed me to conduct fieldwork on forests in French Guyana, putting in perspective the historical research on forest valuation presented in Chapter 2 of this book. The conversations with my colleagues in this project sharpened my take on the problem of valuation; their careful reading of the different chapters of this book was extremely helpful and encouraging.

My research on discounting also benefited from my participation, between 2019 and 2022, in the research project SPIN (Social Pharmaceutical Innovation) funded by the Trans-Atlantic Platform (T-AP). The investigations we conducted together with Vololona Rabeharisoa on value-based pricing greatly enriched my understanding of the operations of discounting in the biopharmaceutical industry presented in Chapter 4, shedding light on the further-reaching implications of the logics of discounting and its peculiar blend of temporality and valuation. Finally, this research benefited from a project on the performativity of the social sciences ("Datos y relatos científico sociales que dan forma a la realidad social de Chile") funded by Fondecyt, the Chilean National Fund for Scientific and Technological Development, as part of which Claudio Ramos Zincke and Fernando Valenzuela invited me to visit the Department of Sociology of Universidad Alberto Hurtado in Santiago, Chili, in January 2015. This visit not only reinvigorated my reflections on the performativity of valuation devices, but also sparked the research on the use of discounting in the calculation of investors' compensations presented in Chapter 5, following the direction indicated by Jorge Pavez.

I am grateful to several colleagues who invited my research on discounting in collective publications: Jens Beckert and Richard Bronk, editors of *Uncertain Futures: Imaginaries, Narratives, and Calculation in the Economy* (2018), Olivier Godechot, editor of *economic sociology_ the european electronic newsletter* (2018), and Jenny Andersson and Sandra Kemp, editors of *Futures* (2021). Their feedback has been crucial for the development of my approach to discounting the future. I have also immensely benefited from the comments and reflections of all the participants in seminars where I presented my research on discounting in the last ten years: the Nordic STS conference (University of Oslo, 2023); the Interdisciplinary Market Studies Workshop (University of Edinburgh, 2023); "Calculating Sovereignty. The Law and Politics of the Valuation of Foreign Investment" (University of Glasgow, 2022); "Technologies du temps: Risque, incertitude, connaissance " (Collège International de Philosophie, 2020); Science Studies Colloquium Series (University of Oslo, 2020); Vienna STS talks (University of Vienna, 2019); "Making Sense of the Copper Value Chain: Mapping the Conceptual Landscape of the Anthropology of Extraction in the Context of Financialization" (University of Zurich, 2018); "The Good Economy: If Valuation Studies and "the Bioeconomy" Meet" (Hamarøy, 2018); "Realising the Future" (Goldsmiths, 2017), Chaire Ethique et Finance (Fondation Maison des Sciences de l'Homme, 2017); "Quant-org: Pratiques et usages de la quantification dans les organisations" (Université Paris Dauphine, 2017); EGOS (European Group for Organizational Studies) Colloquium (Copenhagen, 2017); "Economic Futures: Imaginaries, Narratives, and Calculation" (Institut d'études avancées de Paris, 2016); seminar of the STS group at UNIL (Université de Lausanne, 2015); seminar of the Department of Sociology (University Alberto Hurtado, 2015); "Sociologie économique et économie critique: à la recherche du politique" (Centre Culturel International de Cerisy, 2014); Congrès de l'Association Française de Sociologie—AFS (Nantes, 2013); Meeting of the Society for Social Studies of Science—4S (San Diego, 2013); "Les outils de gestion comme analyseurs du capitalism" (EHESS, 2013); and the Accounting, Organizations and Society seminar (London School of Economics and Political Science, 2012). I would like to thank Kristin Asdal, Alexandre Camus, Vincent-Arnaud Chappe, Eve Chiapello, Will Davies, Max Fochler, Tone Huse, Stefan Leins, Anna Longo, Toni Marzal, and Christian Walter for their invitations.

I was not aware of all the work needed to transform a text into a book. Three people played a key role in this transformation. I had the privilege to be read by Bud Bynack, and I was impressed by the thoroughness and the acuity of his copyediting work. I sincerely thank Bud for the care he took of the manuscript and for the boost he gave to it. Meighan Gale was a wonderful companion throughout the entire publishing process. I thank her in particular for her help with the images in the book. In designing the jacket, Julie Fry visualized the general idea of the book with striking aptness.

My last acknowledgments go to my parents, Danya and Aleksandar Doganovi, to whom I wish to dedicate this book.

Notes

INTRODUCTION

1. Unless otherwise noted, throughout, all translations from non-English-language sources are my own.

2. The ideas presented in this book took shape gradually through a series of articles that I published on discounting in the recent years (Doganova 2011, 2014, 2015, 2018, 2021). Nevertheless, the empirical material on which the book builds and the general arguments that it develops are novel—it took several years and several hundreds of pages to weave them in a meaningful whole.

3. I consider the "de-scription" of discounting—in the tradition of the "de-scription" of technical objects in Science and Technology Studies (Akrich 1992)—as one of the major achievements of the research presented in this book. Akrich writes: "The notion of *de-scription* proposed here ... is the inventory and analysis of the mechanisms that allow the relation between a form and a meaning constituted by and constitutive of the technical object to come into being. These mechanisms of adjustment ... become particularly clear when they work by exclusion, whether or not this exclusion is deiberate" (p. 209).

4. Note that even actors who appear most openly to embrace climate change action can be accused of climate inaction: this was the case of France, against which a suit for "climate inaction" was filed in 2019 by Grande-Synthe, a city in the north of France that considered itself particularly vulnerable to climate change.

5. This way of reasoning may seem quite obvious in arenas such as markets or corporations; for example, an individual buys a share on the stock exchange

imagining the dividends that it will yield later, or a company develops a new product imagining the sales that it will bring later. It may be more troubling when action takes place outside of such arenas. I started with the example of climate policy, but I could have taken the example of the very things of which environmental policies are supposed to take care—the environment, climate, nature. I could have taken the example of other kinds of public policy, such as transportation or social policies. I could have even taken the example of individual decision-making in matters apparently noneconomic, such as personal decisions about what to study and whom to marry. In all these arenas we can observe the idea that action now should be judged by its future effects, translated in terms of costs and benefits and discounted back into the present.

6. Discounting intervenes when government is processed through the mechanics of cost-benefit analysis (CBA), the environment is modelled as "natural capital," and individuals are examined as the locus of formation of "human capital." Take, for example, a student who contemplates the possibility to acquire knowledge as an investment in education that will allow her to achieve higher revenues when she enters the job market, in exchange for a certain cost to be paid now. Or take a ministry that justifies the need for a social program not by the relief that it brings to vulnerable populations, but by the benefits (or "avoided costs") that it will allow for in the national budget when these populations become less vulnerable and start needing less help. This move is particularly visible when social programs are repackaged as "social impact bonds" that bring together for a few years unlikely companions like the unhoused, unemployed, or incarcerated people, the ministries under whose jurisdiction they fall, the NGOs and charities who take care of them, and the international consultancy companies and banks who secure the funding that states complain to be lacking. The help provided to the vulnerable populations becomes a cost; the benefits that justify this cost become changes in individual behavior: find a shelter, get a job, do not repeat offense, do not return to prison. Avoiding future homelessness, unemployment, or recidivism in social policy, becomes akin to avoiding future forest fires in climate policy, when a future event is monetized, discounted, and compared to what it takes to produce it and can thus be justified.

7. As I suggested above, if this way of envisaging actions and things as investments may seem quite straightforward for, say, an agent buying shares on the financial market or a real estate developer buying land, it appears less evident for, say, a state thinking about which climate policy to implement, a student pondering which and how much education to pursue, or a family considering the possibility to acquire a new home. And yet all these situations come to be translated in the terms of investment. Climate action, the *Stern Review* suggested, "must be viewed as an investment." Social action, the promoters of social impact bonds echo, can be viewed as an investment and configured so as to become one. "Schooling, on-the-job training, medical care, vitamin consumption, and acquiring information about the economic system," wrote Gary Becker, the theoretician of human capital, are ways of "investing in human capital": activities that "primarily affect future well-being" (as opposed to "others that have their main impact in the present"), that "improve the physical and mental abilities of people and thereby raise real income prospects" (Becker 1962, p. 9).

8. Real options are proposed as an alternative to discounting. Unlike discounting, they account for managerial flexibility, that is, the possibility for managers to expand, change, or curtail projects based on changing external conditions or new knowledge generated by the project. Their valuation draws on the valuation of options in financial markets.

9. This book project started in 2017 and experienced many delays. I would like once again to express my gratitude to Zone Books and Michel Feher in particular for their patience and their infallible trust in this project which may have seemed never-ending.

10. In *Capitalization: A Cultural Guide* (Muniesa et al. 2017) we analyzed the process of capitalization from a sociological perspective. We envisaged capitalization as form of valuation whose specificity lies in its orientation toward the future and in its related way of considering things as "investments" (p. 11) or "assets" (p. 12). We argued that anthropology and sociology had paid particular attention to other forms of valuation in which things are valued "as they are bought and sold, and hence valued as commodities in the market" (p. 13) and had neglected capitalization, either by naturalizing it or replacing it by "a

chimeric object, 'Capital,' which can represent anything (e.g., power, money, matter, domination, freedom, evil, good, you name it" (p. 13). This observation, fortunately, is becoming less and less true. Together with Fabian Muniesa, we have explored the bifurcation between these two forms of valuation—marketization and capitalization—through its material and historical underpinnings (Doganova and Muniesa 2015; Muniesa and Doganova 2020). Drawing on their respective works (Birch 2017, 2020; Muniesa et al. 2017), Kean Birch and Fabian Muniesa (2020) have expanded the study of capitalization through a related concept—"assetization"—which is attracting growing attention in the literature in sociology, political economy, and science and technology studies. In a similar vein, they contrast the form of the asset to that of the commodity, and argue that the study of the former has been neglected at the expense of the study of the latter. The reason they see for this, however, is related to the newness of assetization. As they put it, "we cannot characterize and analyze technoscientific capitalism solely in commodity terms anymore, not in the era of Uber and Airbnb, Google and Amgen," an era in which "an emerging 'asset form'…has come to replace the commodity as the primary basis of contemporary capitalism" (p. 2). In contrast, this book is interested in the deeper historical origins and the built-in omnipresence of this form of valuation rather than in its recentness and exuberance.

11. I draw a brief presentation of this history from the article devoted to the Panama Canal on Wikipedia: https://en.wikipedia.org/wiki/Panama_Canal.

CHAPTER ONE: WHAT IS DISCOUNTING AND HOW TO STUDY IT?

1. Source: 33 USC 701a: Declaration of policy of 1936 act, https://uscode. house.gov/view.xhtml?req=granuleid:USC-prelim-title33-section701a&num=0&edition=prelim, and An Act Authorizing the Construction of Certain Public Works on Rivers and Harbors for Flood Control, and for Other Purposes, June 22, 1936, R.R. 8455.J., Public, No. 738.J, https://uscode. house.gov/statviewer.htm?volume=49&page=1570#.

2. The Office of Management and Budget (OMB) revised its recommended discount rates from 10 to 7 percent in 1992 and then to 7 or 3 percent in 2003. The European Commission recommends a social discount rate of 3 or 5 percent

for the CBA of major projects. By way of comparison, discount rates used by firms in the pharmaceutical industry appear to be in the range of 10 to 15 percent.

3. For an example in the United States, see the employee saving plan Save More Tomorrow™ designed by Thaler and Benartzi (2004).

4. As we will see, to the list of characters sketched by Peter Miller and Christopher Napier (1993, p. 634)—"the Bookkeeper, the Decision-Maker or the Cost Accountant")—our genealogy of discounting calculations will add the character of "the Investor."

5. On the notion of calculative devices, see the work of Michel Callon and Fabian Muniesa (2005). Their discussion of markets as calculative devices has given rise to the notion of market devices (Callon et al. 2007). Building on their work, but avoiding an exclusive focus on markets, I have proposed the notion of valuation devices for analyzing calculative devices such as discounting that are disseminated in places that can be described as both "in" and "out" of markets (Doganova 2019).

6. I mentioned the influential work of historian Theodore Porter in the Introduction (Porter, 1995). Other works on CBA in STS include (Boudia 2014) and (Øvstebø Tvedten 2022).

7. The term "net present value" (NPV) appears later in the report. When the authors discuss the details of discounting in public policy—or "the theory of social discounting" (p. 197)—they say, "The question for CBA is, what is the appropriate social discount rate for calculating the NPV of public projects?" (OECD 2018, p. 200).

8. In their discussion of the social theory of discounting, the authors mention the possibility to integrate risk into the discount rate, following the example of countries like France, Norway, and the Netherlands, as well as the advances of modern finance theory (with tools like the Capital Asset Pricing Model, to which I refer in Chapter 4).

9. An option is a financial product that gives its holder the right, but not the obligation, to buy or sell something at a predetermined price.

10. I borrow the term "political qualities" from works in science and technology studies that have analyzed the politics of technologies, in particular

Langdon Winner's reply to the provocative question, "Do artifacts have politics?" and Yannick Barthe's analysis of nuclear waste disposal technologies and modes of political decision-making. In Winner's conception of the "political qualities" of technologies, politics involves "arrangements of power and authority in human associations as well as the activities that take place within those arrangements" (Winner 1980, p. 123). In Barthe's terms, the "political qualities" of technologies refer to "the constraints that they impose, the resources that the provide in terms of political action, and finally the mode of government to which they are articulated" (Barthe 2009, p. 119). Studying these political qualities then means "clarifying the problems to which they are supposed to respond, the roles that they attribute to different actors, the scenarios and the hypotheses that they incorporate, and the ways in which these hypotheses are questioned in the course of [controversies]" (Barthe 2009, p. 120). The argument developed in this book can be seen as the extension of Barthe's perspective onto technologies of calculation.

11. In a similar vein, Horacio Ortiz discusses the political nature of the financial industry as it has played "a central role in the distribution of resources, within a global space of financial flows that it has contributed to constitute by administering the inequalities, balance of power and conflicts within it" (Ortiz 2014b, pp. 18–19). The valuation of listed companies, he argues, is both a technical and a political act insofar as it directs credit in a global space (Ortiz 2013).

12. "We should be pricing these medicines on the value they bring to society," claimed the president of the biotechnology start-up that developed Zolgensma (Green 2019), in reaction to the controversies triggered by the price of this drug.

13. For a few varied examples of sociological analyses of such technologies of the future, see (Andersson 2018; Andersson & Prat 2015; Aykut et al. 2019; Brown and Michael 2003; Comi and Whyte 2017; Dahan 2007; Giraudeau 2012).

14. Lawrence Summers was, among other positions, chief economist of the World Bank, treasury secretary in Bill Clinton's administration, and director of the National Economic Council for President Obama, as well as president of Harvard University.

1. For a critical review of the literature on the history of discounting and an attempt at an "accurate reconstruction," see (Scorgie 1996).

2. More narrowly defined, the concept of sustainable management developed by eighteenth-century foresters referred to the ability of the forest to provide a "sustainable yield," that is, a regular annual income in perpetuity. It can remind us of another vision of sustainability that can be encountered today: the idea that activities should be economically sustainable, that is, that they should be able to generate some form of revenue for those on whom they depend and that this revenue should be neither sporadic nor short-lived, if the activity in question is to last. This economic vision of sustainability can be found, for example, in the discourse of social businesses when they attempt to position themselves with respect to other social actors such as NGOs, with arguments such as the following one: a water pump that is donated will not outlive the end of the development project because as soon as the NGO that installed it leaves, there will be no one to maintain it; by contrast, a water pump that is operated as a business will be sustainable because the company that operates it will have an incentive to maintain it. (Of course, this holds only as long as the pump provides revenues.)

3. Earlier applications of discounting to forestry have been documented (Moog and Bösch 2013; Scorgie 1996; Viitala 2006), but the impact of the Faustmann formula has been described as "monumental" due to its many applications in forest management and beyond (Viitala 2006, p. 132).

4. In this chapter, I use Dagobert de Salomon's (1837) translation for Johann Heinrich Cotta's work, and Michael Gane's (1968) translation for E. von Gehren's and Martin Faustmann's articles.

5. Von Gehren distinguished two scenarios: intermittent management and sustained management. I will focus only on intermittent management for it will suffice to illustrate the reasoning of discounting. "Intermittent forestry" focuses on the level of the stand: a forest is established, thinned, and finally clear-cut, then the same cycle is repeated. The forest yields equal revenues and yields from each rotation period. "Sustainable forestry" focuses on the level of the forest. The "normal" forest provides constant annual yields (Viitala 2006).

6. Von Gehren used Georg Ludwig Hartig's normal yield tables. Like Cotta,

Hartig was Gthe founder of a forestry school and the author of yield tables that used past measurements of trees' diameter and height to provide estimates of "normal yields" from thinnings and the final crop according to the age of trees. See, for example (Pretzsch 2001, p. 214).

7. See, for example, Chapter 3 and the argument that discounting is not erroneous but simply not applicable to certain types of projects, in particular, those that are risky.

8. One of the most striking examples of this lack of questioning is the omnipresence of discount rates (be they high or low, positive or negative) in current debates on climate change and sustainable development, which I discussed in the Introduction.

9. This formula is known as Faustmann's soil expectation value formula.

10. This article is signed by "F." and attributed to Faustmann (Viitala 2006). In this section, I rely on Viitala's account of F.'s article.

11. These questions bring forward the problem of the political relationship between generations, which has a long history in political thought. Eighteenth-century revolutionaries, willing to break free from the heritage of the past and to sever the links between past and present generations, argued for strict temporal limits on power and against "the vanity and presumption of governing beyond the grave," as Thomas Paine beautifully put it (quoted in Nordblad, 2021, pp. 367–68). Presentism, as Nordblad (2018, pp. 45–46) shows, which is now pointed out as one of democracy's problems in dealing with climate change, was once part of a political program: political renewal could be imagined only through the disqualification of any right of the present to subject future generations to its laws.

12. A translation of "aménagement" by "management" is not satisfactory because it loses the ideas of layout, organization, and planning that are present in the French term.

13. More precisely, the difference between the coppice and high forests relates to the age and the means of reproduction of trees (Noirot-Bonnet 1842, p. 157). "Taillis" (coppice) is exploited at an earlier age (less than thirty to forty years) and can reproduce itself from its stump and its roots. "Futaie" (high forest) provides high-quality timber for construction purposes. It is exploited at a later age (more

than eighty years), and its reproduction requires growing from seeds.

14. It is through François Vatin's work that I discovered the works of Louis Noirot-Bonnet, Georges-Louis Leclerc Buffon, and Varenne de Phenille, which I then read through the lens of the argument developed in this book. The discussion on the alignment of the general and the individual interest in this section draws on Vatin's analysis and expands it with the ideas of time as cost, investors' impatience, and discounting.

15. Vatin underlines the novelty of this reasoning, in which he sees an early formulation of the economic theory of marginalism.

16. Note that contemporary authors used the notion of the interest rate to refer both to financial and forestry investments. The notion of the discount rate is hence an anachronism that I use in this chapter in order to keep in mind that the equivalence between the discount rate and the interest rate corresponds to a particular moment in history. As we will see in the next chapter, in the middle of the twentieth century, the discount rate was detached from the interest rate and redefined as the cost of capital.

17. For a description of these debates in seventeenth-century England with reference to the case of forests, see chapter 2 in (Tucker 1960).

18. Interview with a French forest economist, Paris, March 1, 2013.

19. Fictitious name.

20. Interview with a North American forest economist, San Francisco, October 3, 2013.

21. Ibid.

22. Interview with a French forest economist, Paris, March 1, 2013.

23. I thank my colleague Béatrice Cointe for sharing this video with me upon her return from the COP27.

24. Coalition for Rainforest Nations, "Gabon: REDD+ Sovereign Carbon Credits," https://www.youtube.com/watch?v=xy-pgRfw8v4.

25. How this changes the definition of the future as a political domain and how discounting intervenes in the process is a question to be explored in a different study.

26. Interview with a North American forest economist, San Francisco, October 3, 2013.

1. The example in this paragraph draws on the description of the transformations undergone by four companies in different industries as they entered the Swedish stock exchange in an article by Kraus and Strömsten (2012).

2. The rhetoric of shareholder value—the claim that what matters for a company is the value that it delivers to its shareholders—is widespread. The literature on financialization has devoted significant attention to the emergence and diffusion of shareholder value (Williams 2000). Its origins can be traced to a consultancy product designed and promoted in the 1980s by US consultants such as Alfred Rappaport, the author of *Creating Shareholder Value* in 1986, and Bennett Stewart, the author of *The Quest for Value* in 1991 (Froud et al. 2000). Shareholder value bloomed on the fertile ground left by a series of transformations that occurred in the 1970s, including the economic difficulties with which US corporations were struggling, the invention of agency theory, and the rise of institutional investors and financial deregulation (Lazonick and O'Sullivan 2000). Among its consequences can be found the short-termism made visible in the example with which I opened this chapter and more broadly the alteration of managers' subjectivity and companies' productive activities (Roberts et al. 2006) and accounting systems (Ezzamel et al. 2008). Kraus and Strömsten (2012) have noted in particular how the information infrastructure describing companies that went public was filtered through accounting categories that fitted the financial analysts' "preconceived conceptualizations" and, of greatest interest for my argument here, their "standard discounted cash flow models" (p. 196).

3. For an insightful analysis of face-to-face meetings between managers and investors and of managers' anticipatory self-discipline, see (Roberts et al. 2006).

4. My approach here echoes Eve Chiapello's (2015) call to complement the study of financialization with a new aspect that she calls the "financialization of valuation," that is, "the gradual colonization [of valuation] by 'financialized' techniques and calculation methods" (p. 15). She identifies three such techniques, one of which is the calculation of NPV through DCF. In her view, DCF is a "financialized" technique because it is part of the "models, instruments,

and representations belonging to the explicit knowledge underpinning the approach and practices of finance professionals," a knowledge that can be found in finance textbooks, for example (p. 17).

5. For the description of an early figure of this manager, see Anthony G. Hopwood's (1992) and Sidney Pollard's (1965b) accounts of Wedgwood's costing and pricing endeavors in the eighteenth century.

6. In his history of profit, Jonathan Levy (2014) identifies four periods marked by different profit regimes and calculations: the commercial balance of income and outgo (before 1850), the operating ratio (1850 to 1920), the rate of return on capital invested, or ROI (1920 to 1980), and the rate of return on equity, or ROE (from 1980 on).

7. The payback period refers to the amount of time it takes to recover the cost of an investment. It is calculated by dividing the cost of the investment by the annual cash flow until the cumulative cash flow is positive, which yields the year the investment is paid back.

8. I take this example from Joel Dean's article. Note the high levels of the discount rate, which are employed without discussion.

9. Note the precocity of this reasoning, which predates the formalization of the Capital Asset Pricing Model (CAPM) and the Weighted Average Cost of Capital (WACC).

10. Quotations in this paragraph come from this article published in the *New York Times* (Wayne 1982).

11. Interview with Robert Hayes, Cambridge, Massachusetts, May 9, 2013. Unless stated otherwise, the quotes in this paragraph are taken from this interview.

12. Ibid.

13. Ibid.

14. Ibid.

15. Ibid.

16. Ibid.

17. "Stewart Myers Biography," *MIT Sloan School of Management*, https:// mitsloan.mit.edu/faculty/directory/stewart-myers.

18. Interview with Stewart Myers, Cambridge, Massachusetts, April 30,

2013. Unless stated otherwise, the quotes in this section are taken from this interview.

19. The authors acknowledge that "the rate of return on capital can be computed in countless ways" (Holland and Myers 1979, p. 4). The methodology that they apply is profoundly influenced by the value theory of discounting: the authors explain that they use capital market data, rather than accounting data, because "the value of the firm is not determined by the cumulative funds invested in it, or by the net replacement cost of its stock of real capital, but by the stream of earnings investors expect it to generate," and the value of this stream can be observed directly in capital markets (p. 5).

20. "Roger G. Ibbitson," *Yale School of Management*, https://som.yale.edu/faculty/roger-g-ibbotson.

21. Lee Fang, "King Rex, A Stock Baron Goes All in on Missouri politics," *Politico*, July/August 2014, https://www.politico.com/magazine/story/2014/06/king-rex-sinquefield-108015.

22. Real options are one example of these new approaches to valuation. Myers has been an active proponent of them.

23. Interview with Stewart Myers, Cambridge, Massachusetts, April, 30, 2013.

24. Ibid.

25. I thank Stine Engen for asking me this question and making me reflect on how to answer it.

CHAPTER FOUR: DISCOUNTING AND THE VALUATION OF DRUG DEVELOPMENT PROJECTS

1. I borrow the notion of "capitalized uncertainty" from McGoey (2009), but use it in a different, less metaphorical sense, as the chapter will explain below.

2. The chapter partly draws on (Doganova 2011, 2015, 2018).

3. Lucien Karpik's sociological analysis surprisingly resonates with the analysis that the economist George Akerlof (1970) made a few decades earlier of the "market for lemons." Using the market for used cars as an example, he showed that uncertainty over the quality of cars and asymmetrical information

between the buyer and the seller are likely to hinder the functioning of the market. The solution he suggested consisted of "counteracting institutions" such as guarantees, brands, or certification.

4. Like Frank Knight and John Maynard Keynes, George Shackle is an economist who used the notion of uncertainty to criticize orthodox economic theories that hypothesize the possibility of rational decision-making.

5. I ask here the same kind of question that Michel Callon asked in his introduction to the edited volume *The Laws of the Markets* (Callon 1998a), which laid the foundations of STS-inspired analyses of the construction of markets by sketching two directions for answering this question: the role of market devices (Callon 2007) and the performativity of economics (MacKenzie et al. 2007).

6. They also remind us that an account of the success of Knight's risk/uncertainty distinction should not be oblivious to his strong institutional position as a director of the Economics Department of the University of Chicago, an influential founding member of the Mont Pelerin Society, and a president of the American Economic Association.

7. Profit is analyzed as the revenue of the entrepreneur, next to salary, which is the revenue of the worker, and rent, which is the revenue of the owner. As Pierre-Charles Pradier and David Teira Serrano interestingly observe, one important implication of Knight's theory of profit is to evacuate the issue of the justice of distribution, which hinges on some kind of correspondence between the contribution provided to economic activity and the reward drawn from it: "Insofar as uncertainty is not measurable either a priori or a posteriori...it is impossible to assess the *true* contribution of the entrepreneur to production. Therefore, it is illusory to seek any sort of 'justice' in the remuneration of entrepreneurs." (Pradier and Serrano 2000, p. 102, emphasis in the original).

8. Interestingly, Knight likens the process of estimating the future to that of remembering the past: "Prophecy seems to be a good deal like memory itself, on which it is based. When we wish to think of some man's name, or recall a quotation which has slipped our memory, we go to work to do it, and the desired idea comes to mind, often when we are thinking about something else—or else it does not come, but in either case there is very little that we can

tell about the operation, very little 'technique.' So when we try to decide what to expect in a certain situation, and how to behave ourselves accordingly, we are likely to do a lot of irrelevant mental rambling, and the first thing we know we find that we have made up our minds, that our course of action is settled" (Knight 1921, p. 211).

9. Consolidation consists in grouping instances into cases in order to reduce their uniqueness, as happens with insurance.

10. These methods refer to the production of knowledge about the present and the past, supposed to enlighten predictions of the future. Knight points out "the existence of highly specialized industrial structures performing the functions of furnishing knowledge and guidance" (p. 260). Information about market and industry conditions is generated and disseminated through market associations, public statistics, trade journals, and statistical bureaus; "instructions for the guidance of conduct" are delivered by experts and consultants who have recently "swarmed" in nearly every department of industrial life (p. 262).

11. I do not comment on this here, but the evocation of "good luck" in the quote nicely illustrates Pradier and Serrano's (2000) point that Knight's theory of uncertainty evacuates the problem of justice from the explanation of entrepreneurs' rewards.

12. The figure of the investor, as we have seen in Chapter 3, has come to encompass that of the manager, giving rise to what I have called the "investing manager" (Doganova 2014).

13. "Innate Pharma and Novo Nordisk announce strategic partnership to research and develop drugs targeting natural killer cells." Press release, April 5, 2006, https://www.innate-pharma.com/sites/default/files/pr_novonordisk_innate06.pdf.

14. Interview with the director of cooperation of a French pharmaceutical company, Paris, France, 2009.

15. This is the "lemmings" approach to the analysis of valuation "under Knightian uncertainty" (p. 14) in Beunza and Garud's (2007) inspiring argument on the role of securities analysts in financial markets.

16. Note that the balance of power may not necessarily be in favor of the pharmaceutical company: the start-up benefits from the lure of "innovation"

that is eagerly sought after by pharmaceutical companies.

17. DCF is also used to value companies in the case of acquisitions (typically, a pharmaceutical company acquiring a biotechnology start-up). Here, I focus on the valuation of drug development projects.

18. Interview with a consultant specialized in valuation in the biopharmaceutical industry, Basel, Switzerland, 2009.

19. Ibid.

20. Ibid.

21. Ibid. The book he refers to is yet another textbook on valuation in the biopharmaceutical industry.

22. Note that the distinction that this author puts forward is different from Knight's classical distinction: for Savage (2012), "uncertainty is an objective feature of the universe, whereas risk is in the eye of the beholder" (p. 52).

23. The BIO-Europe meeting is a major event that gathers actors from the biopharmaceutical industry twice a year. I conducted ethnographic research at two such events: a BIO-Europe meeting in 2012 and a BioPharm America meeting in 2014. The example used here is drawn from an article published by the organizers of another meeting (BIO-Europe 2017) on their website.

24. On the history of Genentech and the invention of the biotech business model, see (Doganova and Muniesa 2015).

25. The seven metrics (selected depending on their relevance and the availability of data to measure them) are the amount of investment required for each product to reach the market, R&D intensity, the amount of time required to take a product from initial inception to market launch, the possibility of complete product failure late in development, the existence of differences in regional regulation, the competitive landscape of the industry, and the importance of patenting.

26. The report builds on the work of Stewart Myers, whom I introduced in Chapter 3 for his work on corporate finance and his defense of DCF in particular. He is listed as one of the principal contractors for the Office of Technology Assessment (OTA) report. (He co-authored a contract report titled "Cost of Capital Estimates for Investment in Pharmaceutical Research and Development" in 1991.) It should be noted that Myers took part in the MIT Program on the

Pharmaceutical industry (POPI) that was founded in 1991. The 1997 annual report of the POPI research stream on "drug discovery and development" explains the major contributions to the pharmaceutical industry in the following terms: "Ongoing POPI work has been central to the industry's own financial understanding. Our researchers have built a financial simulation model which connects the tools of modern finance to a detailed description of the costs, risks, and returns of pharmaceutical R&D—a prototype for financial analysis of R&D investment and a way of understanding the financial structure and performance of the industry. It is POPI research that has identified the cost of developing a successful new drug to be in the vicinity of $450 million, considering actual expenditures on discovery, testing, and the cost of capital" (POPI 1998).

27. One might wonder why, of all risk-averse people, investors are the ones to be rewarded. Or why, while investors are rewarded because they dislike loss, they do not reward in turn because they like gain.

28. Avance newsletter, Discount rates for biotech companies, https://avance.ch/download/discount-rates-in-pharma-and-biotech/

29. Ortiz (2021) beautifully analyzes the "political imaginaries" of the WACC formula and the contradictions between the figures of "the maximizing investor," "the efficient markets," and "the sovereign state" that it implies.

30. We met one of the inventors of the CAPM at the Harvard Business School cafeteria in Chapter 3. The CAPM brought the Nobel Prize in Economics to another of its inventors in 1990.

31. The calculation proceeds as follows. The macro risks affecting a company (the so-called "betas") are estimated based on the past performance of the company's stock and of the overall market. The results of the calculation show, for example, that in 1990, Abbott Laboratories had a "beta" of 1.01 and an expected return on equity (that is, cost of equity capital) of 15.6 percent, while Eli Lilly had a "beta" of 1.24 and an expected return on equity of 17.6 percent. This means, in short, that Abbott Laboratories is an asset that has behaved similar to the market in the last five years and hence has an average risk (beta close to 1), while Eli Lilly is an asset that has a higher risk and therefore requires a higher return. After adding the cost of debt into the calculation, the results

show that the WACC of these two firms (and hence their discount rates) are equal to 15.3 percent for Abbott and 17.3 percent for Eli Lilly. A similar calculation on a subsample of smaller pharmaceutical firms (which in 1989 were the first biotechnology start-ups) shows that, for example, Genentech had a beta of 1.51 and a cost of capital of 20.3 percent and Cetus Corporation had a beta of 1.7 and a cost of capital of 20.7 percent in 1989.

32. Other observers are much more critical of such adjustments. For example, in a newsletter evocatively entitled "Charlatanry in Valuation," the consultancy company I mentioned above quotes "several examples— sometimes funny, sometimes even frightening—of how valuation should not be done." In its line of sight happen to be, for example, the financial manager of a biotechnology start-up according to whom "if one uses success rates, then the attrition risk is already taken into account and pharmaceutical companies' discount rates should be used" and the author of a Harvard Business School article who claims that "value = DCF without success rates (because compounds are not comparable) but discounted with a rate of 50%" (Avance newsletter, Charlantry in Valuation, https://avance.ch/download /funny-valuations/).

33. The MCPM uses the prices of equity options on a company's shares, which are supposed to reflect the market's estimates of the future volatility of these shares.

CHAPTER FIVE:

DISCOUNTING AND THE STATE-INVESTOR RELATIONSHIP

1. Olofsson (2020a) explains how the NPV of projected mines is calculated by mineral "explorationists." However, his interest lies in showing that the "relative certainty" of the NPV as a comprehensive valuation of the projected mine is less solid than it may first appear" (p. 139), insisting on the fragility of the future estimates on which it relies. I discussed this form of critique of discounting in Chapter 4.

2. I will capitalize it, too, in this chapter when I approach discounting from his perspective.

3. I thank Professor Claudio Ramos-Zincke and his colleague Fernando

Valenzuela for their invitation to do a research visit at the Department of Sociology of Universidad Alberto Hurtado as part of their research project on the performativity of the social sciences in Chile.

4. I thank Jorge Pavez for introducing me to the role played by discounting in Chile.

5. This section adopts Enchenque Piñera's point of view, drawing on three types of sources: the text of the mining law; his book explaining the "principles" of this law, *Fundamentos de la Ley Constitucional Minera* (Piñera 1981b) and an article in English that provides a summary of the book, "Wealth through Ownership: Creating Property Rights in Chilean Mining" (Piñera 2004), the text of which was also available on his website until recently; and personal communication through a series of email exchanges I had with Mr. Piñera in the summer of 2018. Unless specified otherwise, the quotes in this section are taken from Piñera's article "Wealth through Ownership."

6. It should be noted that there are several versions of the notion of property that are implied in this chapter. The first version is the one that Piñera wanted to avoid because it would have implied a politically unacceptable privatization. So copper mines remained under public ownership. The second version of property is the one that Piñera invented with the full concession: here, "property" refers to a relationship between the mine and the company that operates it that is so strong that detaching one from the other becomes an instance of "expropriation." A third version, which we will discuss below, refers to the partition of the shares of the mine: the entity that owes a mine is the one that has more than 51 percent of its shares.

7. This latter point, echoing the agreements on maximum profits evoked in the constitution, was a reference to the Cartagena Agreement of May 26, 1969, according to which Chile, Peru, Colombia, Ecuador, and Bolivia limited profits of foreign investors in their countries to 14 percent of invested capital (Fleming 1973).

8. Theodore H. Moran (1974, p. 121) reports that in 1952, when the comptroller general was asked to write a report on the domestic copper industry, he responded that "except for the foreign management of the companies nobody, including himself, had any idea of what was going on in the industry."

9. I will revert to this part of the legislation, known as the Nuevo Trato, below.

10. Here again, unless specified otherwise, the quotes from Piñera are taken from his article "Wealth through Ownership."

11. It should be noted that discounting is not the only economic innovation introduced by "the Chicago Boys" that has persisted in Chile. For José Ossandon and Sebastián Ureta (2019, p. 177), "one of the key dilemmas regarding Chile's recent history" is "the fact that the reforms initiated during the military dictatorship (1973–1989) have resisted decades of left-leaning social democrat governments."

12. Raúl Prebisch was executive secretary of the United Nations Economic Commission for Latin America from 1950 to 1963. His model was published in the commission's report addressing the "principal problems" of economic development of this region (Economic Commission on Latin America 1950) and was based, in particular, on Prebisch's work on Chilean data.

13. According to Moran's research (1974), it is Kennecott itself that proposed to get "Chileanized" even before Eduardo Frei took office. Based on his interviews with Kennecott officials, Moran explains Kennecott's proposal by citing a number of reasons, including their understanding that "long-term guarantees for operations in Chile ... were losing their meaning" (p. 132). In other words, Kennecott was preparing for expropriation. The company also built arrangements with US government agencies and customers, the aim of which, Moran quotes the executive vice-president of Kennecott's Chilean operations whom he interviewed as saying, was "to insure that nobody expropriates Kennecott without upsetting relations to customers, creditors, and governments on three continents" (p. 136).

14. For example, The Libyan American Oil Company, whose concessions were nationalized in 1973 and 1974 by the Libyan Arab Republic, submitted compensation claims to an arbitration tribunal amounting to a total $207 million, of which only $14 million corresponded to the value of its physical plants and equipment, while the rest corresponded to the "loss of profits" that the concession would have yielded to the company over the remaining term of the concession or producing life of the deposits lying within it. The calculation of the profits lost was equal to the present value of the revenues and costs estimated

from 1974 to 1988, discounted at a rate of 12 percent (Libyan American Oil Co. v. Libyan Arab Republic, 20 I.L.M. 1,78-79 [1981]).

CONCLUSION: A PROGRAM FOR THE MINISTRY FOR THE FUTURE

1. I thank Brice Laurent and Kaja Lilleng for pointing to me this chapter relating to discounting in Kim Stanley Robinson's novel.

2. The ideas presented in the conclusion of this book owe a lot to my conversation with Michel Feher.

3. The most comprehensive study of such knowledge-oriented technologies of the future is certainly Jenny Andersson's book *The Future of the World* (Andersson 2018).

4. The claim about environmental degradation is visible, for example, in the Brundtland report, titled "Our Common Future" and known as the one of the first formulations of "sustainable development." While it argued for a "development that meets the needs of the present without compromising the ability of future generations to meet their own needs" (WCED 1987, chapter 2), this report put forward poverty as one of the "symptoms and causes" of "our threatened future": "Those who are poor and hungry will often destroy their immediate environment in order to survive: They will cut down forests; their livestock will overgraze grasslands; they will overuse marginal land; and in growing numbers they will crowd into congested cities" (WCED 1987, chapter 1).

5. In 2003, the United States Office of Management and Budget (OMB) published a circular that revised recommended discount rates, requiring public agencies to provide estimates of CBA using two different discount rates: not only the 7 percent that had been in place since 1992, but also a 3 percent rate in order to account for the "special ethical considerations" that arise when the effects of policies (that is, their benefits and costs) are distant in time and hence span "across generations." The circular acknowledged that the argument that "government should treat all generations equally" is incompatible with the very idea of discounting the future. "Future citizens who are affected by such choices cannot take part in making them, and today's society must act with some consideration of their interest" (OMB circular A-4, 17 September 2003, p. 35). The lower discount rate of 3 percent was a way to do so. However, it was

still justified in terms of investment. While the 7 percent rate was defined as the "rate of return to private capital in the U.S. economy," which "approximates the opportunity cost of capital," the 3 percent rate corresponded to the "rate of return on long-term government debt" as a proxy for "the rate that the average saver uses to discount future consumption" (p. 33).

The report that revised the French discount rate in 2005—the rate set by the Commissariat Général au Plan for public investments (Lebègue 2005)—performs a similar operation. In the preface to the report, signed by the Planning Commissioner Alain Etchegoyen, the discount rate was first defined in a broad and openly political formulation: "it translates the relative price that a community attaches to the present and sets the limit of the effort that this community agrees to make for the future" (p. 3). The need to revise the discount rate, which had remained stable for twenty years, was explained in terms of our changing relationship to the future: "the concern for future generations, the problem of sustainable development and risk management" (pp. 5-6). Its measure, however, was still discussed in terms of "return": here, "the rate of return to public investments." This return, the report explained, "is a democratic requirement, but by its peculiar concept, it shakes up the notions of political or financial rate of return: it suggests the idea of a return to the general interest" (p. 6). The discount rate was supposed to capture this idea. With an evocative play of words, the report construed the discount rate as "a general interest rate [*taux d'intérêt général*]" (p. 6), meaning both a rate of interest that is general and a rate of the general interest.

6. Another obstacle that this critique has encountered lies in the necessity to find alternative temporalities of valuation for the places that should be preserved from discounting. This book has discussed in particular the use of the past as an alternative temporality of valuation. The most telling illustration of this proposition is Salvador Allende's calculation of the compensation to be paid to foreign investors in the case of nationalization. It failed tragically, but this required no less than the intervention of a powerful ally and the establishment of a military dictatorship.

References

AFP Agence France-Presse. 2020. "Climate Economics Nobel May Do More Harm Than Good." *France24*, July 6, https://www.france.24.com/en/20200706-climate-economics-nobel-may-do-more-harm-than-good.

Akerlof, George A. 1970. "The Market for 'Lemons': Quality Uncertainty and the Market Mechanism." *Quarterly Journal of Economics* 84.3, pp. 488–500, https://doi.org/10.2307/1879431.

Akrich, Madeleine. 1992. "The De-scription of Technical Objects." In Wiebe E. Bijker and John Law, eds., *Shaping Technology / Building Society: Studies in Sociotechnical Change*, pp. 205–24. Cambridge, MA: MIT Press.

Allende, Salvador. 1970. Mensaje de Ejecutivo, con el que inicia un proyecto de reforma constitucional que modifica el articulo 10, No. 10, de la Constitución Politica del Estado, Dec. 23, 1970.

———. 1972 "Speech to the United Nations (Excerpts)," https://www.marxists.org/archive/allende/1972/december/04.htm.

Andersson, Jenny. 2018. *The Future of the World: Futurology, Futurists, and the Struggle for the Post Cold War Imagination*. Oxford, UK: Oxford University Press.

Andersson, Jenny, & Prat, P. (2015). "Gouverner le long terme: La Prospective et la production bureaucratique des futurs en France." *Gouvernement et Action Publique* 3, pp. 9–29.

Asdal, Kristin, Béatrice Cointe, Bård Hobæk, et al. 2003. "'The good economy': a conceptual and empirical move for investigating how economies and versions of the good are entangled." *BioSocieties* 18, 1–24, https://doi.org/10.1057/s41292-021-00245-5.

Ashraf, Nava, Dean Karlan, and Wesley Yin. 2006. "Tying Odysseus to the

Mast: Evidence From a Commitment Savings Product in the Philippines." *Quarterly Journal of Economics* 121.2, pp. 635–72, https://do i.org/10.1162/qjec.2006.121.2.635.

Austin, J. L. 1962. *How to Do Things with Words.* edited by J. O. Urmson and Marina Sbisà. Cambridge, MA: Harvard University Press.

Aykut, S., Demortain, D., & Benbouzid, B. 2019. "The Politics of Anticipatory Expertise: Plurality and Contestation of Futures Knowledge in Governance—Introduction to the Special Issue." *Science & Technology Studies. Special Issue: The Politics of Anticipatory Expertise* 32(4), https://doi. org/10.23987/sts.87369

Barthe, Yannick. 2006. *Le pouvoir d'indécision: La mise en politique des déchets nucléaires.* Paris: Economica.

———. 2009. "Les qualités politiques des technologies: Irréversibilité et réversibilité dans la gestion des déchets nucléaires." *Tracés: Revue de Sciences Humaines* 16, pp. 119–37, https://doi.org/10.4000/traces.2563.

Becker, Gary S. 1962. "Investment in Human Capital: A Theoretical Analysis." *Journal of Political Economy* 70.5, pp. 9–49, https://doi.org/10.1086 /258724.

Beckert, Jens. 2016. *Imagined Futures: Fictional Expectations and Capitalist Dynamics.* Cambridge, MA: Harvard University Press.

———, and Richard Bronk, eds. 2018. *Uncertain Futures: Imaginaries, Narratives, and Calculation in the Economy.* Oxford, UK: Oxford University Press.

Beunza, Daniel, and Raghu Garud. 2007. "Calculators, Lemmings or Frame-Makers? The Intermediary Role of Securities Analysts. *Sociological Review* 55.2 supplement, pp. 13–39, https://doi.org/10.1111/j.1467 -954X.2007.00728.x.

Birch, Kean. 2017. "Rethinking *Value* in the Bio-Economy: Finance, Assetization, and the Management of Value." *Science, Technology, and Human Values* 42.3, pp. 460–90, https://doi.org/10.1177/0162243916661633.

———. 2018. "What Is the Asset Condition?" Review of Fabian Muniesa, Liliana Doganova, Horacio Ortiz, Álvaro Pina-Stranger, Florence Paterson, Alaric Bourgoin, Véra Ehrenstein, Pierre-André Juven, David Pontille,

Başak Saraç-Lesavre, and Guillaume Yon, *Capitalization: A Cultural Guide*. Paris, Presses des Mines, 2017. *European Journal of Sociology* 59.3, pp. 500–506, https://doi.org/10.1017/S000397561800036X.

———. 2020. "Technoscience Rent: Toward a Theory of Rentiership for Technoscientific Capitalism." *Science, Technology, and Human Values* 45.1, pp. 3–33, https://doi.org/10.1177/0162243919829567.

———, and Fabian Muniesa, eds. 2020. *Assetization: Turning Things into Assets in Technoscientific Capitalism.* Cambridge, MA: MIT Press.

Bogdan, Boris, and Ralph Villiger. 2007. *Valuation in Life Sciences: A Practical Guide.* Heidelberg: Springer.

Boudia, Soraya. 2014. "7. Gouverner par les instruments économiques: La trajectoire de l'analyse coût-bénéfice dans l'action publique." In Dominique Pestre, ed., *Le gouvernement des technosciences: Gouverner le progrès et ses dégâts depuis 1945*, pp. 231–59. Paris: La Découverte, https://doi.org/10.3917/dec.pest.2014.01.0231.

Bourdieu, Pierre. 1963. "La société traditionnelle: Attitude à l'égard du temps et conduite économique." *Sociologie du travail* 5.1, pp. 24–44, https://www.persee.fr/doc/sotra_0038-0296_1963_num_5_1_1127.

———. 2000. "Pratiques économiques et dispositions temporelles." In Pierre Bourdieu, *Esquisse d'une théorie de la pratique*, pp. 377–85. Paris: Seuil.

———. 2005. *The Social Structures of the Economy.* Trans. Chris Turner. Cambridge, UK: Polity.

Brackenborough, Susie, Tom McLean, and David Oldroyd. 2001. "The Emergence of Discounted Cash Flow Analysis in the Tyneside Coal Industry c.1700–1820." *British Accounting Review* 33.2, pp. 137–55, https://doi.org/10.1006/bare.2001.0158.

Brealey, Richard A., and Stewart C. Myers. 1988. *Principles of Corporate Finance.* Third edition. New York: McGraw-Hill.

Brigham, Eugene F. 1975. "Hurdle Rates for Screening Capital Expenditure Proposals." *Financial Management* 4.3, pp. 17–26.

Bronk, Richard. 2009. *The Romantic Economist: Imagination in Economics.* Cambridge, UK: Cambridge University Press.

Brown, N., & Michael, M. 2003. "A Sociology of Expectations: Retrospecting

Prospects and Prospecting Retrospects." *Technology Analysis & Strategic Management* 15(1), pp. 3–18. https://doi.org/10.1080/0953732032000046024

Bryan, Dick, and Michael Rafferty, 2013. "Fundamental Value: A Category in Transformation." *Economy and Society* 42.1, pp. 130–53, https://doi.org/10.1080/03085147.2012.718625.

Bryan, Gharad, Dean Karlan, and Scott Nelson. 2010. "Commitment Devices." *Annual Review of Economics*, 2.1, pp. 671–98, https://doi.org/10.1146/annurev.economics.102308.124324.

Buchanan, J., Chai, D. H. and Deakin, S. 2012. *Hedge Fund Activism in Japan: The Limits of Shareholder Primacy*. Cambridge: Cambridge University Press.

Buffon, Georges-Louis Leclerc, Comte de. 1739. *Mémoire sur la conservation et le rétablissement des forêts*. Paris: Mémoire de l'Académie royale des sciences.

Burrows, Geoffrey. H. 2013. "Gordon Shillinglaw: Economist, Consultant, and Management Accounting Scholar." *Accounting Horizons* 27.3, pp. 647–58, https://doi.org/10.2308/acch-10348.

Callon, Michel. 1981. "Struggles and Negotiations to Define What Is Problematic and What Is Not." In Karin D. Knorr, Roger Krohn, and Richard Whitley, eds., *The Social Process of Scientific Investigation: Sociology of the Sciences. A Yearbook*, vol .4, pp. 197–219. Dordrecht: Springer, https://doi.org/10.1007/978-94-009-9109-5_8.

_____, ed. 1998a. *The Laws of the Markets*. Oxford, UK: Blackwell / The Sociological Review.

_____. 1998b. "Introduction: The Embeddedness of Economic Markets in Economics." *Sociological Review* 46.1 supplement, pp. 1–57, https://doi.org/10.1111/j.1467-954X.1998.tb03468.x.

_____. 2007. "What Does It Mean to Say That Economics Is Performative?" In Donald MacKenzie, Fabian Muniesa, and Lucia Siu, eds., *Do Economists Make Markets? On the Performativity of Economics*, pp. 311–57. Princeton, NJ: Princeton University Press.

_____. 2009. "Civilizing Markets: Carbon Trading between *in Vitro* and *in*

Vivo Experiments." *Accounting, Organizations and Society* 34.3-4, pp. 535-48, https://doi.org/10.1016/j.aos.2008.04.003.

———, Yuval Millo, and Fabian Muniesa, eds. 2007. *Market Devices*. Malden: Blackwell / The Sociological Review.

———, and Fabian Muniesa. 2005. "Peripheral Vision: Economic Markets as Calculative Collective Devices." *Organization Studies* 26.8, pp. 1229-50, https://doi.org/10.1177/0170840605056393.

Cha, Myong, Bassel Rifai, and Pasha Sarraf. 2013. "Pharmaceutical Forecasting: Throwing Darts?" *Nature Reviews Drug Discovery* 12.10, pp. 737-38, https://doi.org/10.1038/nrd4127.

Chesbrough, Henry. 2006. *Open Innovation: The New Imperative for Creating And Profiting from Technology*. Boston, MA: Harvard Business School Press.

Chiapello, Eve. 2015. "Financialisation of Valuation." *Human Studies* 38.1, pp. 13-35, https://doi.org/10.1007/s10746-014-9337-x.

Chile's Constitution of 1980 with Amendments through 2012. Trans. A. I. Vellvé Torras, A. Staines, and J. J. Ruchti, https://www.constituteproject.org/constitution/Chile_2012.pdf.

Christensen, Clayton. M., Stephen P. Kaufman, and Willy C. Shih. 2008. "Innovation Killers: How Financial Tools Destroy Your Capacity to Do New Things." *Harvard Business Review* 86.1, pp. 98-105 and 137.

Coalition for Rainforest Nations, "Gabon: REDD+ Sovereign Carbon Credits," https://www.youtube.com/watch?v=xy-pgRfw8v4.

Collier, Stephen J. 2014. "Neoliberalism and Natural Disaster: Insurance as Political Technology of Catastrophe." *Journal of Cultural Economy* 7.3, pp. 273-90, https://doi.org/10.1080/17530350.2013.858064.

Comi, Alice, and Jennifer Whyte. 2017. "Future Making and Visual Artefacts: An Ethnographic Study of a Design Project." *Organization Studies* 39.8, pp. 1055-83, https://doi.org/10.1177/0170840617717094.

Comptroller General. 1971. Comptroller General's Resolution on Compensation: Determination of the Compensation to the Nationalized Copper Enterprises, Resolution No. 529, Oct. 11, 1971. *International Legal Materials* 10.6, pp. 1240-53.

Cournot, Antoine-Auguste. 1863. *Principes de la théorie des richesses*. Paris: Vrin.

Dahan, A., ed. 2007. *Les modèles du futur*. La Découverte.

D'Ambrosio, Charles A., and Stewart D, Hodges. 1988. *Study Guide to Accompany Brealey and Myers Principles of Corporate Finance*. New York: McGraw-Hill.

Day, George, and Liam Fahey. 1990. "Putting Strategy into Shareholder Value Analysis." *Harvard Business Review* 68.2, pp. 156–62.

De Onis, Juan. 1971. "Allende Accuses U.S. Copper Interests." *The New York Times*, July 12, p. 1.

De Salomon, Dagobert, and Johann Heinrich Cotta. 1837. *Traité de l'aménagement des forêts: Enseigné à l'Ecole royale forestière*, vols. 1–2. Paris: Au Bureau de l'Almanach du commerce.

Dean, Joel. 1951. *Capital Budgeting: Top-Management Policy on Plant, Equipment, and Product Development*. New York: Columbia University Press.

———. 1953. "Better Management of Capital Expenditures Through Research." *Journal of Finance* 82.2, pp. 119–28, https://doi.org/10.2307/2976334.

———. 1954. "Measuring the Productivity of Capital." *Harvard Business Review* 32.1, pp. 120–13.

Decree Concerning Excess Profits of Copper Companies. 1971. *International Legal Materials* 106, September 28, pp. 1235–40.

Deloitte. 2014. *High Value, High Uncertainty: Measuring Risk in Biopharmaceutical Research and Other Industries Investing in the Future of Health*. Zaventem: Deloitte Belguim.

Deringer, William. 2018. "Compound Interest Corrected: The Imaginative Mathematics of the Financial Future in Early Modern England." *Osiris* 33.1, pp. 109–29, https://doi.org/10.1086/699236.

DiMasi, Joseph A., Ronald W. Hansen, and Henry G. Grabowski. 2003. "The Price of Innovation: New Estimates of Drug Development Costs." *Journal of Health Economics* 22.2, pp 151–85, https://doi.org/10.1016/S0167-6296 (02)00126-1

———. 2016. "Innovation in the Pharmaceutical Industry: New Estimates of R&D Costs." *Journal of Health Economics* 47, pp. 20–33, https://doi.org

/10.1016/j.jhealeco.2016.01.012

Doganova, Lilana. 2011. "Necessarily Untrue: On the Use of the Discounted Cash Flow Formula in Valuation of Exploratory Projects." Paper presented at the 7th Critical Management Studies Conference, CMS7, July 11–13, Naples, Italy, https://hal-mines-paristech.archives-ouvertes.fr/hal-00652887/document.

———. 2013. "Transfer and Exploration: Two Models of Science-Industry Intermediation." *Science and Public Policy* 40.4, pp. 442–52, https://doi.org/10.1093/scipol/scto33.

———. 2014. "Décompter le futur: La formule des flux actualisés et le manager-investisseur." *Sociétés contemporaines* 93.1, pp. 67–87, https://doi.org/10.3917/soco.093.0067.

———. 2015. "Que vaut une molécule? Formulation de la valeur dans les projets de développement de nouveaux médicaments." *Revue d'anthropologie des connaissances* 9.1, pp. 17–38, https://www.cairn.info/revue-anthropologie-des-connaissances-2015-1-page-17.htm.

———. 2018. "Discounting and the Making of the Future: On Uncertainty in Forest Management and Drug Development." In Jens Beckert and Richard Bronk, eds., *Uncertain Futures: Imaginaries, Narratives, and Calculation in the Economy*, pp. 278–97. Oxford, UK: Oxford University Press.

———. 2019. "What Is the Value of ANT Research into Economic Valuation Devices?" In Anders Blok, Ignacio Farias, and Celia Roberts, eds., *The Routledge Companion to Actor-Network Theory* pp. 256–63. London: Routledge, https://doi.org/10.4324/9781315111667-28.

———. 2021. "Discounting the Future: A Political Technology." In Jenny Andersson and Sandra Kemp, eds., *Futures*, pp. 380–94. Oxford, UK: Oxford University Press.

———, and Marie Eyquem-Renault. 2009. "What Do Business Models Do? Innovation Devices in Technology Entrepreneurship." *Research Policy* 38.10, pp. 1559–70, https://doi.org/10.1016/j.respol.2009.08.002.

———, and Peter Karnoe. 2015. "Clean and Profitable: Entangling Valuations in Environmental Entrepreneurship." In Ariane Berthoin Antal, Michael Hutter, and David Stark, eds., *Moments of Valuation: Exploring Sites of*

Dissonance, pp. 229–48. Oxford, UK: Oxford University Press, https://doi. org/10.1093/acprof:oso/9780198702504.003.0012.

_____, and Brice Laurent. 2019. "Carving Out a Domain for the Market: Boundary Making in European Environmental Markets." *Economy and Society* 48.2, pp. 221–42, https://doi.org/10.1080/03085147.2019.162407 1.

_____, and Fabian Muniesa. 2015. "Capitalization Devices: Business Models and the Renewal of Markets." In Martin Kornberger, Lisa Justesen, Anders Koed Madsen, and Jan Mouritsen, eds., *Making Things Valuable*, pp. 109–25. Oxford, UK: Oxford University Press.

_____, and Vololona Rabeharisoa. 2022. "Price as an Epistemic and a Political Object: An inquiry into 'the Most Expensive Drug Ever.'" Paper presented at EGOS conference 2022, panel "Valuation and Critique in the 'Good Economy'," Vienna, Austria.

Dupoy, Georges. 1983. *La chute d'Allende*. Paris: Éditions Robert Laffont.

Economic Commission on Latin America. 1950. *The Economic Development of Latin America and Its Principal Problems*. United Nations, Department of Economic Affairs.

Espeland, Wendy Nelson, and Mitchell L. Stevens. 1998. "Commensuration as a Social Process." *Annual Review of Sociology* 24.1, pp. 313–43, https:// doi.org/10.1146/annurev.soc.24.1.313.

Esposito, Elena 2011. *The Future of Futures: The Time of Money in Financing and Society*. Cheltenham, UK: Edward Elgar.

Etchegaray, Javier. 2017. "Towards a Historiography of the 1973 Nationalization of Chilean Copper." *Ex Post Facto* 26, pp. 9–33.

Ezzamel, Mahmoud, Hugh Willmott, and Frank Worthington. 2008. "Manufacturing Shareholder Value: The Role of Accounting in Organizational Transformation." *Accounting, Organizations and Society* 33.2, pp. 107–40, https://doi.org/10.1016/j.aos.2007.03.001.

Falcoff, Mark. 1989. *Modern Chile: 1970–1989: A Critical History*. New Brunswick, NJ: Transaction Publishers.

Faulhaber, Gerald R., and William J. Baumol. 1988. "Economists as Innovators: Practical Products of Theoretical Research." *Journal of Economic Lit-*

erature 26.2, pp. 577–600, https://www.jstor.org/stable/2726363.

Faustmann, Martin. 1849. "Berechnung des Werthes, welchen Waldboden, sowie noch nicht haubare Holzbestände für die Waldwirtschaft besitzen." *Allgemeine Forst- und Jagdzeitung* 15, pp. 441–55

———. 1968. "Calculation of the Value Which Forest Land and Immature Stands Possess for Forestry." In Michael Gane, ed., *Martin Faustmann and the Evolution of Discounted Cash Flow: Two Articles from the Original German of 1849*, pp. 27–55. Oxford, UK: Commonwealth Forestry Institute, University of Oxford.

Feher, Michel. 2009. "Self-Appreciation; or, The Aspirations of Human Capital." *Public Culture* 21.1, pp. 21–41, https://doi.org/10.1215/08992363 -2008-019.

———. 2017. *Le temps des investis: Essai sur la nouvelle question sociale.* Paris: La Découverte.

———. 2018. *Rated Agency: Investee Politics in a Speculative Age.* Trans. Gregory Elliott. New York: Zone Books.

Fisher, Irving. 1906. *The Nature of Capital and Income.* New York: Macmillan.

———. 1907. *The Rate of Interest: Its Nature, Determination and Relation to Economic Phenomena.* New York: Macmillan.

Fleming, John. 1973. "The Nationalization of Chile's Large Copper Companies in Contemporary Interstate Relations." *Villanova Law Review* 18.4, pp. 593–647, https://digitalcommons.law.villanova.edu/vlr/vol18/iss4/2.

Folkers, Andreas. 2020. "Air-Appropriation: The Imperial Origins and Legacies of the Anthropocene." *European Journal of Social Theory* 23.4, pp. 611–30, https://doi.org/10.1177/1368431020903169.

Fortin, Carlos. 1975. "Compensating the Multinationals: Chile and the United States Copper Companies." *Institute of Development Studies Bulletin* 7.1, pp. 23–29, https://doi.org/10.1111/j.1759-5436.1975.mp7001005.x.

Foucault, Michel. 2004. *Sécurité, territoire, population: Cours au Collège de France, 1977–1978.* Paris: Le Seuil.

———. 2008. *The Birth of Biopolitics: Lectures at the Collège de France 1978–1979.* Trans. Graham Burchell. New York: Palgrave Macmillan.

Freeman, Christopher. 1982. *The Economics of Industrial Innovation*. 2nd ed. London: Frances Pinter.

Fressoz, Jean-Baptiste. 2012. *L'apocalypse joyeuse: Une histoire du risque technologique*. Paris: Le Seuil.

Friedman, H. K. 1982. "Disputes over the Hayes and Abernathy Gospel." Letter to the business editor, *The New York Times*, June 1, https://www.nytimes.com/1982/06/13/business/l-disputes-over-the-hayes-and-abernathy-gospel-206020.html.

Froud, Julie, Colin Haslam, Sukdev Johal, and Karel Williams. 2000. "Shareholder Value and Financialization: Consultancy Promises, Management Moves." *Economy and Society* 29.1, pp. 80–110, https://doi.org/10.1080/030851400360578.

Gane, Michael. 1968. Introduction to Michael Gane, ed., *Martin Faustmann and the Evolution of Discounted Cash Flow: Two Articles from the Original German of 1849*, pp. 5–16. Oxford, UK: Commonwealth Forestry Institute, University of Oxford.

Garfinkel, Harold. 1967. *Studies in Ethnomethodology*. Englewood Cliffs, NJ: Prentice-Hall.

Geiger, Susi, and John Finch. 2016. "Promissories and Pharmaceutical Patents: Agencing Markets through Public Narratives." *Consumption Markets and Culture* 19.1, pp. 71–91, https://doi.org/10.1080/10253866.2015.1067199.

Giraudeau, M. 2012. "Imagining (The Future) Business: How to Make Firms with Plans?" In P. Quattrone, N. Thrift, & F.-R. Puyou, eds., *Imagining Organizations: Performative Imagery in Business and Beyond*, pp. 223–39. New York: Routledge Routledge. https://doi.org/10.4324/9780203807903-19

Goulder, Lawrence H., and Roberton C, Williams III. 2012. "The Choice of Discount Rate for Climate Change Policy Evaluation." *Climate Change Economics* 3.4, p. 1250024, https://doi.org/10.1142/S2010007812500248.

Grab, Denise. 2017. "Trump's Alternative Economics of Climate Change." *The Regulatory Review*, April 24, https://www.theregreview.org/2017/04/24/grab-trumps-alternative-economics-climate-change.

Graham, J. R., and Harvey, C. R. 2001. "The Theory and Practice of Corporate Finance: Evidence from the Field." *Journal of Financial Economics* 60.2-3, pp. 187-243, https://doi.org/10.1016/S0304-405X0100044-7.

Green, Adam. 2019. "Biotech Companies Defend Prices of One-Off Gene Therapy." *Financial Times*, December 9, https://www.ft.com/content/edd639fc-9755-11e9-98b9-e38c177b152f.

Haka, Susan F. 2006. "A Review of the Literature on Capital Budgeting and Investment Appraisal: Past, Present, and Future Musings." In *Handbooks of Management Accounting Research*. Vol. 2, pp. 697-728, https://doi.org/10.1016/S1751-3243(06)02010-4.

Harrington, Scott E. 2012. "Cost of Capital for Pharmaceutical, Biotechnology, and Medical Device Firms." In Patricia M. Danzon and Sean Nicholson, eds., *The Oxford Handbook of the Economics of the Biopharmaceutical Industry*, pp. 75-99. New York: Oxford University Press.

Harrison, Robert Pogue. 1992. *Forests: The Shadow of Civilization*. Chicago: University of Chicago Press.

Hartog, François. 2003. *Régimes d'historicité: Présentisme et expériences du temps*. Paris: Seuil.

Hay, Michael., David W. Thomas, John L. Craighead, Celia Economides, and Jesse Rosenthal. 2014. "Clinical Development Success Rates for Investigational Drugs." *Nature Biotechnology* 32.1, pp. 40-51, https://doi.org/10.1038/nbt.2786.

Hayes, Robert H., and William J. Abernathy. 1980. "Managing Our Way to Economic Decline." *Harvard Business Review* 58.4, pp. 67-77.

———. 2007. "Managing Our Way to Economic Decline (HBR Classic)." *Harvard Business Review*, July 1, https://store.hbr.org/product/managing-our-way-to-economic-decline-hbr-classic/R0707L.

———, and David A. Garvin. 1982. "Managing As If Tomorrow Mattered." In *Managerial Excellence: McKinsey Award Winners from the Harvard Business Review, 1980-1994*, pp. 51-66. Cambridge, MA: Harvard Business Review Press.

———, and Ramchandran Jaikumar. 1988. "Manufacturing's Crisis: New

Technologies, Obsolete Organizations." *Harvard Business Review* 66.5, pp. 77–85.

Holden, Stein T., Bekele Shiferaw, and Mette Wik. 1998. "Poverty, Market Imperfections and Time Preferences: Of Relevance for Environmental Policy?" *Environment and Development Economics* 3.1, pp. 105–30, https://doi.org/10.1017/S1355770X98000060.

Holland, Daniel M., and Stewart C. Meyers. 1979. "Trends in Corporate Profitability and Capital Costs." In Robert Lindsay, ed., *The Nation's Capital Needs: Three Studies*, pp. 103–88. New York: Committee on Economic Development.

———. 1980. "Profitability and Capital Costs for Manufacturing Corporations and All Nonfinancial Corporations." *American Economic Review* 70.2, pp. 320–25.

Hölzl, Richard. 2010. "Historicizing Sustainability: German Scientific Forestry in the Eighteenth and Nineteenth Centuries." *Science as Culture* 19.4, pp. 431–60, https://doi.org/10.1080/09505431.2010.519866.

Hopwood, Anthony G. 1992. "Accounting Calculation and the Shifting Sphere of the Economic." *European Accounting Review* 1.1, pp. 125–43, https://doi.org/10.1080/09638189200000007.

Houston Durrant, Tracy, Daniele de Rigo, and Giovanni Caudullo. n.d. S.v. "Pinus sylvestris in Europe: Distribution, Habitat, Usage and Threats." In Jesus San-Miguel-Ayanz, Daniele de Rigo, Giovanni Caudullo, Tracy Houston Durrant, and Achille Mauri, eds., *European Atlas of Forest Tree Species*, pp. 132–33. Publication Office of the European Union, Luxembourg, https://ies-ows.jrc.ec.europa.eu/efdac/download/Atlas/pdf/Pinus_sylvestris.pdf.

Hull, Cordell. 1938. The Secretary of State to the Mexican Ambassador (Castillo Nájera), July 21, 1938. US Department of State, Office of the Historian, Foreign Relations of the United States Diplomatic Papers, 1938, The American Republics. Volume 5, 812.52/2939a, https://history.state.gov/historicaldocuments/frus1938v05/d662.

Ibbotson, Roger G., and Rex A. Sinquefield. 1976. "Stocks, Bonds, Bills, and Inflation: Year-by-Year Historical Returns 1926–1974." *Journal of Business*

49.1, pp. 11–47.

———. 1982. *Stocks, Bonds, Bills and Inflation: The Past and the Future*. Charlottesville, VA: Financial Analysts Research Foundation.

Indap, Sujeet. 2013, "Discounted Cash Flow: Seeing the Future." *Financial Times*, July 28, https://www.ft.com/content/33bb726c-f0bc-11e2-929c-00144feabdc0.

Innerarity, Daniel. 2012. *The Future and Its Enemies: In Defense of Political Hope*. Trans. Sandra Kingery. Stanford, CA: Stanford University Press.

Istvan, Donald F. 1961. "The Economic Evaluation of Capital Expenditures." *Journal of Business* 34.1, pp. 45–51.

Jefferson, Michael. 2012. "Shell Scenarios: What Really Happened in the 1970s and What May Be Learned for Current World Prospects." *Technological Forecasting and Social Change* 79.1, pp. 186–97, https://doi.org/10.1016/j.techfore.2011.08.007.

Jensen, Michael C., and William H. Meckling. 1976. "Theory of the Firm: Managerial Behavior, Agency Costs and Ownership Structure." *Journal of Financial Economics* 3.4, pp. 305–60, https://doi.org/10.1016/0304-405X(76)90026-X.

Johnson, H. Thomas, and Robert S. Kaplan. 1987. *Relevance Lost: The Rise and Fall of Management Accounting*. Boston, MA: Harvard Business School Press.

Kahneman, Daniel, and Amos Tversky. 1979. "Prospect Theory: An Analysis of Decision under Risk." *Econometrica* 47.2, pp. 263–91, https://doi.org/10.2307/1914185.

Kaplan, Robert S. 1986. "Must CIM be Justified by Faith Alone?" *Harvard Business Review* 64.2, pp. 87–95.

Karopka, Manuel, and Mirjam Milad. 2007. "The Scots Pine—Tree of the Year 2007." *Waldwissen.Net*, February 26, https://www.waldwissen.net/wald/baeume_waldpflanzen/nadel/fva_waldkiefer/index_EN.

Karpik, Lucien. 1989. "L'économie de la qualité." *Revue Française de Sociologie* 30.2, pp. 187–210.

———. 2010. *Valuing the Unique: The Economics of Singularities*. Princeton, NJ: Princeton University Press.

Kelleher, J. Paul. 2017. "Descriptive versus Prescriptive Discounting in Climate Change Policy Analysis." *Georgetown Journal of Law and Public Policy* 15, pp. 957–77, https://philarchive.org/rec/JPADVP.

Kennecott Copper Corp. 1971. *Expropriationof El Teniente, the Worlds Largest Underground Copper Mine.* Reprinted in Richard B. Lillich, ed., *The Valuation of Nationalized Property in International Law.* Vol. 3. Charlottesville: University Press of Virginia, 1975.

Keynes, John Maynard. 1936. *The General Theory of Employment, Interest and Money.* London: Palgrave Macmillan.

———. 1937. "The General Theory of Emplyment." *Quarterly Journal of Economics* 51.2, pp. 209–23, http://www.jstor.org/stable/1882087.

Klammer, Thomas. 1972. "Empirical Evidence of the Adoption of Sophisticated Capital Budgeting Techniques." *Journal of Business* 45.3, pp. 387–97, http://dx.doi.org/10.1086/295467.

Klemick, Heather, and Mahmud Yesuf. 2008. "Do Discount Rates Change Over Time? Experimental Evidence from Ethiopia." Environment for Development Discussion Paper Series, https://ideas.repec.org/p/rff/dpaper/dp-08-06-efd.html.

Knight, Frank H. 1921 [1964]. *Risk, Uncertainty and Profit.* New York: Kelley Reprint of Economic Classics.

Knights, David, and Theodore Vurdubakis. 1993. "Calculations of Risk: Towards an Understanding of Insurance as a Moral and Political Technology." *Accounting, Organizations and Society* 18.7, pp. 729–64, https://doi.org/10.1016/0361-3682(93)90050-G.

Kohn, Eduardo. 2013. *How Forests Think: Toward an Anthropology beyond the Human.* Berkeley: University of California Press.

Kola, Ismail, and John Landis. 2004. "Can the Pharmaceutical Industry Reduce Attrition Rates?" *Nature Reviews Drug Discovery* 3.8, pp. 711–16, https://doi.org/10.1038/nrd1470.

Koselleck, Reinhart. 1985. *Futures Past: On the Semantics of Historical Time.* Trans. Keith Tribe. New York: Columbia University Press.

———. 2016. "Raccourcissement du temps et accélération." *Écrire l'histoire* 16, pp. 27–48, https://doi.org/10.4000/elh.1052.

Krasts, Aivars. 1982. "More Gospel." Letter to the busisness editor, *The New York Times*, June 20, https://www.nytimes.com/1982/06/20/business/l-more-gospel-223215.html.

Kraus, Kalle, and Torkel Strömsten. 2012. "Going Public: The Role of Accounting and Shareholder Value in Making Sense of an IPO." *Management Accounting Research* 23.3, pp. 186–201, https://doi.org/10.1016/j.mar.2012.05.003.

La Fontaine, Jean de. 1882. *The Fables of La Fontaine*. Trans. Elizur Wright. *Full Text Archive*, https://cdn.fulltextarchive.com/wp-content/uploads/wp-advanced-pdf/1/The-Fables-of-La-Fontaine.pdf.

Laurent, Brice. 2017. *Democratic Experiments: Problematizing Nanotechnology and Democracy in Europe and the United States*. Cambridge, MA: MIT Press.

Lauterpacht, Eli. 1990. "Issues of Compensation and Nationality in the Taking of Energy Investments." *Journal of Energy and Natural Resources Law* 8.1–4, pp. 241–50, https://doi.org/10.1080/02646811.1990.11433693.

Law 17450, Reforma la Constitucion Politica del Estado, 16-07-1971, https://www.bcn.cl/leychile/navegar?i=29026.

Law 18097, Ley Organica Constitucional sobre Concesiones Mineras, 21-01-1982, https://www.bcn.cl/leychile/navegar?idNorma=29522.

Lazonick, William, and Mary O'Sullivan. 2000. "Maximizing Shareholder Value: A New Ideology for Corporate Governance." *Economy and Society* 29.1, pp. 13–35, https://doi.org/10.1080/030851400360541.

Le Monde. 2022. "En Gironde, Elisabeth Borne annonce un 'renfort de moyens' face aux feux de forêt, 'liés au dérèglement climatique'." *Le Monde*, August 11, https://www.lemonde.fr/politique/article/2022/08/11/feux-de-foret-on-sait-tres-bien-qu-ils-sont-lies-au-dereglement-climatique-declare-elisabeth-borne_6137787_823448.html.

Le Roy, G. 1757. S.v. "Forêt." In Denis Diderot and Jean le Rond d'Alembert, eds., *Encyclopédie, Dictionnaire raisonné des sciences, des arts et des métiers, par une Société de Gens de lettres*, https://encyclopedie.uchicago.edu.

Lebègue, Daniel. 2005. *Révision du taux d'actualisation des investissements publics*. Paris: Commissariat Général au Plan.

Lemkin, Jack. 1982. "Disputes over the Hayes and Abernathy Gospel." Letter to the business editor, *The New York Times*, June 13, https://www.nytimes.com/1982/06/13/business/l-disputes-over-the-hayes-and-abernathy-gospel-203649.html.

Levy, Jonathan. 2014. "Accounting for Profit and the History of Capital." *Critical Historical Studies* 1.2, pp. 171–214, https://doi.org/10.1086/677977.

———. 2017. "Capital as Process and the History of Capitalism." *Business History Review* 91.3, pp. 483–510, https://doi.org/10.1017/S0007680517001064.

Leyshon, Andrew, and Nigel Thrift. 2007. "The Capitalization of Almost Everything: The Future of Finance and Capitalism." *Theory, Culture and Society* 24.7–8, pp. 97–115, https://doi.org/10.1177/0263276407084699.

Libyan American Oil Co. v. Libyan Arab Republic, 20 I.L.M. 1,78-79 1981, https://jusmundi.com/en/document/decision/en-libyan-american-oil-company-v-the-government-of-the-libyan-arab-republic-award-tuesday-12th-april-1977.

Lillich, Richard B., ed. 1975. *The Valuation of Nationalized Property in International Law*. Vol. 3. Charlottesville: University Press of Virginia.

Linebaugh, Peter. 1976. "Karl Marx, the Theft of Wood, and Working Class Composition: A Contribution to the Current Debate." *Social Justice* 40.1–2, pp. 137–61.

Lordon, Frédéric. 2000. "La 'création de valeur' comme rhétorique et comme pratique: *Généalogie et sociologie de la 'valeur actionnariale.'*" *L'Année de La Régulation* 4, pp. 117–65.

Lowood, Henry E. 1991. "The Calculating Forester: Quantification, Cameral Science and the Emergence of Scientific Forestry Management in Germany." In Torre Frängsmyr, J. L. Heilbronn, and Robin E. Rider, eds., *The Quantifying Spirit in the 18th Century*, pp. 315–42. Berkeley: University of California Press.

Lynch, Michael. 2012. "Revisiting the Cultural Dope." *Human Studies* 35.2, pp. 223–33, https://doi.org/10.1007/s10746-012-9227-z.

MacKenzie, Donald. 2003. "An Equation and Its Worlds: Bricolage, Exemplars, Disunity and Performativity in Financial Economics." *Social Stud-*

ies of Science 33.6, pp. 831–68, https://doi.org/10.1177/0306312703336002.

———. 2004. "The Big, Bad Wolf and the Rational Market: Portfolio Insurance, the 1987 Crash and the Performativity of Economics." *Economy and Society* 33.3, pp. 303–34, https://doi.org/10.1080/0308514042000225680.

———. 2006. *An Engine, Not a Camera: How Financial Models Shape Markets.* Cambridge, MA: MIT Press.

———, and Yuval Millo. 2003. "Constructing a Market, Performing Theory: The Historical Sociology of a Financial Derivatives Exchange." *American Journal of Sociology* 109.1, pp. 107–45, https://doi.org/10.1086/374404.

———, Fabian Muniesa, and Siu Leung-Sea, eds. 2007. *Do Economists Make Markets? On the Performativity of Economics.* Princeton, NJ: Princeton University Press.

———, and Taylor Spears. 2014a. "'The Formula That Killed Wall Street': The Gaussian Copula and Modelling Practices in Investment Banking." *Social Studies of Science* 44.3, pp. 393–417, https://doi.org/10.1177 0306312713517157.

———. 2014b. "'A Device for Being Able to Book P&L': The Organizational Embedding of the Gaussian Copula." *Social Studies of Science* 44.3, pp. 418–40, https://doi.org/10.1177/0306312713517158.

Mann, Geoff. 2022. "Check Your Spillover: The Climate Colossus." *London Review of Books* 44.3, February 10. Review of William D, Nordhaus, *The Spirit of Green: The Economics of Collisions and Contagions in a Crowded World* (Princeton, NJ: Princeton University Press, 2021), https://www.lrb.co.uk/the-paper/v44/n03/geoff-mann/check-your-spillover.

Mårald, Erland, and Erik Westholm. 2016. "Changing Approaches to the Future in Swedish Forestry, 1850–2010." *Nature and Culture* 11.1, pp. 1–21, https://www.jstor.org/stable/26430609.

Marx, Karl. 1904. *A Contribution to the Critique of Political Economy.* Trans N. I. Stone. Chicago: Charles Kerr.

———. 1842. "Proceedings of the Sixth Rhine Province Assembly. Third Article. Debates on the Law of Thefts of Wood." *Rheinische Zeitung* 298, 300, 303, 305, and 307, https://www.marxists.org/archive/marx/works/download/Marx_Rheinishe_Zeitung.pdf

Marzal, Toni. 2021. "Quantum (In)Justice: Rethinking the Calculation of Compensation and Damages in ISDS." *Journal of World Investment and Trade* 22.2, pp. 249–312, https://doi.org/10.1163/22119000-12340209.

Mazzucato, Mariana. 2018. *The Value of Everything: Making and Taking in the Global Economy.* London: Allen Lane.

McGoey, Linsey. 2009. "Pharmaceutical Controversies and the Performative Value of Uncertainty." *Science as Culture* 18.2, pp. 151–64, https://doi.org/10.1080/09505430902885474.

McNulty, James J., Tony D. Yeh, William S. Schultze, and Michael H. Lubatkin. 2002. "What's Your Real Cost of Capital?" *Harvard Business Review* 80.10, pp. 114–21.

Merlin, Julien, Brice Laurent, and Yann Gunzburger. 2021. "Promise Engineering: Investment and Its Conflicting Anticipations in the French Mining Revival." *Economy and Society* 50.4, pp. 590–617, https://doi.org/10.1080/03085147.2021.1903772.

Miller, Peter. 1991. "Accounting Innovation beyond the Enterprise: Problematizing Investment Decisions and Programming Economic Growth in the U.K. in the 1960s." *Accounting, Organizations and Society* 16.8, pp. 733–62, https://doi.org/10.1016/0361-36829190022-7.

———, and Christopher Napier. 1993. "Genealogies of Calculation." *Accounting, Organizations and Society* 18.7, pp. 631–47, https://doi.org/10.1016/0361-3682(93)90047-A.

———, and Nikolas Rose. 1990." Governing Economic Life." *Economy and Society* 19.1, pp. 1–31, https://doi.org/10.1080/03085149000000001.

Montagne, Sabine, and Horacio Ortiz. 2013. "Sociologie de l'agence financière: Enjeux et perspectives. Introduction." *Sociétés contemporaines* 92.4, pp. 7–33, https://doi.org/10.3917/soco.092.0007.

Montgomery, Catherine. M. 2017. "From Standardization to Adaptation: Clinical Trials and the Moral Economy of Anticipation." *Science as Culture* 26.2, pp. 232–54, https://doi.org/10.1080/09505431.2016.1255721.

Moog, Martin, and Matthias Bösch. 2013. "Interest Rates in the German Forest Valuation Literature of the Early Nineteenth Century." *Forest Policy and Economics* 30, pp. 1–5, https://doi.org/10.1016/j.forpol.2013.03.004.

Moran, Theodore H. 1974. *Multinational Corporations and the Politics of Dependence: Copper in Chile*. Princeton, NJ: Princeton University Press.

Muniesa, Fabian, Liliana Doganova, Horacio Ortiz, Florence Paterson, Alaric Bourgoin, Véra Ehrenstein, Pierre-André Juven, David Pontille, Basak Saraç-Lesavre, and Guillaume Yon. 2017. *Capitalization: A Cultural Guide*. Paris: Presses des Mines.

———, and Liliana Doganova. 2020. "The Time That Money Requires: Use of the Future and Critique of the Present in Financial Valuation." *Finance and Society* 6.2, pp. 95–113, https://doi.org/10.2218/finsoc.v6i2.5269.

Myers, Stewart C. 1984. "Finance Theory and Financial Strategy." *INFORMS Journal on Applied Analytics* 14.1, pp. 126–37, https://doi.org/10.1287/inte.14.1.126.

———, and Lakshmi Shyam-Sunder. 1996. "Measuring Pharmaceutical Industry Risk and the Cost of Capital." In Robert B. Helms, ed. *Competitive Strategies in the Pharmaceutical Industry*, pp. 208–37. Washington, DC: AEI Press.

———, and Stuart M. Turnbull. 1977. "Capital Budgeting and the Capital Asset Pricing Model: Good News and Bad News." *Journal of Finance* 3.22, pp. 321–33, https://doi.org/10.1111/j.1540-6261.1977.tb03272.x.

Nixon Tapes. n.d.. http://nixontapes.org/chile.html.

Noirot-Bonnet, Louis. 1842. *Théorie de l'aménagement des forêts 1840*. 2nd ed. Paris: Bouchard-Huzard.

Nordblad, Julia. 2016. "Time for Politics: How a Conceptual History of Forests Can Help Us Politicize the Long Term." *European Journal of Social Theory* 20.1, pp. 164–82, https://doi.org/10.1177/1368431016653241.

———. 2018. "Historicising the Question of Democracy's Presentism: The Concept of Interest and Political Languages of the Future in France, 1830–1850." *Redescriptions: Political Thought, Conceptual History and Feminist Theory* 21.4, pp. 44–70, http://doi.org/10.7227/R.21.1.4.

———. 2021. "Concepts of Future Generations: Four Contemporary Examples." In Jenny Andersson and Sandra Kemp, eds., *Futures*, pp. 364–79. Oxford, UK: Oxford University Press.

Nordhaus, William. 2007. "Critical Assumptions in the Stern Review on

Climate Change." *Science* 317.5835, pp. 201–202, https://doi.org/10.1126/science.1137316.

Novitski, Joseph. 1971, "Chile Nullifies Payments for Seized Copper Mines." *The New York Times*, September 29, https://www.nytimes.com/1971/09/29/archives/chile-nullifies-payments-for-seized-copper-mines-chile-nullifies.html.

Novoa Monreal, Eduardo. 1972. *La nacionalización chilena del cobre: Comentarios y documentos.* Also titled *La batalla por el cobre.* Santiago: Ediciones Quimantú.

OECD. 2018. *Cost-Benefit Analysis and the Environment: Further Developments and Policy Use.* Paris: OECD Publishing, https://doi.org/10.1787/9789264085169-en

Olofsson, Tobias. 2020a. "Mining Futures: Predictions and Uncertainty in Swedish Mineral Exploration." PhD diss., Uppsala University.

———. 2020b. "Imagined Futures in Mineral Exploration." *Journal of Cultural Economy* 13.3, pp. 265–77, https://doi.org/10.1080/17530350.2019.1604399.

Ortiz, Horacio. 2013. "La 'valeur' dans l'industrie financière: Le prix des actions cotées comme 'vérité' technique et politique." *L'année sociologique* 63.1, pp. 107–36, https://doi.org/10.3917/anso.131.0107.

———. 2014a. "The Limits of Financial Imagination: Free Investors, Efficient Markets, and Crisis." *American Anthropologist* 116.1, pp. 38–50, http://www.jstor.org/stable/24028891.

———. 2014b. *Valeur financière et vérité: Enquête d'anthropologie politique sur l'évaluation des entreprises cotées en Bourse.* Paris: Les Presses de Sciences Po.

———. 2022. "Political Imaginaries of the Weighted Average Cost of Capital: A Conceptual Analysis." *Valuation Studies* 8.2, pp. 5–36, https://doi.org/10.3384/VS.2001-5992.2021.8.2.5-36.

Ossandón, José, and Sebastián Ureta. 2019. "Problematizing Markets: Market Failures and the Government of Collective Concerns." *Economy and Society* 48.2, pp. 175–96, https://doi.org/10.1080/03085147.2019.1576433.

Øvstebø Tvedten, Irene. 2022. "Distributed Accountability: Picking a Carbon Price for Cost–Benefit Analysis." *Journal of Cultural Economy* 15.3, pp. 358–72, https://doi.org/10.1080/17530350.2022.2028649.

Pandey, Mohan. 2003." Investment Decisions in Pharmaceutical R&D Projects." *Drug Discovery Today* 8.21, pp. 968–71, https://doi.org/10.1016/S1359-6446(03)02731-4.

Perrings, Charles. 1989. "An Optimal Path to Extinction? Poverty and Resource Degradation in the Open Agrarian Economy." *Journal of Development Economics* 30.1, pp. 1–24, https://doi.org/10.1016/0304-3878(89)90048-5.

Petty, J. William, David F. Scott, and Monroe M. Bird. 1975. "The Capital Expenditure Decision-Making Process of Large Corporations." *Engineering Economist* 20.3, pp. 159–72, https://doi.org/10.1080/00137917508965140.

Peyron, Jean-Luc, and Jacques Maheut. 1999. "Les fondements de l'économie forestière moderne: Le rôle capital de Faustmann, il y a 150 ans, et celui de quelques-uns de ses précurseurs et successeurs." *Revue Forestière Française* 51.6, pp.679–98, http://dx.doi.org/10.4267/2042/5479.

Pezet, Anne. 1997. "The Development of Discounted Cash Flow and Profitability of Investment in France in the 1960s." *Accounting, Business and Financial History* 7.3, pp. 367–80, https://doi.org/10.1080/095852097330685.

Piñera Echenique, José. 1981a. "Anuncio de aprobación de la Ley Constitucional Minera," *La revolución chilena*, December 2, http://www.josepinera.org/RevChilena/chile_mineria_discurso.htm.

———. 1981b. *Fundamentos de la Ley Constitucional Minera, josepinera.org*, http://www.josepinera.org/zrespaldo/leyminera.pdf.

———. 2004. "Wealth through Ownership: Creating Property Rights in Chilean Mining." *Cato Journal* 24.3, pp. 295–301.

Pisano, Gary P. 2006. *Science Business: The Promise, the Reality, and the Future of Biotech*. Cambridge, MA: Harvard Business Review Press.

Pollard, Sidney. 1965. *The Genesis of Modern Management: A Study of the Industrial Revolution in Great Britain*. Cambridge, MA: Harvard University Press.

POPI. 1998. "Report of Research and Educational Activities." MIT's Program on the Pharmaceutical Industry, *MIT*, June, http://web.mit.edu/popi/annrpt97.html.

Porter, Theodore M. 1995. *Trust in Numbers: The Pursuit of Objectivity in Science and Public Life*. Princeton, NJ: Princeton University Press.

Pottage, Alain. 2019. "Holocene Jurisprudence." *Journal of Human Rights and the Environment* 10.2, pp. 153–75, https://doi.org/10.4337/jhre.2019.02.01.

Pottier, Antonin. 2018. "Climat: William Nordhaus est-il bien sérieux?" *Alternatives Economiques*, October 9, https://www.alternatives-economiques.fr/climat-william-nordhaus-bien-serieux/00086544.

Pradier, Pierre-Charles, and David Teira Serrano. 2000. "Frank H. Knight: Le risque comme critique de l'économie politique." *Revue de Synthèse* 121.1, pp. 79–116, https://doi.org/10.1007/BF02962737.

Pretzsch, H. 2001. "Models for Pure and Mixed Forests." In J. Evans, ed., *The Forests Handbook, Volume 1: An Overview of Forest Science* , vol. 1, pp. 210–28). Hoboken, NJ: Blackwell Science.

PwC. 2017. *PwC International Arbitration Damages Research—2017 update*, https://www.pwc.co.uk/forensic-services/assets/pwc-international-arbitration-damages-research-2017.pdf.

Radkau, Joachim. 2007. *Holz: Wie ein Naturstoff Geschichte schreibt*. Munich: Oekom.

———. 2008. *Nature and Power: A Global History of the Environment*. Cambridge, UK: Cambridge University Press.

Razgatis, Richard. 1999. *Early-Stage Technologies: Valuation and Pricing*. New York: Wiley.

Righetti, Erin. 2017. "Mounting Uncertainty Threatens Research and Innovation in Medicines." *Informaconnect*, July 15, https://informaconnect.com/mounting-uncertainty-threatens-research-and-innovation-in-medicines.

Roberts, John, Paul Sanderson, Richard Barker, and John Hendry. 2006. "In the Mirror of the Market: The Disciplinary Effects of Company/Fund Manager Meetings." *Accounting, Organizations and Society* 31.3, pp. 277–

94, https://doi.org/10.1016/j.aos.2005.02.001.

Rosa, Harmut. 2013. *Social Acceleration: A New Theory of Modernity*. Trans. Jonathan Trejo-Mathys. New York: Columbia University Press.

Rubinstein, Mark. 2003. "Great Moments in Financial Economics: I. Present Value." *Journal Of Investment Management* 1.1, pp. 7–13.

Sallman, Doug, Erin Flanigan, Krista Jeannote, Chris Hedden, and Dororthy Morallos. 2012. *Operations Benefit/Cost Analysis Desk Reference* FHWA-HOP-12-028. U.S. Department of Transportation, Federal Highway Administration, https://ops.fhwa.dot.gov/publications/fhwahop12028/fhwahop12028.pdf.

Samuelson, Paul A. 1976. "Economics of Forestry in an Evolving Society." *Economic Inquiry* 14.4, pp. 466–92, https://doi.org/10.1111/j.1465-7295.1976.tb00437.x.

Savage, Sam L. 2012. *The Flaw of Averages: Why We Underestimate Risk in the Face of Uncertainty*. Hoboken, NJ: Wiley.

Scorgie, Michael E. 1996. "Evolution of the Application of Present Value to Valuation of Non-Monetary Resources." *Accounting and Business Research* 26.3, pp. 237–48, https://doi.org/10.1080/00014788.1996.9729514.

Scott, James C. 1998. *Seeing Like a State: How Certain Schemes to Improve the Human Condition Have Failed*. New Haven, CT: Yale University Press.

Seibt, Sébastian. 2022. "As France Battles Wildfires, Experts Call for a Rethink of Forest Management. *France24*, July 19, https://www.france24.com/en/europe/20220719-as-france-battles-wildfires-experts-call-for-a-rethink-of-forest-management.

Seligman, Martin E. P., Peter Railton, Roy F. Baumeister, and Chandra Sripada. 2016. *Homo prospectus*. Oxford, UK: Oxford University Press.

Shabecoff, Philip. 1985. "Budget Office Attacked over Rules for Asbestos." *The New York Times*, October 4, www.nytimes.com/1985/10/04/us/budget-office-attacked-over-rules-for-asbestos.html.

Shackle, G. L. S. 1972. *Epistemics and Economics: A Critique of Economic Doctrine*. New Brunswick, NJ: Transaction Publishers.

Shillinglaw, Gordon. 1959. "Managing Capital Expenditures: Appraisal of Specific Proposals." *Engineering Economist* 4.3, pp. 1–21, https://doi.

org/10.1080/00137915908968391.

Simmons, Joshua B. 2013. "Valuation in Investor-State Arbitration: Toward a More Exact Science." In John Norton Moore, ed., *International Arbitration: Contemporary Issues and Innovations*, pp. 53–114. Leiden: Martinus Nijhoff.

Smith, Gerald W. 1967. "A Brief History of Interest Calculations." *Journal of Industrial Engineering* 18, pp. 569–74.

Spathelf, Peter, and Christian Ammer. 2015. "Forest Management of Scots Pine (*Pinus sylvestris L*) in Northern Germany: A Brief Review of the History and Current Trends." *Forstarchiv* 86.3, pp. 59–66, https://www.researchgate.net/publication/281735726_Forest_management_of _scots_pine_Pinus_sylvestris_L_in_northern_Germany-a_brief_ review_of_the_history_and_current_trends.

Spilimbergo, Antonio. 1999. *Copper and the Chilean Economy, 1960–98.* IMF Working paper, https://www.imf.org/en/Publications/WP/ Issues/2016/12/30/Copper-and-the-Chilean-Economy-196098-2993.

Stanley Robinson, Kim. 2020. *The Ministry for the Future*. New York: Orbit Books.

Stein, Rob. 2019. "At $2.1 Million, New Gene Therapy Is the Most Expensive Drug Ever." *Npr*, May 24, https://www.npr.org/sections/health-shots/2019/05/24/725404168/at-2-125-million-new-gene-therapy-is-the -most-expensive-drug-ever?t=1609368038973.

Stern, Nicholas. 2007. *The Economics of Climate Change: The Stern Review.* Cambridge, UK: Cambridge University Press.

Sunder Rajan, Kaushik. 2006. *Biocapital: The Constitution of Postgenomic Life*. Durham, NC: Duke University Press.

Svetlova, Ekaterina. 2012. "On the Performative Power of Financial Models." *Economy and Society* 41.3, pp. 418–34, https://doi.org/10.1080/03085147.2 011.616145.

Thaler, Richard. 1981. "Some Empirical Evidence on Dynamic Inconsistency." *Economics Letters* 8.3, pp. 201–207, https://doi. org/10.1016/0165-1765(81)90067-7.

_____, and Shlomo Benartzi. 2004. "Save More Tomorrow™: Using Behavioral Economics to Increase Employee Saving." *Journal of Political Economy* 112.1, part 2, pp. 164–87, https://doi.org/10.1086/380085.

Thomas, David W., Justin Burns, John Audette, Adam Carroll, Corey Dow-Hygelund, and Michael Hay. 2016. *Clinical Development Success Rates 2006–2015*. Amplion, Inc., https://www.bio.org/sites/default/files/legacy/bioorg/docs/Clinical%20Development%20Success%20Rates%202006-2015%20-%20BIO,%20Biomedtracker,%20Amplion%202016.pdf.

United Nations General Assembly Resolution 1803, adopted on December 14, 1962, on Permanent Sovereignty Over Natural Resources. n.d., https://www.ohchr.org/en/instruments-mechanisms/instruments/general-assembly-resolution-1803-xvii-14-december-1962-permanent.

US Congress, Office of Technology Assessment. 1993. *Pharmaceutical R&D: Costs, Risks and Rewards* OTCambridge: A-H-522, https://ota.fas.org/reports/9336.pdf.

Valdes, Juan. Gabriel. 1995. *Pinochet's Economists: The Chicago School of Economics in Chile*. Cambridge, UK: Cambridge University Press.

Varenne de Fenille, Philibert-Charles-Marie. 1791. *Observations sur l'aménagement des forêts, et particulièrement des forêts nationales présentées à l'Assemblée nationale, par la Société royale d'agriculture, le 9 juin 1791*. Paris: Feuille du Culvateur.

Vatin, François. 2005. "Aménagement forestier et métaphysique économique XVIIIe–XIXe siècles: Le premier débat sur le 'développement durable'." In Jean-Paul Maréchal and Béatrice Quenault, eds., *Le développement durable: Une perspective pour le XXIe siècle*, pp. 51–67. Rennes: Presses universitaires de Rennes.

_____. 2008. "L'esprit d'ingénieur: Pensée calculatoire et éthique économique." *Revue Française de Socio-Économie* 1.1, pp. 131–52, https://doi.org/10.3917/rfse.001.0131.

_____. 2012. *L'espérance-monde: Essai sur l'idée de progrès à l'heure de la mondialisation*. Paris: Albin Michel.

_____. 2013. "Le produit de la nature et le temps des hommes: Don, service et rendement." *Revue du MAUSS* 42.2, pp. 221–45, https://doi.org/10.3917/

rdm.042.0221.

Vidalou, Jean-Baptiste. 2017. *Être forêts: Habiter des territoires en lutte.* Paris: La Découverte.

Viitala, E.-J. 2006. "An early contribution of Martin Faustmann to natural resource economics." *Journal of Forest Economics* 12(2), pp. 131–44, https://doi.org/10.1016/j.jfe.2006.04.001

von Gehren, E. 1849. "Ueber Geldwerthbestimmung des holzleeren Waldbodens." *Allgemeine Forst- und Jagdzeitung* 15, pp. 361–66.

———. 1968. "On the Determination of the Money Value of Bare Forest Land." In Michael Gane, ed., *Martin Faustmann and the Evolution of Discounted Cash Flow: Two Articles from the Original German of 1849*, pp. 19–26. Oxford, UK: Commonwealth Forestry Institute, University of Oxford.

Warde, Paul. 2006. *Ecology, Economy and State Formation in Early Modern Germany.* Cambridge, UK: Cambridge University Press.

———. 2011. "The Invention of Sustainability." *Modern Intellectual History* 8.1, pp. 153–70, https://doi.org/10.1017/S1479244311000096.

Wayne, Leslie. 1982. "Management Gospel Gone Wrong." *The New York Times*, May 30, https://www.nytimes.com/1982/05/30/business/management-gospel-gone-wrong.html.

World Commission on Environment and Development (WCED). 1987. *Our Common Future: Report of the World Commission on Environment and Development*, https://sustainabledevelopment.un.org/content/documents/5987our
-common-future.pdf.

Weisbach, David A., and Cass R. Sunstein. 2009. "Climate Change and Discounting the Future: A Guide for the Perplexed." *Yale Law and Policy Review* 27, pp. 433–57, https://openyls.law.yale.edu/handle/20.500.13051/17104?show=full.

Weller, James. W. 1986. "International Parties, Breach of Contract, and the Recovery of Future Profits." *Hofstra Law Review* 15.2, pp. 323–51.

Westapher, Geoff. 2013. "Details of Your Incompetence Do Not Interest Me." *Beer Business Unplugged*, March 5, http://www.beerbusinessunplugged.com/?p=130.

Weszkalnys, Gisa. 2014. "Anticipating Oil: The Temporal Politics of a Disaster Yet to Come." *Sociological Review* 62.1 supplement, pp. 211–35, https://doi.org/10.1111/1467-954X.12130.

Williams, Karel. 2000. "From Shareholder Value to Present-Day Capitalism." *Economy and Society* 29.1, pp. 1–12, https://doi.org/10.1080/030851400360532.

Winner, Langdon. 1980. "Do Artifacts Have Politics?" *Daedalus* 109.1, pp. 121–36, http://www.jstor.org/stable/20024652.

World Bank. 1996. *A Mining Strategy for Latin America and the Caribbean.* World Bank Technical Paper no. 345, https://documents.worldbank.org/pt/publication/documents-reports/documentdetail/650841468087551845/a-mining-strategy-for-latin-america-and-the-caribbean.

Zeff, Stephen A. 2008. "The Contribution of the Harvard Business School to Management Control, 1908–1980." *Journal of Management Accounting Research* 20.1, pp. 175–208, https://doi.org/10.2308/jmar.2008.20.s-1.175.

Zelizer, Viviana A. 1994. *Pricing the Priceless Child: The Changing Social Value of Children.* Princeton, NJ: Princeton University Press.

Index

Innerarity, Daniel, 18, 23, 248, 263.
Instantness, 21, 98–99, 104, 107.
Interdependency, 154–55.
Interest rate: and discounting, 10–11, 29; linkage between capital and income, 44–45; market, 117–18; "natural," 45. *See also* Present value.
Internal rate of return, 143, 145, 174, 198.
International law, 217, 229, 231, 238, 249.
International Monetary Fund, 220.
Investment, 15; and consequences of discounting, 150.
Investors, 15, 19–20, 49, 73, 77–78, 80, 129, 165, 262; and cost of capital, 29, 48–49, 133, 143–44; expectations of, 143, 241–42, 249; forest owners as, 86, 88–89, 104, 109, 110, 120, 125–26; government or state as, 51, 89; international, and national governments, 215, 217, 230; monopolistic positions of, 244; and regulatory risk, 242; state compensation for (in) action of, 250; and states, 218, 226, 245–46, 250; and uncertainty, 183, 240–41; views of, embedded in discounting, 49, 142. *See also* Financialization of discounting.
Iran-United States Claims Tribunal, 225.
IRR. *See* Internal rate of return.
Irreversibility, 154–55.
Istvan, D. F., 145.

JAIKUMAR, RAMCHANDRAN, 157, 158, 165.
Janssen, 197.
Japan, 150, 153, 154, 167.
Jefferson, Thomas, 248.
Joel Dean Associates, 141, 142, 144.
Johnson, H. Thomas, 139–40.

KABYLE TRADITIONAL SOCIETY, 75, 256.
Kahneman, Daniel, 170.
Kaplan, Robert S., 139–40, 165, 166.
Karpik, Lucien, 177, 257, 282 n.3.
Kennecott, 227, 229, 232, 233–34, 235, 243–44.
Keynes, John Maynard, 175–76, 178.
Kissinger, Henry, 238.
Klammer, Thomas, 146.
Knight, Frank, 173, 175, 179–83, 193, 195, 209; theory of knowledge, 173, 179, 181–82, 195, 209; theory of profit, 173, 179, 181–82, 209.
Korean War, 245.
Koselleck, Reinhart, 74–76.

LA FONTAINE, JEAN DE, 99, 103.
Laws of the Markets (Callon), 55, 257.
Le Roy, Georges, 109.
Levy, Jonathan, 31, 139–40.
Life annuities, 81.
Linebaugh, Peter, 106.
London Metal Exchange, 245.
London Stock Exchange, 77, 78.
Lordon, Frédéric, 41.

MACKENZIE, DONALD, 54–55.
Managerial Economics (Dean), 136.
Managers, US, 129, 140, 147, 151–56, 158, 165; and influence of finance theory, 155–56; investment behavior of, 58–59, 130, 133, 136–37, 142, 143–44, 148–49, 163; and marketing, 155; and misuse of financial tools, 160–61; and rationalization of decision-making, 29, 132, 136–37, 153, 155.
Managing Our Way to Economic Decline (Hayes and Abernathy), 154, 159.
Mann, Geoff, 14–15.
Marginal analysis, 82.

Market, the: and judgment devices, 177; as site of veridiction, 66–67; social mechanisms in, 170, 177–78, 257; sociological accounts of, 257. *See also* Instantness.

Market-derived capital pricing model, 208, 287 n.33.

Market prices, and valuation, 92–93, 98.

Marx, Karl, 21, 53, 105, 107.

Marzal, Toni, 225, 226, 230, 241–43.

Massé, Pierre, 135.

McGoey, Linsey, 201, 282 n.1.

McKinsey, 196.

McKinsey Award, 150.

MCPM. *See* Market-derived capital pricing model.

Mémoire sur la conservation (Buffon), 85–86.

Merck, 201.

Miller, Peter, 28, 41, 67, 68, 133, 134–35.

Ministry for the Future, 253, 259, 266.

Ministry for the Future (Stanley), 252–53, 266.

MIT, 132, 141, 144, 158, 159, 161, 268, 285 n.26.

Montagne, Sabine, 77.

Moog, Martin, 117.

Moran, Theodore, 243–44, 245.

Myers, Stewart, 158, 160–63, 164, 205.

NAPIER, CHRISTOPHER, 28, 41, 275 n.4.

National Economic Development Council (UK), 69.

Nationalization, 72, 135, 230, 238. *See also under* Copper mines, of Chile.

National Mining Enterprise (Chile), 232.

Natural resources, state sovereignty over, 84, 229–31, 242.

Nature of Capital and Income (Fisher), 24, 42–43.

Neoliberalism, American, 69–71, 78–79, 216.

Net present value, 16, 17, 30, 36, 39, 49, 143, 145, 146, 172, 188, 250; formula for, 47; risk-adjusted, 189. *See also* Cost-benefit analysis.

New York Commodity Exchange, 245.

New York Times, 18, 37, 148, 149, 154, 229.

Nixon, Richard, 238.

Noirot-Bonnet, Louis, 86, 102–104, 113–15.

Nordblad, Julia, 20, 82, 248, 262.

Nordhaus, William, 13–14, 119, 265.

Normal profits, 232, 233, 238.

Novartis, 211.

Novoa, Eduardo, 237.

NPV. *See* Net present value.

OBSERVATIONS SUR L'AMÉNAGEMENT DES FORÊTS (Varenne de Fenille), 86, 110.

Office of Management and Budget, 37, 71, 274 n.2.

Office of Technology Assessment, 199, 213.

"Old Man and the Three Young Ones" (La Fontaine), 99–100.

OMB. *See* Office of Management and Budget.

"On the Determination of the Money Value" (von Gehren), 85, 86, 87, 88–93.

Open innovation, 168.

Opportunity cost, 111; of capital, 48, 51, 160. *See also* Rate of return.

"An Optimal Path to Extinction?" (Perrings), 255.

Organisation for Economic Co-operation and Development, 50.

Ortiz, Horacio, 66, 77, 266.

Overpasses. *See* Bridges, politics of.

PANAMA CANAL, 26, 27, 44, 52, 62, 214, 247.
Payback, for project evaluation, 145–47.
Performativity, 53–54; Austinian, 55; of discounting, 55–57, 59, 60, 97; of economics, 56, 216.
Petty, J., 147.
"Pharmaceutical Forecasting: Throwing Darts?," 196.
Pharmaceutical industry. *See* Bio-pharmaceutical industry.
Pharmaceutical R&D, 16, 33–34, 62, 65, 171, 183–90, 199–201.
Piñera, José, 215–16, 218–24, 227, 235, 239–40, 249.
Pinochet, Augusto, 30, 215, 218, 222, 226.
Pollard, Sidney, 138, 255.
Poor, the, 21, 86, 107, 259–60; and economic irrationality, 254; inability to look to the future, 107.
Porter, Theodore, 35–36.
Poverty, 39, 62; and individual discount rates, 38, 40, 254–55, 259–60; instantness of, 104, 107; and resource degradation, 255; social effects of, 61.
Poverty alleviation programs, 38, 39.
Pradier, Pierre-Charles, 180, 283 n.7, 284 n.11.
Prebisch model of declining terms, 244.
Precapitalist societies, 255–56, 261–62.
Presentism, 18, 19, 278 n.11.
Present value, 11, 16–17, 20, 30, 33–35, 45, 64, 66, 90. *See also* Copper mines, of Chile; Cost-benefit analysis.
PricewaterhouseCoopers, 227.
Pricing, value-based, 211, 250.
Principles of Corporate Finance (Brealey and Myers), 159.

Principles of the Basic Constitutional Law (Piñera), 218.
Private ownership, 20, 73, 76, 86, 103, 104, 107, 109–10, 113, 220.
Progressive disinvestment, 152.
Public eye, the, 129, 130.
Public policy: cost-benefit analysis, 35–37, 39, 50, 250; discounting in, 39, 47, 50–51, 250, 258; short-termism in, 64.
PV. *See* Present value.

RAILROADS, 81, 131, 141.
Rancagua, Chile, 229.
Rate of Interest (Fisher), 44, 45.
Rate of return, 48, 50, 142, 144, 145–47.
Rationality, critique of, 169–70, 175, 177–79.
Rationalization of managerial decision-making, 29, 132, 136–37, 153, 155.
Real options valuation, 17, 186, 188, 273 n.8.
REDD+ sovereign carbon credits, 124–25.
Regulatory reform, 197.
Resources: allocation of, 64, 77, 166–67; degradation of, 255; and present value, 64, 66.
Return on equity, 140, 281 n.6, 286 n.31.
Return on investment, 139–40, 142, 144, 146.
Rewards, 29, 48–49, 51, 73, 80, 104, 167; in biopharmaceutical industry, 198–200, 207; commensurate with uncertainty, 182–83, 198, 201–202; and discounting, 113, 124, 130, 136, 144, 167, 172–74, 196, 201–202; and entrepreneur, 183; justification of, 179–80, 182–83, 196, 201; and rate of interest, 138.
Rhine Province Assembly, 106–107.
Rio Tinto. *See* Kennecott.

Near Futures series design by Julie Fry
Typesetting by Meighan Gale
Printed and bound by Maple Press